Microlearning

Eugenia Smyrnova-Trybulska
Piet Kommers • Martin Drlík • Ján Skalka
Editors

Microlearning

New Approaches To A More Effective Higher Education

Editors
Eugenia Smyrnova-Trybulska
Department of Humanistic Education
University of Silesia
Katowice, Poland

Piet Kommers
Department of Media,
Communication & Org.
University of Twente
Enschede, Overijssel, The Netherlands

Martin Drlík
Constantine the Philosopher
University in Nitra
Nitra, Slovakia

Ján Skalka
Constantine the Philosopher
University in Nitra
Nitra, Slovakia

ISBN 978-3-031-13361-9 ISBN 978-3-031-13359-6 (eBook)
https://doi.org/10.1007/978-3-031-13359-6

This Springer imprint is published by the registered company Springer Nature Switzerland AG
The registered company address is: Gewerbestrasse 11, 6330 Cham, Switzerland

Contents

Microlearning and Automated Assessment – A Framework Implementation of Dissimilar Elements to Achieve Better Educational Outcomes

Ján Skalka

1 Introduction

Writing the source code of programmes is currently one of the basic skills of a modern employee. Many support systems of various levels, content and quality have been created to support the teaching of programming (Crow et al., 2018). Many researchers seek to focus on the narrow field of programming as such and explore the modern learning environment in a broader context, often in the interconnection of STEM/STEAM area (Çetin & Demircan, 2020; Smyrnova-Trybulska et al., 2017).

The research trends of the last few years are aimed at predicting success or failure in education (Kabathova & Drlik, 2021; Drlik & Munk, 2019). However, the most crucial element of education is the content, form, and distribution to the student (Carlon et al., 2020). Several frameworks have been designed and implemented in recent years to optimise content, distribution, and retain student attention (Halvoník & Kapusta, 2020; Sharma et al., 2012).

Mobile applications are gradually becoming the most important distribution channel due to their ease of use and availability anytime and anywhere (Baldwin & Ching, 2020). The use of mobile applications in education, research in the field of personalisation (Moon et al., 2020; Morze et al., 2021; Bartolomé et al., 2018) and monitoring of user behaviour (Halvoník & Kapusta, 2019) has also intensified.

The article deals with the search for an answer to whether it is possible to combine two effective approaches in teaching programming – microlearning and automated assessment. Methodologies of their use are developed in many sources, and their isolated use is currently a frequent subject of pedagogical research. However, the combination of both approaches is unique and represents an additional

J. Skalka (✉)
Constantine the Philosopher University in Nitra, Nitra, Slovakia
e-mail: jskalka@ukf.sk

E. Smyrnova-Trybulska et al. (eds.), *Microlearning*,
https://doi.org/10.1007/978-3-031-13359-6_1

combination of obtaining basic information and its practical use for writing programs in different programming languages.

In addition to the design and presentation of an educational environment combining learning in small units and tools designed for automatic evaluation of source codes, the article also includes evaluating the perception of the environment and the educational approaches used by students.

The article main aim of the article is to present architecture, current state, and experience with the pilot deployment of virtual learning environment *Priscilla* (Skalka & Drlik, 2018a, b), developed based on the conceptual framework for teaching and learning programming (Skalka et al., 2021).

This environment effectively combines contemporary promising educational approaches, including microlearning (Hug, 2005) and automatically evaluated source codes (automated assessment) (Ala-Mutka, 2005; Fernández Alemán, 2011). The balanced combination of these approaches allows effectively managing the time required for learning theory, applying the obtain knowledge immediately, minimising the time for source code evaluation, and providing immediate feedback, which is important for learning programming.

The research questions are defined as follow:

- RQ1: *What is the effective software architecture covering the needs of the framework defined for learning and teaching programming in introductory courses.*
- RQ2: *How do students perceive the methods of microlearning, and how, according to them, does it contribute to the improvement of their programming skills and knowledge.*
- RQ3: *How do students perceive the method of automated assessment, and how, according to them, does it contribute to the improvement of their programming skills and knowledge.*

The article has the following structure. The second part summarises information about selected information systems for teaching programming and web portals used in programming learning. The third part presents the introductory conceptual model and implementation of the backend and front-end parts. This section also describes the most important framework modules implemented in the *Priscilla* system. The fourth chapter deals with studying the perception of the system by students who completed one semester of study. Finally, the article concludes with a discussion, a description of the current state and future work.

2 Introductory Programming Learning Environments

Despite the relatively extensive research in introductory programming courses, the specific research focused on developing proprietary solutions used by universities is rare. Many universities use plugins or modules implemented in Learning Management Systems (LMS). Skalka et al. (2019) used the LMS plugin implemented by Rodríguez-del-Pino et al. (2012) for LMS Moodle to support automated evaluation of source codes in the introductory programming course of Java.

The following examples of original solutions and software systems for the teaching of programming are considered very promising.

Vesin et al. (2018), Blažeska-Tabakovska et al. (2017) presented Programming Tutoring System (ProTuS) with a cross-platform architecture that aggregates and harmonises study analyses from different systems and quantifies student performance through a set of indicators. Learning is based on a combination of explanations, interactive examples, interactive challenges and coding exercises.

Brusilovsky et al. described the use of the Python Grids System (Brusilovsky et al., 2018) as a tool that provides access to four types of interactive tutorial content for learning Python: annotated examples, animated examples, semantic code evaluation problems, and code construction problems.

Buffardi & Edwards (2014) introduced CodeWorkout – an online training system with course management functions. It hosts an online repository of questions and assignments that teachers can incorporate into their courses. It also provides tools for creating new items so that the exercises can be adapted to the class's needs.

Many courses provided through MOOC portals such as Coursera, Edx, Udemy often contain various types of "camps" that allow writing, running and evaluating codes, either at the automatic level or through peer-review (Chauhan, 2014; Johnston, 2015).

University solutions are complemented by various categories of public portals and applications which offer free courses for the public and life-long learning. Each of them is specific, often closely oriented on technically skilled students without implemented standard didactical methodology. The simplest category of portals provides an essential source of information, where the popular *w3schools.com* was chosen as a typical example. The second category covers portals supporting the development of programming skills by writing programs with the support of many programming languages. Here it is assumed that the user already has basic knowledge and educational content is usually not available (*Hackerrank*, *Codewars*). The next category consists of portals providing content in the microlearning form with various types of competitions. It is assumed that the user achieves the course goals based on internal motivation, ensured by various competitions and strong gamification (*Sololearn*). The last category is represented by portals intended for the youngest users. They can replace writing code by automatically entering entire commands or block-based language depending on age.

Table 1 compares the presented *Priscilla* portal, as a portal based on microlearning and automated assessment with other solutions.

In addition to the portals listed in Table 1, which offer educational content for multiple programming languages, many other portals are focused on a specific programming language. Many solutions make it possible to integrate selected parts of the content into teaching or use web portals as a suitable supplement for practising educational content.

Table 1 Popular free web portals focused on programming learning compared with a real implementation of the presented framework by system PRISCILLA

Portal/property	w3schools.com	codewars.com/ qualified.io	sololearn.com	freecodecamp.org	hackerrank.com	codeavengers.com	code.org	PRISCILLA
Age category	Teens, adults	Teens, adults	Teens, adults	Teens, adults	Teens, adults	5+	4+	Teens, adults
Supported languages	JavaScript, HTML/CSS; PHP in simple form	All language types	All language types	JavaScript, HTML/CSS, python	All language types	JavaScript, HTML/ CSSweb languages, python	Primary block-based visual programming	All language types
Content	Basic	–	Yes	Basic	As part of tasks	Yes	In a specific form	Complex in microcontent
Micro-content	–	–	Yes	–	–	–	–	Yes
Quizzes	Basic	–	Yes	–	–	Yes	–	Yes
Automatic code evaluation	Yes	Yes	–	Yes	Yes	Yes	Yes	Yes
Sandbox or own code space	Yes	–	Yes	–	–	–	–	In preparation
Learning paths/ courses	Basic	–	Yes	Yes	Yes	Yes	Yes	Yes
Competitions	–	Yes	Yes	–	Yes	–	–	Yes
Gamification	–	Yes	Yes	–	Yes	Yes	In a specific form	Yes
Teaching	–	Yes	Create content	–	–	Yes	In a specific form	Yes

3 Learning Environment Concept

Successful and sustainable implementation of the framework requires coverage of introductory programming courses and activities intended for future educational environment development and content development. Taking care of content updates and creation and updating design following modern design trends can be covered by educational activities in advanced engineering courses. Students will work on the development of an environment that they know because they studied in it the basics of programming.

The implementation of the framework (Skalka & Drlík, 2018a, b) defines the concept and learning processes into independent systems preceded by the implementation in the *LMS Moodle* environment (Skalka et al., 2021). Typical tests in *Moodle* with quiz questions of various types were used to cover the needs of microlearning. Prepared tests consist of simple answers through the selection of options to complete the source code. Automatic code evaluation was provided by the *Virtual Programming Lab* supporting automatic source code evaluation in many programming languages (Rodríguez-del-Pino et al., 2012).

Using *Moodle* during implementation has resulted in the need to address many limitations and did not produce the expected results in the user interface. The most problematic places were the static structure of the course, which does not support the efficient display of a large number of course objects and the complicated integration of gamification elements into the system. Support for user activity logging and support for learning analytics, which are the essential features of a system for understanding the learning process, did not provide detailed information on user behaviour. It has also been laborious for users to obtain detailed information about fixes and source improvements. The ability to adapt the user's view of the educational content was low, etc.

The form of programming new modules in *LMS Moodle* is precisely given, and module programmers require a thorough knowledge of the LMS system and the use of spaghetti code in *PHP*. The complicated development has significantly reduced the potential for sustainable system development due to lower motivation and higher demands on students in advanced programming courses.

The logical step was to create a stand-alone, fully adaptable system in-house that primarily supports the requirements of the framework and is based on new popular and widely used technologies.

Following the positive experience with microlearning activities and exercises based on automated source code evaluation in *LMS Moodle* (Skalka & Drlik, 2020) and requirement of conceptual design presented above and in (Skalka & Drlik, 2018a, b), the concept of a software architecture proposal of a system called *Priscilla* (PRogressIve System for interaCtIve (programming) Learning and Learning Assistance) was designed. Its structure and implementation are presented in this section.

3.1 Framework Architecture

The conceptual model of *Priscilla* presented in Fig. 1 is structured as three-layered architecture, which contains an independent front-end part (presentation/client module) and separate backend parts integrated into the server infrastructure. The communication between front-end and backend is realised via the API interface, and particular features use web sockets.

The front-end part can be implemented as a web, mobile or desktop application. The user's interaction with the application is fluent because the network traffic is very low after the first application launch in a web browser.

The front-end part provides the educational content in three forms:

- Micro-content represents the content in the form of text, short source codes, images, etc. This type of activity is designed as an HTML container, and the content is transmitted as a package containing formatted text (headings, text, source code, images, tables, etc.).
- Microlearning activities are interactive objects that require the user to solve simple tasks. A typical example is filling in the correct code result, filling a gap in the code by typing or drag-and-dropping the right parts, reordering shuffled lines of source code, and so on. Interactive activities are combined with content activities (usually 1:1 or in favour of interactive activities) in lessons and chapters. Tasks in interactive activities are focused on the information contained in previous content activities – the content structure is developed concerning microlearning principles.

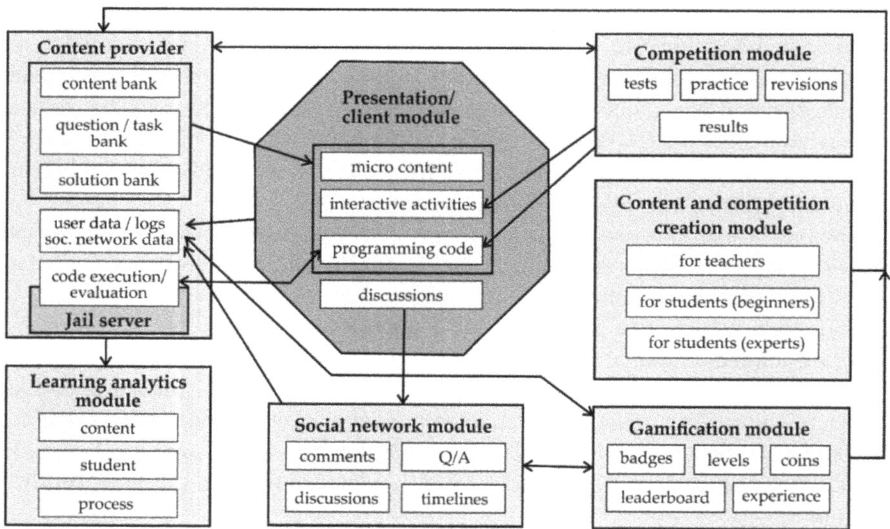

Fig. 1 Simplified conceptual model of PRISCILLA-2.0 based on the PRISCILLA model presented in (Skalka & Drlik, 2018a, b)

- Activities aimed at acquiring programming skills are focused on writing, executing and validating the program code. The student completes the developed programs or writes complete codes in a user-friendly editor adapted to the selected language. After writing the code, the student sends the program to the validation system, which evaluates its correctness. The response may contain compiler errors (syntax errors) or code accuracy, which depends on comparing the submitted code results with the expected results.

The front-end part allows the student to use the discussion module to communicate with their classmates, rate the content and activities and report errors or inaccuracies in the content. Each user's action causes a connection to the API interface and records the action type and user identification. Many activities require an educational system response implemented by RPC (Request-Response Protocol) using the JSON format.

Responses are generated on the backend part, which is divided into two physical and several logical segments. Two independent systems present the physical parts:

- The educational system is implemented as a web application working with data stored in a database system. This structure will be described later.
- The jail-system is implemented as an independent Linux system designed to verify the source code. Because program code verification is often based on program execution, the system must be resistant to attacks, malicious code, and system errors and must be self-healing. The *Priscilla* system uses the jail-server developed for the *Virtual programming Lab* in Moodle (Rodríguez-del-Pino et al., 2012), which can evaluate dozens of programming languages. The jail-system creates a new temporary user with low privileges for every task, and after reading the results, the user is removed from the system. The restrictions defined for program activities are derived from *Linux* user permissions.

The logical structure of the backend reflects the education system functions and the ideas presented in the previous section. It is designed so that the individual parts cover all the functions of the system. The parts are closely linked with each other, as activity in one part often causes related activity in the other part. The backend has the following components:

- *The Content provider* provides access to all educational content. The main part of the content is divided into lessons and chapters organised in educational courses. Extended content is intended for tests, exercises, revisions and competitions. Each question, task or assignment is accompanied by tips, hints and correct answers or authoring solutions of the programs. *The Content provider* processes the requests from the client interface and sends the content or evaluation results. All evaluation algorithms are implemented in the backend part to prevent hacker attacks. The *User data module* is a part of the *Content provider* containing information about all activities, attempts, and users' results in the system. This part of the data is primarily intended for the *Learning analytics module*.

- *The Content and competition creation module* is determined for content building. This section is intended for administrators or content creators, and the typical user is not authorised to use the features of this module. The module provides functions for competitions, courses, chapters and lesson structure creating. Content, questions and assignments can fill built elements.
- *The Competition module* ensures the realisation of activities aimed at testing students (in organised education) or competitions of students with each other. It offers prepared content in educational objects (matches, tests, revisions, etc.) and keeps track of time defined for them. The module also includes the evaluation of test results as a whole and the ordering of competitors. The structure of the questions is identical to the items used in the learning part. Two main areas are used in competitions – users can compete in answering questions or writing programs (rated for writing speed, execution speed, or code effectiveness).
- *The Social network module* is a layer that provides task-related discussions, commenting, micro-object evaluation, bug reporting, and general discussion management. Each discussion post can be evaluated (positively or negatively), and the author can get feedback, which is also used in the gamification part.
- *The Gamification module* monitors user activities and processes the collected data into gamification elements. The most frequent gamification components of the *Priscilla* system are badges in many categories (different types of experience with the learning process, experience with competition, evaluation, and activities in discussions, contribution to the system, etc.). Badges are also graded according to performance into several levels (bronze, silver, gold, diamond, etc.). Each action in the system triggers event processing in the *Gamification module* and changes the monitored user parameters.
- *The Learning analytics module* is designed to analyse and evaluate the user's behaviour and educational outcomes, identify problematic parts of the content and predict the user's preferences and success. This module does not create new data; it only processes the data of *the Content provider* and displays it based on the teacher or administrator's defined views. The module helps to tune and optimise the parameters of the system.

3.2 Backend Implementation

Typical attributes of modern software systems are permanent availability, fast processing of many parallel requests, and orientation to the data provided through services. Complex systems usually consist of related services that work independently and can be developed in isolation. Increased flexibility gained by adopting paradigms such as API-oriented architecture is associated with creating robust and complex systems (Brosig et al., 2014). The communication between the front-end and the backend is provided via web services. This architecture allows the development of various front-end applications: web-client, mobile application, or desktop application.

The core of the *Priscilla* system based on the conceptual model is implemented as a server application developed in the PHP framework *Laravel Lumen* intended to develop applications based on microservices. The current database system is *MySQL*. The communication is realised via REST API using application/JSON format.

The backend part of the system processes front-end requests in several layers and is depicted in Fig. 2:

- The first layer verifies the user's identity. Only the requests of the authorised and logged-in user will be moved for further processing. Authentication is provided by OAuth components (Ferretti et al., 2017).
- The API layer identifies the request and selects the correct service to process or provide the data.
- Service is usually a single-purpose method for providing communication with a database or simple request processing. The services can be combined and typically write a record of the operation in a database recording the user's behaviour and results.

Services can be divided into three types: services for processing anonymous activities (login, registration, visits to the main page of the system, etc.), activities with

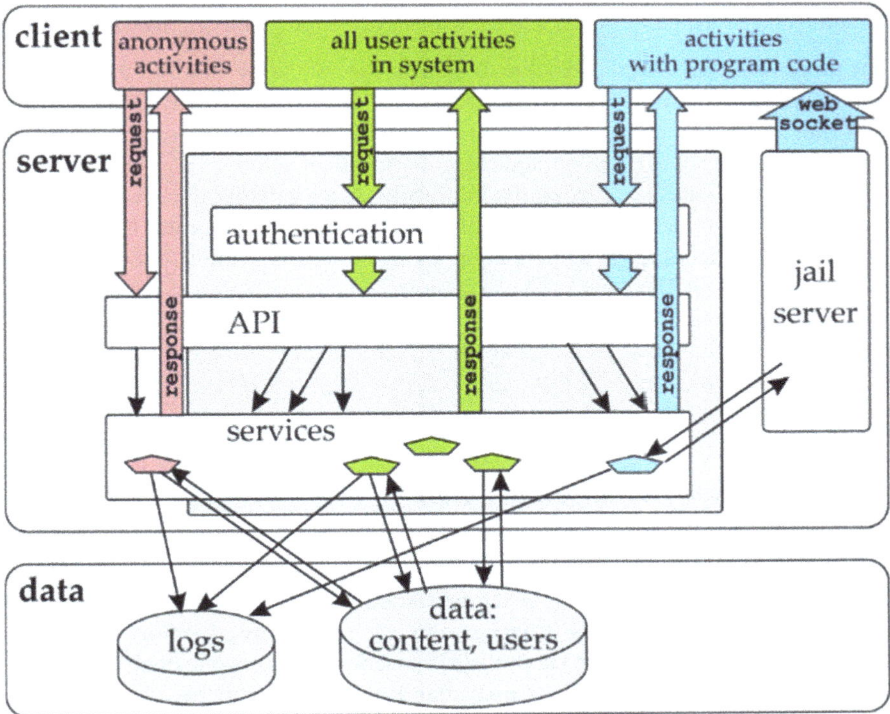

Fig. 2 The software structure of PRISCILLA implementation based on microservices

program codes that are specific and all other activities performed by the logged-in user in the system.

Anonymous activities skip the authorisation layer and process requests directly. The answer may also include data from the database.

Activities with automatic source code evaluation are specific because it is necessary to ensure communication with the jail server. The communication of the application as a whole with the jail-server is realised as follows:

- the user in the front-end asks to check the correctness of his program,
- the service invoked in the backend stores code of the delivered program into the database and prepares the request to the jail server,
- the backend sends a request to the jail-server and, in response, immediately receives a token representing the jail-server process executing the source code,
- the obtained token is sent as a response (to the demand of the code verification) to the front-end,
- the front-end gets a token and opens a web-socket to the jail-server; jail-server has meanwhile started the execution of the program delivered from backend,
- front-end reads the changes on the jail-server via the socket, and if the jail-server reaches one of the final states (error, long program execution time, program completion, etc.), the front-end sends a request to the backend to read the results,
- the jail-server results are read by the backend service and written to the database; at the end of the process, the service sends evaluation results to the front-end.

The process is a bit complicated due to the decrease of server load and the elimination of cheating. Direct communication with the jail-server is realised only on the backend. The time-consuming operation of monitoring the running program's activity on the jail-server is again implemented on the client side.

All other activities are carried out uniformly: After defining the application client's request parameters and calling the appropriate microservice, the backend realises user authentication, authorisation verification (user, admin), and subsequent request processing. The standard services cover common CRUD operations, evaluation of the solution's correctness, logging of activities, gamification and use of social network elements. Task evaluation is performed exclusively on the server to eliminate cheating.

3.3 The Front-end Implementation

The current version of the application's front-end part was developed in the *VueJS* environment with the definition of the appearance based on the rules of *Material design* of *Google*. The system is designed to teach many programming languages, and the structure of the system supports their teaching in one application. The example of used courses, languages and user interface is presented in Fig. 3.

Language support depends primarily on language interpreters (compilers) and then on advanced content (defined usually by content developers or teachers). Each

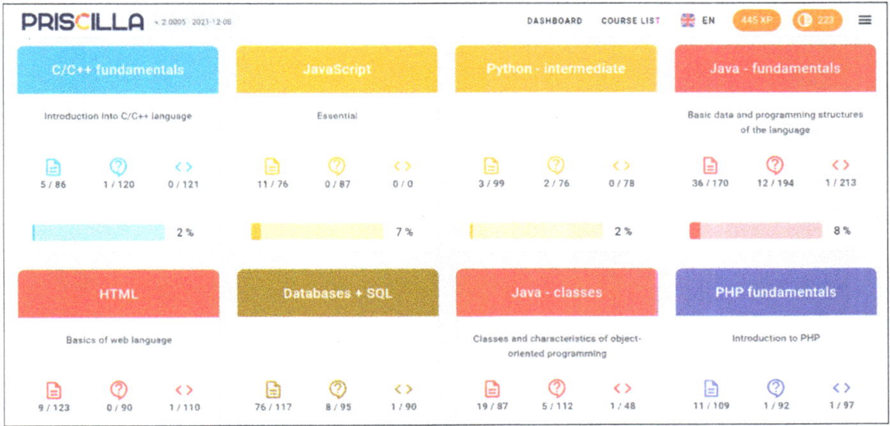

Fig. 3 The user's view of the dashboard and his opened courses in the PRISCILLA system

language has defined a default lesson path consisting of microlearning activities (tasks) and programming tasks (code).

3.3.1 Content Structure

The essential idea in successful introductory programming courses is to leave students some freedom to choose the order of activities they should complete in the programming course. The programming courses were designed following the classical educational structures, and the order of defined chapters is in line with the didactics of teaching programming. Still, they do not force the student to proceed linearly. Almost every chapter contains a combination of tasks and programs, which students complete based on their preferences. Each task can be repeated as many times as a student needs. Students can return to the place of explanation of the issue, if necessary – the system's goal is not to evaluate but to teach.

The basic information displayed to the student is the progress of completed questions and submitted programs that are part of each chapter. An overview of the open course Java – fundamental (Skalka et al., 2020a) is shown in Fig. 4.

Each chapter displays an icon indicating whether it should be started or whether the user should solve more tasks in the previous chapter. The recommendation is calculated to a 50% success rate of tasks and programs in the previous chapter. No chapter is locked; there are only recommendations, and the user can study any chapter at any time.

The panel on the right side contains information about the last completed activity in the course, the achieved score and the amount of currency gained, and other gamification objects.

All interactive activities are dynamically generated based on data obtained from the backend part of the system and a standard universal template.

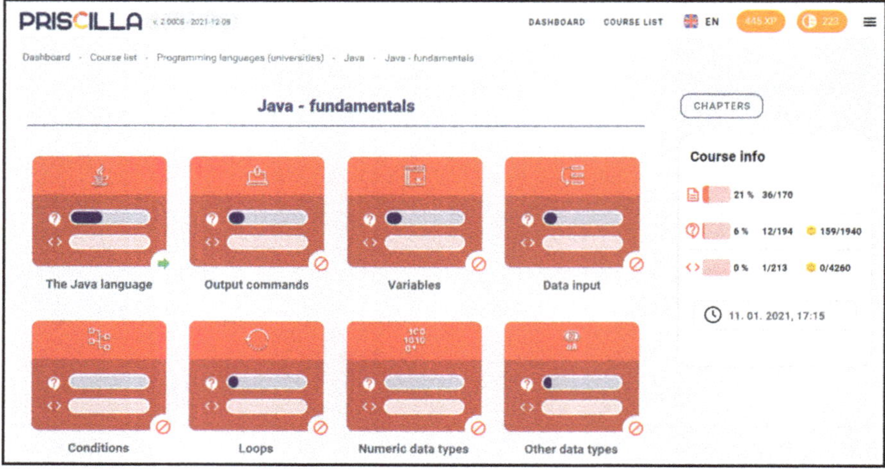

Fig. 4 User's view of the Java course content

A combination of micro-content and micro-tasks realises the implementation of microlearning in the system. The micro-content contains brief information, and the micro-task follows it and contains a question ensuring the repetition or consolidation of the presented information. It is advisable to alternate micro-content and micro-tasks within the lessons in a ratio of 1:1 or more (one content and at least one task). The specific content of micro-content and micro-task are presented in Figs. 5 and 6.

Support for building skills in several ways is based on a combination of different types of tasks. There are available the following task types covering the following activities:

- typical domain verification tasks (short answer, choice of options),
- placing code snippets,
- supplementing the writing of commands or parts of code,
- finding the results of subroutines,
- rearranging lines of source code,
- different types of writing programs (in whole or part).

3.3.2 Automatic Source Code Evaluation

Exercises based on automatic source code evaluation consist of three basic types.

The most used and simplest type for the content creator automatically evaluates programs based on comparing the program's correct outputs with the outputs of the user program (I/O approach). The definition of evaluated inputs has a typical structure compatible with the definition of inputs and expected results in the VPL

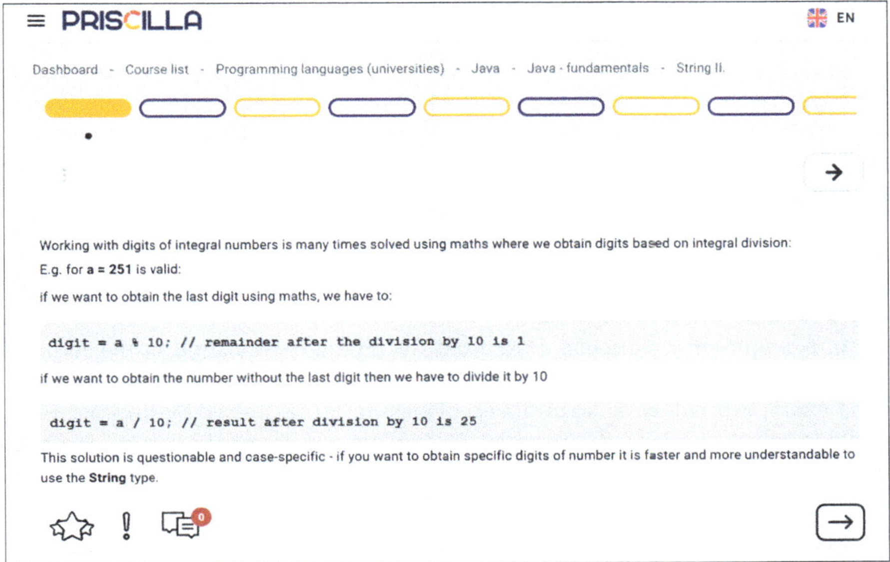

Fig. 5 Example of micro-content in the educational system PRISCILLA

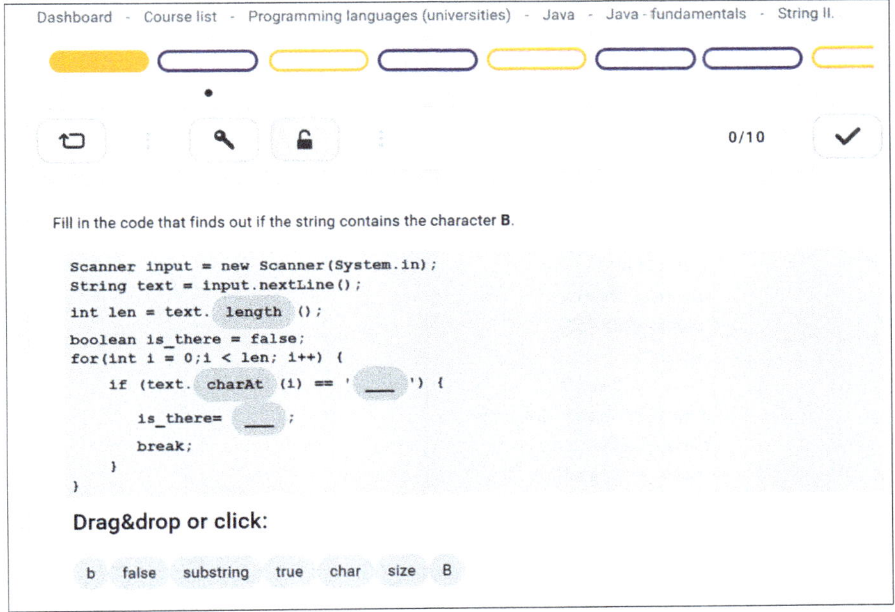

Fig. 6 Example of micro-task in the educational system PRISCILLA

environment (Rodríguez-del-Pino et al., 2012). The example of test cases and their use is presented in Figs. 7 and 8.

Based on *xUnit* testing ideas, the second approach is typical for tasks designed to learn object-oriented programming. It uses automated tests principles, and its implementation depends on the creators' abilities and habits. Each content creator can implement their testing methods. The easiest way is to use the *xUnit* libraries, where the creator has set the tested methods and the correct outputs.

The system is also open to unique approaches. The content creator can create his random generators for selecting a sequence of methods, selecting input values, and using the author's solution as a sample solution, with the results of which the student's solution will be compared.

An example of a particular class used for program evaluation in the form of another class defined in the assignment is shown in Fig. 9. The definition uses an input matrix that will be set as attributes of class instances passed by students. Each attribute and method should be tested for random and threshold values. The user output has the same design as the *Execution info* section in Fig. 8.

The last type of automatic evaluation is a static evaluation used in any programming language of varying complexity and difficulty. Its simple version based on content (not structure) analysis is used, for example, in HTML courses. The idea is based on defining the rules and evaluating their fulfilment. *Priscilla* contains several rules that can be used to varying degrees to validate a document (text). The rules are defined to check the existence, position, or order of text patterns. A simple example is presented in Fig. 10.

```
case = Test1
input=here-there
output=10
case = Test2
input=MOTHER.
output=7
case = Test3
input=Winter is coming.
output=18
case = Test4
input=springspringspringspringspringspring
output=36
```

Fig. 7 Test cases definition for code that should print the number of characters in a defined string

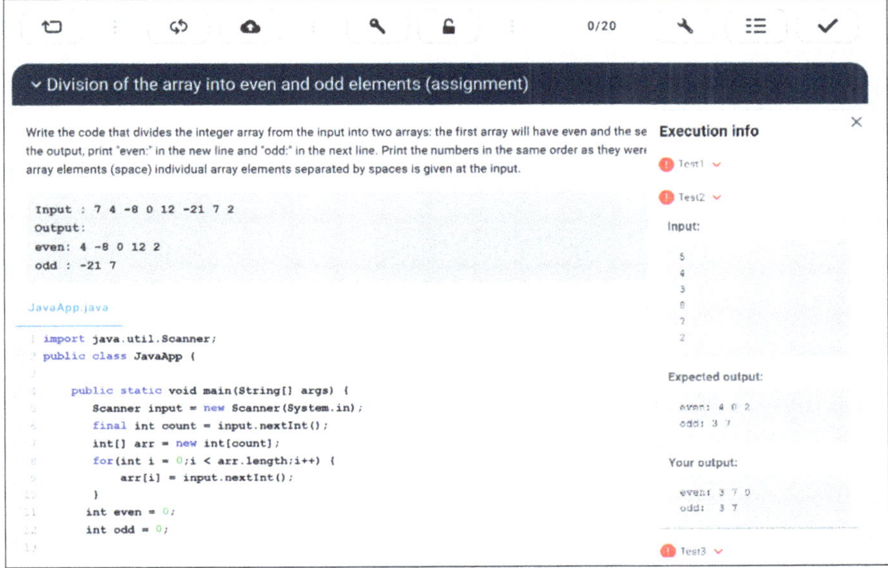

Fig. 8 The result of program code evaluation in the implementation of the presented framework in the educational system PRISCILLA. The Execution info section shows the inputs and outputs of test cases in which the expected and obtained values do not match

3.3.3 Learning and Teaching Support

For each task, the template provides the ability to invoke help or unlock an answer, add a discussion post, report errors, and rate the quality of the question. The activities dedicated to programming are extended by sending the program to evaluate and display compiler messages or test results. The views of activities are presented in Fig. 11.

The user interface for competitions (test, revisions etc.) uses the same templates and activity types, but the time to prepare answers for tasks and programs is limited. After the set time has elapsed, all the tasks (including unfinished ones) are automatically submitted and evaluated.

The educational environment includes gamification tools – levelling, awarding badges, rewarding selected activities and rankings for individual courses or programming languages.

A teacher role has been created in the *Priscilla* system to support the use of blended activities. This role can be acquired by any user who sets up a study group, where the students join by the key. The teacher has permission to monitor students activity and results in his group, and he can participate in solving course activities.

```
public class Evaluate {

    public String doTests(Object[][] cases) {
        String output = "";
        int correct_count = 0;
        for(int i = 0; i < cases.length; i++) { // number of tests, test cases
            int value1 = 0;
            int value2 = 0;
            switch (((String)cases[i][0])) {
                case "P": value1 = (int)(Math.random()*1000); break;
                case "N": value1 = -(int)(Math.random()*1000); break;
                case "Z": value1 = 0; break;
                case "R": value1 = -100000+(int)(Math.random()*200000); break;
            }
            switch (((String)cases[i][1])) {
                case "P": value2 = (int)(Math.random()*1000); break;
                case "N": value2 = -(int)(Math.random()*1000); break;
                case "Z": value2 = 0; break;
                case "R": value2 = -100000+(int)(Math.random()*200000); break;
            }
            // tested class and author solution
            MyClass tested = new MyClass();
            MySolution correct = new MySolution();

            int result_test = tested.getMax(value1, value2);
            int result_correct = correct.getMax(value1, value2);
            // results comparison
            if (result_test != result_correct) {
                output = output + "!--- result: " + TEXT_ERROR + "\n";
            } else {
                output = output + "!--- result: OK\n";
                correct_count++;
            }
            ...
```

Fig. 9 A simple example of a class designed to compare the results of students classes with the original solution. The assignment was simple – create a method for the sum of two real values. Test cases are defined by string constants – P (positive values), N (negative values), R (random values) and Z (zero). The randomisation of input values minimises the risk of false positives

4 Students' Perception of the Elements of the Priscilla System

Priscilla was first deployed in the winter semester of 2020/2021 as the primary teaching tool for Java courses and a complementary database and SQL learning tool. Other courses were used to support additional activities in the voluntary preparation of students.

The research focused on the perception of elements of the system by students was carried out after the end of the semester. Answers of the Java course students

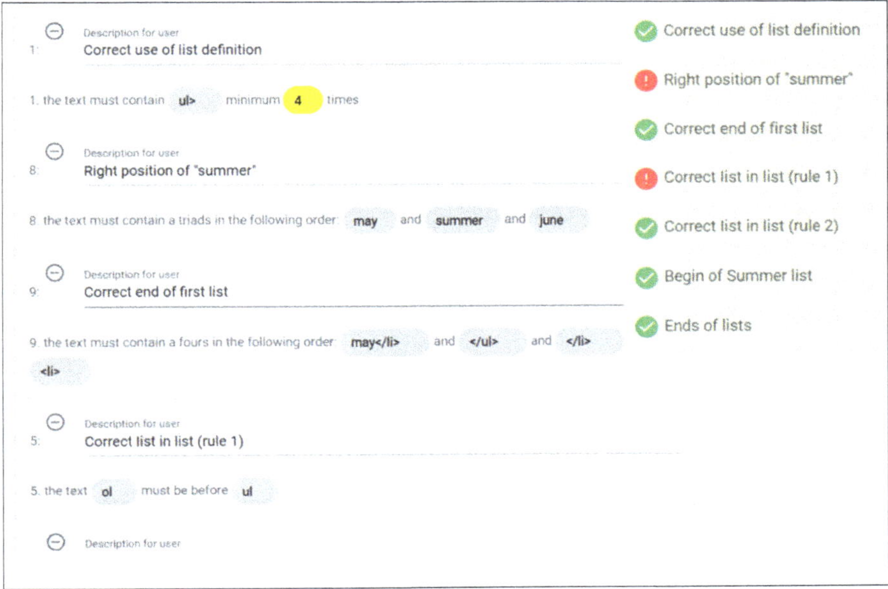

Fig. 10 Example of static automated evaluation of HTML program code in the implementation of the educational system PRISCILLA. The rules are defined in the admin interface, and the user views only a simple window after evaluation

were collected not anonymously to find dependency between students results and their perception of the educational process. The questionnaire was focused comprehensively, the coverage of the topics of lessons by micro-content and automatically evaluated programs was identified. A series of similar questions focused on perception by students was devoted to individual elements of the environment.

The questionnaire respondents were students of the first year of the study program of applied informatics aged 20–23 years.

Table 2 presents the perceptions of micro-lessons by students. The course content was created to evenly cover all the topics covered in the introductory course of programming. The perception of the compliance of the content of micro-lessons and lectures realised in 2020 in online form expresses mastery and understanding of content by students. If students perceive that the taught and the practised content are the same, they are likely to understand the context or at least paid sufficient attention to the content. The first question in the questionnaire finds out this fact.

The second group of questions focuses on identifying the role of micro-content through the Likert scale. The role of micro-content is expressed in questions at different levels:

- Micro-content and micro-questions helped students understand the curriculum.
- Micro-content and micro-questions helped students practice previously understood curriculum content.

(a)

10/10

Complete the command to output the text:

```
class Cat {
  public static void main(String[ ] args) {
    System.out.   ("Miau!");      // output Miau!
  }
}
```

(b)

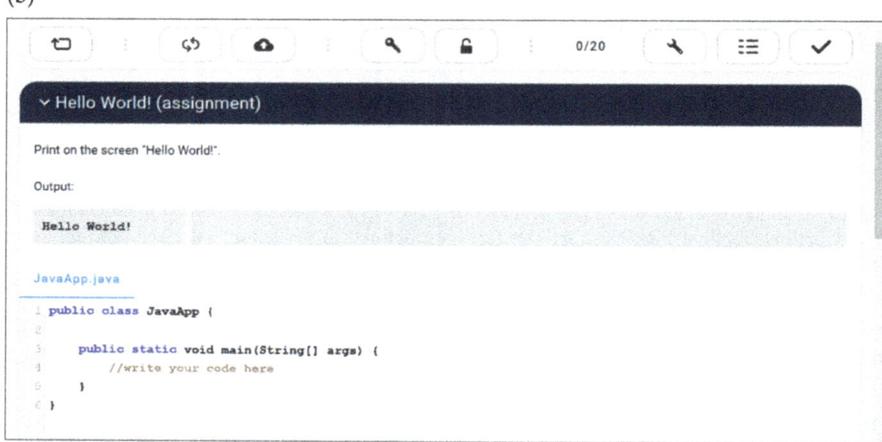

Fig. 11 Functions implemented in interactive (**a**) and programming (**b**) activities. There are shared functions on the header toolbar – get help, buy the correct answer and in the program activity: show/hide the compiler message and show/hide the execution information. The footer of each activity contains icons for rating assignments, bug reports, and discussion views

- Micro-content helped students with a comprehensive mastery of the curriculum – the student used it as a primary source of learning.

It can be observed that majority of students perceived microlearning positively to very positively.

Table 3 presents the perceptions of automated assessment by students. The most important characteristics of educational content are students understanding and the teacher's (or course creator's) ability to assign a task clearly and accurately. The first question focuses on identifying the unambiguity and comprehensibility of the assignment.

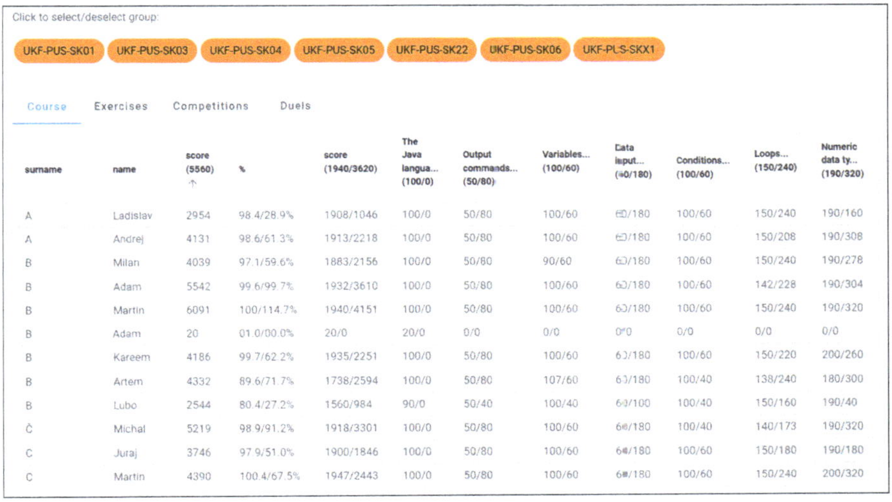

Click to select/deselect group:

UKF-PUS-SK01 UKF-PUS-SK03 UKF-PUS-SK04 UKF-PUS-SK05 UKF-PUS-SK22 UKF-PUS-SK06 UKF-PUS-SKX1

Course Exercises Competitions Duels

surname	name	score (5560) ↑	%	score (1940/3620)	The Java langua... (100/0)	Output commands... (50/80)	Variables... (100/60)	Data input... (60/180)	Conditions... (100/60)	Loops... (150/240)	Numeric data ty... (190/320)
A	Ladislav	2954	98.4/28.9%	1908/1046	100/0	50/80	100/60	60/180	100/60	150/240	190/160
A	Andrej	4131	98.6/61.3%	1913/2218	100/0	50/80	100/60	60/180	100/60	150/208	190/308
B	Milan	4039	97.1/59.6%	1883/2156	100/0	50/80	90/60	60/180	100/60	150/240	190/278
B	Adam	5542	99.6/99.7%	1932/3610	100/0	50/80	100/60	60/180	100/60	142/228	190/304
B	Martin	6091	100/114.7%	1940/4151	100/0	50/80	100/60	60/180	100/60	150/240	190/320
B	Adam	20	01.0/00.0%	20/0	20/0	0/0	0/0	0/0	0/0	0/0	0/0
B	Kareem	4186	99.7/62.2%	1935/2251	100/0	50/80	100/60	60/180	100/60	150/220	200/260
B	Artem	4332	89.6/71.7%	1738/2594	100/0	50/80	107/60	60/180	100/40	138/240	180/300
B	Lubo	2544	80.4/27.2%	1560/984	90/0	50/40	100/40	60/100	100/40	150/160	190/40
Č	Michal	5219	98.9/91.2%	1918/3301	100/0	50/80	100/60	60/180	100/40	140/173	190/320
C	Juraj	3746	97.9/51.0%	1900/1846	100/0	50/80	100/60	60/180	100/60	150/180	190/180
C	Martin	4390	100.4/67.5%	1947/2443	100/0	50/80	100/60	60/180	100/60	150/240	200/320

Fig. 12 Monitoring of student activities in teacher defined groups

Table 3 Perceptions of automated assessment by students in the winter semester of 2020/2021

Question	1 (disagree)	2	3	4	5	6	7 (agree)
Clarity and accuracy of assignments	4	2	8	15	**18**	**18**	**10**
Help to understand	3	1	6	9	**16**	**17**	**23**
Practice understood content	4	0	2	10	**13**	**22**	**24**

Table 2 Perceptions of micro-lessons by students in the winter semester of 2020/2021

Question	1 (disagree)	2	3	4	5	6	7 (agree)
Compliance of micro-lessons and lectures	4	0	2	9	**8**	**27**	**25**
Help to understand	3	0	7	11	**13**	**21**	**20**
Practice understood content	3	2	4	8	**11**	**23**	**24**
Primary source of learning	2	4	5	17	**16**	**17**	**14**

The following questions focus on identifying the role of automated assessment through the Likert scale again. The roles of automated assessment were expressed at two levels:

- The automated assessment helped students understand the curriculum.
- The automated assessment helped students practice previously understood content.

The majority of respondents perceived automated assessment positively.

The results of two continuous tests aimed at identifying students' ability to write entire programs independently were used to inspect the relationship between students' answers and their learning outcomes. The maximum score of this pair of tests was 1000 points (500 per test). The histogram in Fig. 13 presents the distribution of the results. Questionnaire respondents who were evaluated in a different way (external study) were omitted from the sample.

The correlations between students' results and the answers to the questionnaire questions are presented in Table 4. The dependence was identified using the Pearson correlation coefficient.

The dependence between characteristics is proven in the case of a value greater than 0.4. The evaluation results demonstrate that there is no dependence between the results of students and their perception of individual types of educational objects.

5 Discussion

The answers to the research questions can be summarised as follows

- RQ1: *What is the effective software architecture covering the needs of the framework defined for learning and teaching programming in introductory courses.*

The software architecture was designed to be able to cover the needs of the framework defined in (Skalka & Drlik, 2018a, b) and at the same time bring a user and research design that is better than its implementation presented in (Skalka et al., 2021). The essential feature of the system is open to any front-end implementations covering the creation of the web, mobile and desktop applications on the same back-end kernel.

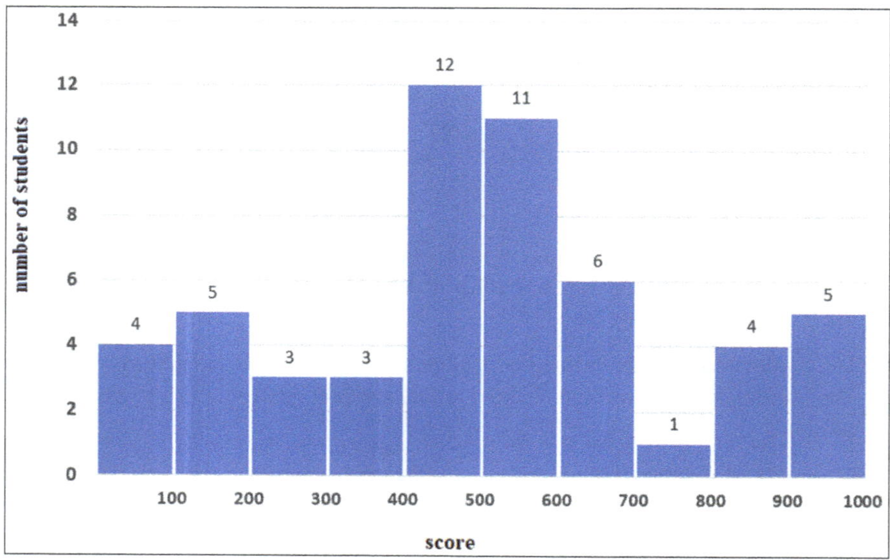

Fig. 13 Histogram of student test results

Table 4 Correlations between student results and questionnaire questions

Activity/questions	Pearson correlation coefficient
Compliance of micro-lessons and lectures	0.22
Micro-lessons helped to understand	0.17
Micro-lessons helped to practice the understood content	0.12
Micro-lessons were a primary source of learning	0.01
Clarity and accuracy of assignments in automated assessment	0.26
The automated assessment helped to understand	0.35
The automated assessment helped practice understood content	0.26

The functionality of the backend kernel ensures the control of responses and the evaluation of source codes. This approach is standard, implemented in several similar systems (Chen et al., 2018; Silva et al., 2017) and, thanks to its isolation from user activities on the front end, also relatively secure (Liebenberg & Jarke, 2020).

Based on conceptual framework ideas, the presented system covers an educational concept implemented as an essential tool for teaching programming at five European universities. The educational system is used to cover the first framework phases defined for building knowledge and skills. *Priscilla* provides an environment to offer content availability, instant feedback in all types of assignments, the ability to communicate between users, and the support of a full-time study of learning programming.

It covers many activities needed to educate programmers at novice levels. There are 24 courses in 8 languages implemented to cover Java, Python, C, HTML, CSS, JavaScript, PHP and SQL. Every course is localised into English, Spanish, Slovak, Czech and Polish languages.

Currently, the system has about 1500 unique active users, so it can be concluded that the proposed concept is functional and successful.

- RQ2: *How do students perceive the methods of microlearning, and how, according to them, does it contribute to the improvement of their programming skills and knowledge.*
- RQ3: *How do students perceive the method of automated assessment, and how, according to them, does it contribute to the improvement of their programming skills and knowledge.*

A pair of research questions were answered through a questionnaire with the following results based on the evaluation of the feedback obtained after the end of the semester on a sample of 75 first-year students. It can be stated that:

- micro-lessons **help students understand** new content and are sufficient for 72% of students as a basic source of information, 13% disagree with this statement,
- 77% of respondents say that microlearning **helped them practice** educational content, and 12% are negative about the claim,
- 63% of students can accept micro-lessons as the **primary source** of information when learning programming, 15% disagree with the statement,

- automated assessments help students **understand** new content for 75% of students, 13% disagree with this statement,
- automated assessments help students **practice** content and are sufficient for 79% of students, 8% disagree with this statement,

The dependence between students' educational results and their perception of micro-content and automated assessment has not been proven. This finding is quite important because it does not favour micro-lessons or automated assessment only for a selected group of students. Statistically, students with better and students with weaker results perceive it in the same way.

6 Conclusion and Future Work

The next phases of students' education focus on developing advanced skills and knowledge use the education system as an environment whose content and modules can students develop. As part of the verification of the framework concept, the following activities will be implemented in the next part of their study:

- Students will be involved in creating new questions and tasks after completing the introductory courses. Creating new assignments expands the educational content provided by the system. Discussion and analysis of new content will create an area for students better to understand the relationships between elements of their acquired knowledge. Self-expression skills and skills for building code and writing test classes or scripts will also be improved. This activity will be covered by students' obligation to create new tasks and provide tools for their verification within the advanced subjects dedicated to application development. Feedback and quality evaluation of the new elements will be provided on two levels. The first level will be covered by user evaluation, which is a part of all micro-units. It will be a subjective part of the evaluation. The evaluation's objective aspect will be realised by learning analytics tools, which can identify outliers from students' average results for individual types of tasks. If students' success in newly added assignments is significantly higher or significantly lower than the average of works of the same type and level, the assignment will be replaced or removed from the system.
- Involving advanced students in discussions on tasks in introductory programming courses will be a versatile benefit. First, it relieves teachers of the tedious work of answering elementary questions and allows them to tackle more complex tasks. It will bring advanced students new experience from working with less experienced colleagues and ensure their communication skills and patience. Simultaneously, advanced students will learn to accept criticism in case of inconsistent or inaccurate answers. We also anticipate developing relationships between groups of students, which may be used later in study or work for team building. Finally, the benefit for novices will be to get the answer to the question

faster, often in a language that is closer to that of the students' generation than to the teachers' generation.

The final part of the framework is focused on mastering the development environments used by employers and building soft skills in general.

- The most challenging task in the advanced phases defined by the framework is to create new types of activities in the system. A prerequisite for implementing new tasks is a mastery of the technologies by which the system is built. Therefore, students will not create new activities at the beginning of specialised courses but later -- after completing a set of school tasks and at least one complex project. It is assumed that students who complete their education in an educational environment and create content for younger colleagues know the system appropriately. Knowledge of the system functionalities is the first condition for the possibility of its development. In parallel, the possibility of using students' creativity in designing completely new types of activities will be utilised not only for programming but also for other areas forming IT professionals' skills and knowledge (mathematics, artificial intelligence, etc.).
- Developing new applications or upgrading applications to new, more modern environments that will gain a foothold in the application development market in the future is a complex task that requires the involvement of development teams. As part of IT specialists training, courses devoted to team cooperation and communication or leadership skills are usually part of the study. These courses content will be updated and extended by tasks supporting the implemented system's upgrade and development. The tasks will be focused on advancing the existing functionalities to a newer environment or building partial applications using the deployed system's backend infrastructure (e.g., C language lessons, 30 days with Java language). Mobile, web or desktop applications can be created – communication with the backend via the API interface will enable any technology communicating via the HTTP protocol. An alternative design of mobile and web applications has great potential in educational activities in developing new types of activities. Students gain knowledge and practical skills in developing applications in the real world with immediate feedback from users.

Implementing the model and the system described creates a space for further research and verification of many educational theories focused on and verified only within the isolated teaching programming problems. It can be assumed that successful implementation will increase the quality of training of IT specialists.

One of the most important educational system goals is identifying problem students and the early detection of the risk of early course (or study) termination. Therefore, a goal in the near future is to implement algorithms that can detect this group of students and then implement functions and modules that will allow them to overcome the unfavourable situation.

Integration with other education systems and collecting data through other education systems to gain a more accurate and detailed view of the student have been developed and described in (Drlík et al., 2017; Skalka et al., 2020b).

Some ideas for future research based on natural language processing (NLP) focused on automation and artificial intelligence functions have been published in (Skalka, 2018). A valuable technique for preparing new lessons from complex content (e.g., book, articles) is a summary that analyses the content and chooses essential information. The summary techniques can extract whole sentences or unit information from the text, which will become the basis of microlessons or questions. Elements of NLP will create coherent sentences, enabling the generation of meaningful content.

Another logical direction from the collected content is feedback generation for program errors (syntactic and semantic). It is possible to categorise the mistakes and identify the reasons for errors using machine learning methods (Keuning et al., 2018). The data for categorisation is obtained from the submitted correct and incorrect source codes. Submitted source code with errors can be classified, and the system will guide students in correcting the code.

Another exciting element is implementing question-answering methods enabling answer generation based on the educational content, via, for example, questions posted to the student's discussion.

Integrating these ideas requires developing additional software modules based on artificial intelligence tools and prepared and optimised content.

Acknowledgements This research was funded by European Commission under the ERASMUS+ Programme 2018, KA2, grant number: 2018-1-SK01-KA203-046382 "Work-Based Learning in Future IT Professionals Education", Ministry of Education of Slovakia, grant number 004UKF-2-1/2021 "Preparation and development of teaching courses in English with a focus on artificial intelligence in the form of blended-learning", and Ministry of Education of Slovakia, grant number: 2020/8148:34-A1101 "Support for the development of practical skills of UKF students in Nitra".

References

Ala-Mutka, K. M. (2005). A survey of automated assessment approaches for programming assignments. *Computer Science Education, 15*(2). https://doi.org/10.1080/08993400500150747

Baldwin, S. J., & Ching, Y. H. (2020). Guidelines for designing online courses for mobile devices. *TechTrends, 64*(3). https://doi.org/10.1007/s11528-019-00463-6

Bartolomé, A., Castañeda, L., & Adell, J. (2018). Personalisation in educational technology: The absence of underlying pedagogies. *International Journal of Educational Technology in Higher Education, 15*(1). https://doi.org/10.1186/s41239-018-0095-0

Blažeska-Tabakovska, N., Ivanović, M., Klašnja-Milićević, A., & Ivković, J. (2017). Comparison of E-learning personalization systems: Protus and PLeMSys. *International Journal of Emerging Technologies in Learning, 12*(1). https://doi.org/10.3991/ijet.v12i01.6085

Brosig, F., Huber, N., & Kounev, S. (2014). Architecture-level software performance abstractions for online performance prediction. *Science of Computer Programming, 90*. https://doi.org/10.1016/j.scico.2013.06.004

Brusilovsky, P., Malmi, L., Hosseini, R., Guerra, J., Sirkiä, T., & Pollari-Malmi, K. (2018). An integrated practice system for learning programming in python: Design and evaluation.

Research and Practice in Technology Enhanced Learning, 13(1). https://doi.org/10.1186/s41039-018-0085-9

Buffardi, K., & Edwards, S. H. (2014). Introducing CodeWorkout. https://doi.org/10.1145/2538862.2544317.

Carlon, M. K. J., Keerativoranan, N., & Cross, J. S. (2020). Content type distribution and readability of MOOCs. In *L@S 2020 – Proceedings of the 7th ACM conference on learning @ Scale*. Retrieved from https://doi.org/10.1145/3386527.3405950.

Çetin, M., & Demircan, H. Ö. (2020). Empowering technology and engineering for STEM education through programming robots: A systematic literature review. *Early Child Development and Care*. https://doi.org/10.1080/03004430.2018.1534844

Chauhan, A. (2014). Massive Open Online Courses (MOOCS): Emerging trends in assessment and accreditation. *Digital Education Review*. https://doi.org/10.1344/der.2014.25.7-17

Chen, H. M., Chen, W. H., & Lee, C. C. (2018). An automated assessment system for analysis of coding convention violations in Java programming assignments*. *Journal of Information Science and Engineering, 34*(5). https://doi.org/10.6688/JISE.201809_34(5).0006

Crow, T., Luxton-Reilly, A., & Wuensche, B. (2018). Intelligent tutoring systems for programming education: A systematic review. In *ACM International conference proceeding series*. Retrieved from https://doi.org/10.1145/3160489.3160492.

Drlik, M., & Munk, M. (2019). Understanding time-based trends in stakeholders' choice of learning activity type using predictive models. *IEEE. Access, 7*. https://doi.org/10.1109/ACCESS.2018.2887057

Drlík, M., Švec, P., Kapusta, J., Munk, M., Noskova, T., Pavlova, T., et al. (2017). Identification of differences in university e-environment between selected EU and non-EU countries using knowledge mining methods: Project IRNet case study. *International Journal of Web Based Communities, 13*(2). https://doi.org/10.1504/IJWBC.2017.084416

Fernández Alemán, J. L. (2011). Automated assessment in a programming tools course. *IEEE Transactions on Education, 54*(4). https://doi.org/10.1109/TE.2010.2098442

Ferretti, L., Marchetti, M., & Colajanni, M. (2017). Verifiable delegated authorization for user-centric architectures and an OAuth2 implementation. In *Proceedings – International computer software and applications conference* (Vol. 2). Retrieved from https://doi.org/10.1109/COMPSAC.2017.260.

Halvoník, D., & Kapusta, J. (2019). Identifying problematic e-courses content based on students behaviour. In *Lecture notes in electrical engineering* (Vol. 489). Retrieved from https://doi.org/10.1007/978-3-319-75605-9_27.

Halvoník, D., & Kapusta, J. (2020). Framework for E-learning materials optimization. *International Journal of Emerging Technologies in Learning, 15*(11). https://doi.org/10.3991/IJET.V15I11.12721

Hug, T. (2005). Microlearning: A new pedagogical challenge. In *Proceedings of microlearning conference 2005*.

Johnston, T. (2015). Lessons from Moocs: Video lectures and peer assessment. *Academy of Educational Leadership Journal, 19*(2).

Kabathova, J., & Drlik, M. (2021). Towards predicting student's dropout in university courses using different machine learning techniques. *Applied Sciences (Switzerland), 11*(7). https://doi.org/10.3390/app11073130

Keuning, H., Jeuring, J., & Heeren, B. (2018). A systematic literature review of automated feedback generation for programming exercises. *ACM Transactions on Computing Education, 19*(1). https://doi.org/10.1145/3231711

Liebenberg, M., & Jarke, M. (2020). Information systems engineering with digital shadows: Concept and case studies: An exploratory paper. In *Lecture notes in computer science (including subseries lecture notes in artificial intelligence and lecture notes in bioinformatics)* (Vol. 12127 LNCS). Retrieved from https://doi.org/10.1007/978-3-030-49435-3_5.

Moon, J., Do, J., Lee, D., & Choi, G. W. (2020). A conceptual framework for teaching computational thinking in personalized OERs. *Smart Learning Environments, 7*(1). https://doi.org/10.1186/s40561-019-0108-z

Morze, N., Varchenko-Trotsenko, L., Terletska, T., & Smyrnova-Trybulska, E. (2021). Implementation of adaptive learning at higher education institutions by means of Moodle LMS. In *Journal of physics: Conference series* (Vol. 1840). Retrieved from https://doi.org/10.1088/1742-6596/1840/1/012062.

Rodríguez-del-Pino, J. C., Rubio-Royo, E., & Hernández-Figueroa, Z. (2012). A virtual programming lab for moodle with automatic assessment and anti-plagiarism features. *Conference on E-Learning, E-Business, entreprise information systems, & E-Government.*

Sharma, R., Banati, H., & Bedi, P. (2012). Adaptive content sequencing for E-learning courses using ant colony optimization. In *Advances in intelligent and soft computing* (Vol. 131 AISC). Retrieved from https://doi.org/10.1007/978-81-322-0491-6_53.

Silva, T. R., Hak, J. L., & Winckler, M. (2017). A behavior-based ontology for supporting automated assessment of interactive systems. In *Proceedings – IEEE 11th international conference on semantic computing, ICSC 2017*. Retrieved from https://doi.org/10.1109/ICSC.2017.73.

Skalka, J. (2018). Data processing methods in the development of the microlearning-based framework for teaching programming languages. *Divai 2018: 12th international scientific conference on distance learning in applied informatics*. Retrieved from https://publons.com/publon/18895954.

Skalka, J., & Drlik, M. (2018a). Conceptual framework of microlearning-based training mobile application for improving programming skills. *Advances in Intelligent systems and computing* (Vol. 725). Retrieved from https://doi.org/10.1007/978-3-319-75175-7_22.

Skalka, J., & Drlik, M. (2018b). Priscilla – Proposal of system architecture for programming learning and teaching environment. *IEEE international conference on application of information and communication technologies*. Retrieved from https://publons.com/publon/27387754.

Skalka, J., & Drlik, M. (2020). Automated assessment and microlearning units as predictors of at-risk students and students' outcomes in the introductory programming courses. *Applied Sciences (Switzerland), 10*(13). https://doi.org/10.3390/app10134566

Skalka, J., Drlik, M., & Obonya, J. (2019). Automated assessment in learning and teaching programming languages using virtual learning environment. *Proceedings of ieee global engineering education conference (EDUCON2017)*. Retrieved from https://doi.org/10.1109/EDUCON.2019.8725127.

Skalka, J., Benko, Ľ., Boryczka, M., Landa, J., & Rodríguez-del-Pino, J. C. (2020a). *Java fundamental*. Retrieved from https://doi.org/10.17846/2020-java1.

Skalka, J., Drlik, M., Obonya, J., & Capay, M. (2020b). Architecture proposal for micro-learning application for learning and teaching programming courses. In *IEEE global engineering education conference, EDUCON* (Vol. 2020–April). Retrieved from https://doi.org/10.1109/EDUCON45650.2020.9125407.

Skalka, J., Drlik, M., Benko, L., Kapusta, J., Del Pino, J. C. R., Smyrnova-Trybulska, E., et al. (2021). Conceptual framework for programming skills development based on microlearning and automated source code evaluation in virtual learning environment. *Sustainability (Switzerland), 13*(6). https://doi.org/10.3390/su13063293

Smyrnova-Trybulska, E., Morze, N., Kommers, P., Zuziak, W., & Gladun, M. (2017). Selected aspects and conditions of the use of robots in STEM education for young learners as viewed by teachers and students. *Interactive Technology and Smart Education, 14*(4). https://doi.org/10.1108/ITSE-04-2017-0024

Vesin, B., Mangaroska, K., & Giannakos, M. (2018). Learning in smart environments: User-centered design and analytics of an adaptive learning system. *Smart learning. Environments, 5*(1). https://doi.org/10.1186/s40561-018-0071-0

Microlearning as an Educational Technology: Information Requests and Bibliometric Analysis

Olena Kuzminska, Nataliia Morze, and Eugenia Smyrnova-Trybulska

1 Introduction

Digital technologies are not only changing our lives but also our traditions, particularly those related to communication and learning. According to Digital 2021: Global Overview Report, a user of modern gadgets spends more than 4 h a day on a smartphone, and a user of social networks spends 2 h and 25 min every day on these platforms (Digital 2021: Global Overview Report). Most young people use TikTok, which contains entertaining content. It is easier for company employees to spend 10–20 min a day on training than to spend a few days on training. Students use more videos and infographics to learn the basics of a given subject. Most Internet users do not read large texts but watch up to 10 min of video (Digital 2021: Global Overview Report). All these features are related to micro-learning technologies, which has become one of the most popular pedagogical trends, especially during the introduction of e-learning (Alqurashi, 2017).

Microlearning, as a set of educational technologies defines three main characteristics (Buchem & Hamelmann, 2010): short duration of units of educational content; focus on a specific learning outcome, content granulation; multiformat and multiplatform. The peculiarities of the implementation of microlearning include

O. Kuzminska
Faculty of Information Technologies, National University of Life and Environmental Sciences of Ukraine, Kyiv, Ukraine
e-mail: o.kuzminska@nubip.edu.ua

N. Morze
Borys Grinchenko Kyiv University, Kyiv, Ukraine
e-mail: n.morze@kubg.edu.ua

E. Smyrnova-Trybulska (✉)
Department of Humanistic Education, University of Silesia in Katowice, Katowice, Poland
e-mail: esmyrnova@us.edu.pl

E. Smyrnova-Trybulska et al. (eds.), *Microlearning*,
https://doi.org/10.1007/978-3-031-13359-6_2

(Pandurov, 2021): the division of educational materials into micro-modules of 5–10 min, which uses modern digital tools and technologies in the process of mastery, the student goes through phases of reflection, processing and evaluation of data and information. The latter makes it possible to gain knowledge faster and respond to changing educational requirements (flexibility); to study at a convenient time and convenient place (mobility); maintain motivation and involvement in learning (simplicity, short time, confidence); improving learning ability and performance (Wang et al., 2021). As MarketsandMarket forecasts that the global microlearning market will grow by $2.7 billion by 2024 (Churbanova, 2021), this technology can be confidently attributed to current educational trends.

Although micro-learning was mainly used in the corporate sector via nonacademic providers and non-formal education, in particular on MEP platforms, the COVID-19 outbreak highlighted the need to provide quality university education in uncertain times, especially considering the form of educational organization (Gill et al., 2020). The flexibility of microcredentials—which can be offered online, in person, or hybrid models combining in-person and online instruction—may also be a contributing factor to the growing microlearning trend in HEI (EDUCAUSE Horizon Report is a registered trademark of EDUCAUSE, 2021), as evidenced by some successful practices (Bannister et al., 2020) within various industries (technical, educational, engineering, etc.).

A good example of the practical implementation of microlearning as an educational technology is the FITPED project (www.fitped.eu). "The project was focus[ed] on activities which support innovative methods and pedagogical approaches, as well as develop digital educational resources and tools. Applied approaches can be considered innovative because they have not been researched yet in detail" (Drlik et al., 2019). The project researchers stressed that „an implemented educational model was utilized [as one of] the positive features of microlearning, [along with] automated programming code assessment, interactivity and immediate feedback. Consequently, the innovative strategy based on the application of the WBL approach to the advanced educational topics was applied" (p. 13).

It should be noted that any scientific knowledge has not only substantive but also methodological content, as it is associated with a critical review of the existing conceptual framework, prerequisites and approaches to the interpretation of the material being studied. For this purpose, in particular, the methods of bibliometric analysis are used (Wormell, 2000).

The purpose of this study—the study is based on the analysis of information needs and scientific publications to determine the state of development of the problem of microlearning as an educational technology and promising areas of further research.

We asked the following research questions:

- What is the trend in the information needs of scientists and educators regarding the concept of microlearning and its use?
- Is the publishing activity of scientists from different countries and organizations on microlearning technologies different?

Task:

1. Carry out a bibliometric analysis to identify trends and patterns of publishing activity on the use of microlearning by scientists from different countries. The obtained quantitative data can be used by researchers to determine the state of development of a particular subject area in general and the following different Research Areas, countries of publication and qualitative analysis of research to determine their effectiveness.
2. To determine the thematic focus of research in a particular subject area of microlearning. The obtained results can be used by both individual researchers and project managers to plan areas for further research.

2 Research Design

In the study, we relied on the methodological foundations of the literature review process as a research method (Creswell, 2014); research on a systematic literature review of personalized learning terms (Shemshack and Spector, 2020), review of the trend of microlearning (Leong et al., 2021); Bibliometric Analysis of COVID-19 across Science and Social Science Research Landscape (Aristovnik et al., 2020), as well as experience using VOSviewer for science mapping (Smyrnova-Trybulska et al., 2018, 2019).

To implement the first task of the study to identify existing trends and patterns in the publishing activity of scientists from different countries, we used the method of bibliographic analysis, which was used both in the context of educational sciences (consider microlearning as an educational technology) and more broadly—in the context of interdisciplinary research, for the following keywords: "microlearning", "micro-learning" and "micro learning".

To determine the dynamics of the studied objects, scientific publications in scientometric databases Scopus (https://www.scopus.com) and Web of Science Core Collection (www.webofknowledge.com) were analyzed. In order to select the most up-to-date and relevant research, it was decided to introduce additional restrictions, namely: articles in periodicals and scientific conference proceedings published over the past 10 years, i.e. from 2010 to 2021. For a more thorough analysis, we searched the fields "TITLE-ABS-KEY" (Scopus) and "Topic" (Web of Science), as well as in the field TITLE, which produced eight data sets. Below are their characteristics.

By searching for prominent keywords in the titles of publications in the Web of Science Core Collection and Scopus, we form two sets: W1 and S1, respectively. Because the Scopus and Web of Science Core Collection web services provide powerful search functionality, two other datasets were created by filtering data from W1 and S1 sets by subject area/category to provide data for microscience analysis in education: W2 as a narrowing of the subject area to the category of Education Educational Research Area, and S2—selection of publications from the Social Sciences Area. The following query was used to select metadata from the Scopus database to form the S2 dataset (given as an example): TITLE (microlearning) OR TITLE (micro-learning) OR TITLE (micro AND learning)) AND (LIMIT-TO, PUBYEAR, 2021) OR LIMIT-TO (PUBYEAR, 2020) OR LIMIT-TO (PUBYEAR, 2019) OR LIMIT-TO (PUBYEAR, 2018) OR LIMIT-TO (PUBYEAR, 2017) OR LIMIT-TO (PUBYEAR, 2016) OR LIMIT-TO (PUBYEAR, 2015) OR LIMIT-TO (PUBYEAR, 2014) OR LIMIT-TO (PUBYEAR, 2013) OR LIMIT-TO (PUBYEAR, 2012) OR LIMIT-TO (PUBYEAR, 2011) OR LIMIT-TO (PUBYEAR, 2010))) AND (LIMIT-TO (PUBSTAGE, "final")) AND (LIMIT-TO (DOCTYPE, "ar") OR LIMIT-TO (DOCTYPE, "cp")) AND (LIMIT-TO) (SUBJAREA, "SOCI")).

The next four groups were formed from sets of publications selected for similar queries, but the search was not by name, but by:

- "Topic" in the Web of Science Core Collection (search query: https://www.webofscience.com/wos/alldb/summary/4659821d-f7aa-4edc-a2c3-bba0806c75f9-010d57a0/relevance/1), resulting in a data set—W3 and its subset W4 containing publications from the Educational Research Area;
- "TITLE-ABS-KEY" in Scopus created a data set S3 and its subset of the Social Sciences Area—S4.

Based on the collected data sets under certain approaches to the quantification of information flows as a method of bibliometric analysis, we determined the dynamics of the studied objects by the time of publication, countries and affiliation of their authors, types of publications, Research Area, open access initiative, etc. This allowed for a comprehensive study of a particular subject area from the standpoint of the effectiveness of the research (evaluated quantitative indicators of publication activity of researchers) and contributed to the transparency and reproducibility of our research. And the reproducibility of the research and the reuse of the obtained results are among the key features of the systematic review of the literature in scientific and business research (Fisch and Block, 2018).

We used science mapping to determine the relationships between objects, their classification, and to study the structure and dynamics of a particular subject area (Smyrnova-Trybulska et al., 2017). The analysis was performed separately for each of the eight datasets using VOSviewer (https://www.vosviewer.com/), the functionality of which allows for clustering and network analysis of bibliometric data.

To prepare data for analysis by VOSviewer, metadata—the results of the selection of data sets of groups W and S were exported from the relevant scientometric databases to files with the extension .txt (Web of Science) and .csv (Scopus).

The co-occurrence method was chosen as the main method of data analysis using VOSviewer as a method of clustering keywords by frequency of use in one work. Thus, thematic clusters are formed from sets of keywords. On "science maps", clusters are marked in different colours, the size of each keyword is determined by the indicator "total link strength", i.e. the strength of the link of this keyword with all others, and the lines reflect the links between two separate keywords (Van Eck et al., 2010; Van Eck & Waltman, 2010). To build scientometric maps (built separately for each of the eight selected data sets W1-W4, S1-S4), we took only those keywords that occur in the sample at least five times (standard "suggestion" VOSviewer) for all sets and additionally for sets W3, W4, S3, S4–15 times, deliberately excluding query terms, because they are present in almost all documents and distort clustering. A comparison of thesauri and analysis of the created maps forms the basis for determining the directions of research (relevant and promising), both in the field of educational sciences and in the context of interdisciplinary research.

3 The Results of the Study

3.1 *Findings Related to the Analysis of Publication Trends of Microlearning*

Analysis of data from sets W1-W4, S1-S4 shows the prevalence of this area in recent years (Table 1): there is a tendency to increase the number of scientific publications indexed in two leading scientometric databases.

Although there is a slight decline in publication activity in 2020 according to the analysis of sets W3 and W4 as well as its subsets, this does not affect the general trend. Moreover, the growing number of citations (Fig. 1) indicates a stable scientific interest in the topic of microlearning.

Moreover, if in the publication (Leong et al., 2021) the authors identified that conference proceedings were the main source of publications for "micro-learning" and on this basis suggested that "micro-learning" is a relatively new topic, the analysis of publications in this study, is a reason to assume that this topic has already been researched more fully, as the number of publications in scientific journals and conference proceedings is about the same: 54% are articles in the set W1, 43%–W2, 67%–W3, 58%–W4, 52%–S1, 48%–S2, 56%–S3, 49%–S4. It should be noted a slight decrease in the percentage of scientific publications in the category of educational sciences, which is observed in the analysis of data selected from both scientometric databases. The latter may indicate a lack of development of this topic as educational technology, as the journal article is usually a more comprehensive and in-depth study than the conference proceedings, or fewer journals indexed in

Table 1 The number of related publications over time

	2010	2011	2012	2013	2014	2015	2016	2017	2018	2019	2020	2021
W1 (582)	12	11	12	23	23	39	67	71	77	89	96	62
S1 (633)	22	16	13	23	25	28	51	55	80	117	129	74
W2(138)	2	2	3	11	1	10	21	20	21	14	21	12
S2 (148)	7	1	3	7	6	10	20	14	14	20	28	18
W3 (9161)	287	349	341	481	538	735	889	980	1172	1404	1321	664
S3 (8643)	301	336	331	426	480	465	643	760	1032	1428	1630	815
W4 (1843)	50	85	69	107	110	181	226	232	236	254	201	92
S4 (1937)	80	90	100	130	124	127	201	173	219	260	309	124

Source: Own research

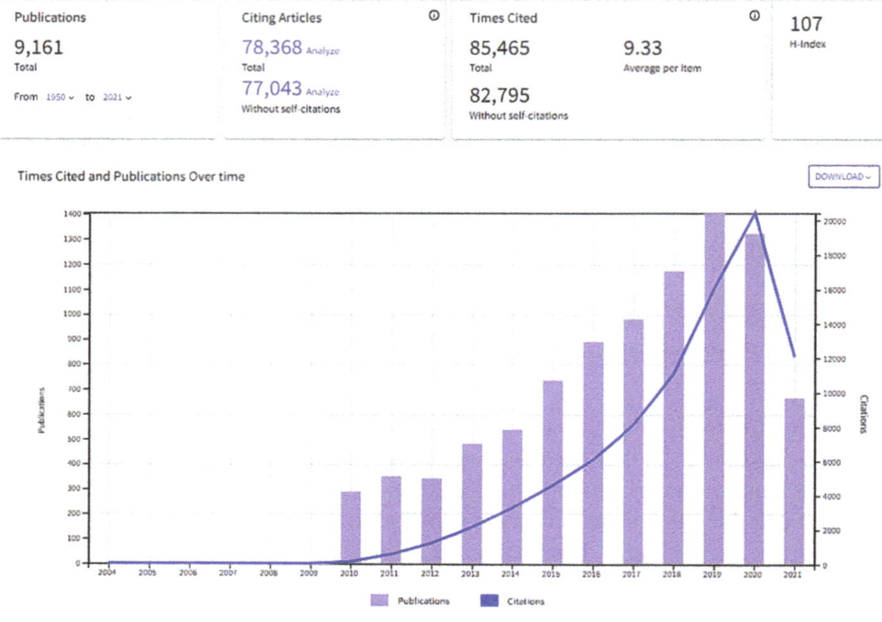

Fig. 1 Report on citation of publications from the data set W3. Source: Own research

Table 2 Distribution of authors Research Areas

	Computer science	Engineering	Education educational research	Social sciences	Mathematics
W1 (582)	66 (11.3%),	185 (21.5%)	138 (23.7%)		
S1 (633)	352 (39.8%)	238 (37.6%)		148 (23.4%)	
W3 (9161)	4494 (49%)	3406 (37.1%)	1843(20.1%)		1754 (19.1%)
S3 (8643)	4220 (48.8%)	2935 (34.0%)		1937 (24.4%)	1195 (13.8%)

Source: Own research

Education Educational Research (Web of Science Core Collection) and Social Sciences (Scopus), compared to other Research Areas. Concerning Research Areas, in addition to the category of educational sciences, we identified the most relevant Areas—those that cover more than 20% of the total number of publications (Table 2). As we can see, the main subject areas are Computer Science, Engineering, and Education Educational Research (Social Sciences), which indicates a comprehensive study of the application and support of microlearning. Moreover, the category of educational sciences is the least represented, which can be considered as a promising area of research. It should also be noted that considering microlearning as an interdisciplinary phenomenon and searching by topic (sets W3, S3), the number of publications in the field of mathematics is approaching 20% of the threshold. This may indicate the high manufacturability of a particular subject area and the actualization of the strengthening of the mathematical apparatus to ensure it.

An analysis of research on the countries of their publication (Table 3) has allowed for the revealing of a number of the countries to which it is necessary to pay primary attention to the qualitative research of experience of the realization of microlearning. Summarizing the contributions of authors (Table 3) who had ten or more publications over a period, the leaders are China and the United States—on average, scientists from each of these countries are the authors of about 20% of all publications in each of our outstanding sets. Other countries account for less than 10% each. Each set contains publications whose authors are from England, and researchers from India and Germany are also actively researching the topic of microlearning. However, with the narrowing of the field of research to educational (social) sciences, there are studies of scientists from the Czech Republic, Spain and Australia (data sets W2, W4). The analysis of the S4 data set is the basis for a more thorough study of the scientific achievements of researchers from Germany as authors of 464 publications (22.4%)—this level of participation is the highest among all countries. On the other hand, it is worth conducting repeated research, as the landscape of scientific publications is very dynamic and it is likely that some of the data we obtained for this study are not systemic.

Understanding the importance of supporting the open access initiative for the development of science, we analyzed the selected data sets by the level of access to publications (Table 4).

In general, there is a tendency for researchers to support the open access initiative. For example, 55% of the publications in the W1 dataset and 62% of the S1 are publicly available, with 42% fully supporting open access (135 of the 320 open access publications in the W1 dataset) and 44% in the S1 dataset, where the open access initiative is supported by the authors of 395 publications, and full openness

Table 3 Distribution of authors by countries

	China	USA	England	Germany	India
W1 (582)	167 (28.694%)	111 (19.072%)	33 (5.670%)	33 (5.670%)	31 (5.326%)
S1 (633)	166 (26.2%)	116 (18.3%)	44 (UK)–7%	39 (6.2%)	36 (5.7%)
W2 (138)	33 (23.9%)	17 (12.3%)	8 (5.8%)	CZ 7 (5.1%)	
S2 (148)	18 (12.2%)	19 (12.8%)	15 (10.1%)	9 (6.1%)	6 (4.1%)
W3 (9161)	2034 (23.3%)	2208 (24,1%)	698 (7,6%)	531(5.8%)	548 (6%)
S3 (8643)	1824 (21.1%)	1970 (22.8%)	694 (8%)	434 (5%)	651 (7.5%)
W4 (1843)	336 (18.2%)	372 (20.2%)	137 (7.4%)	Australia 117 (6.3%)	Spain 106 (5.8%)
S4 (1937)	171 (8.8%)	426 (22.0%)	211 (10.9%)	434 (22.4%)	Australia 116 (6.0%)

Source: Own research

Table 4 The number of related publications over Open Access

	All Open Access	Gold	Hybrid Gold	Bronze	Green
W1 (582)	135	73	16	27	69
S1 (633)	174	68	9	42	102
W2 (138)	20	11	3	6	4
S2 (148)	29	13	1	8	17
W3 (9161)	2632	1287	371	517	1535
S3 (8643)	2633	1037	213	537	1696
W4 (1843)	418	183	72	99	253
S4 (1937)	526	210	58	81	334

Source: Own research

by 174 (Table 3). However, these data do not give a complete picture, because, for example, in the process of analyzing the metadata of the W3 set by Web of Science, the system issued the following message: "6529 record (s) (71.270%) do not contain data in the field being analyzed".

Thus, analyzing publications from different scientometric databases (Tables 3–4) we can conclude the relevance and effectiveness (assessed by quantitative bibliometric indicators) of research on a particular topic, which does not depend on a specific scientometric base or policy of the publisher: also, there are the same general trends in the analysis of different sets of groups W and S. Although there are some "non-critical" differences, their detection in the process of this study may be random.

3.2 *Findings on Thematic Publications Employing VOSviewer*

With the help of VOSviewer, the thematic orientation of publications was studied, which allowed for the building of terminological maps based on terms found in the titles, keywords and annotations of articles from the data sets of groups W and S. For each group separately using VOSviewer tools:

- a keyword analysis was performed, based on the results of which it is possible to assess the intensity of use of one term with others;
- a special thesaurus has been compiled to combine similar terms and eliminate mistakes in the spelling of keywords;
- build a scientific map by keywords (Fig. 2), which highlighted clusters (denoted by different colours), combining key concepts (the size of the circle reflects the frequency in the use of a particular term, its "total link strength") by thematic proximity; within the clusters, the closeness of the connections between the corresponding terms (the closer, the closest) and the different variants of combinations of terms both within the clusters and between them (the width of the lines reflects the so-called "link strength" between pairs of terms).

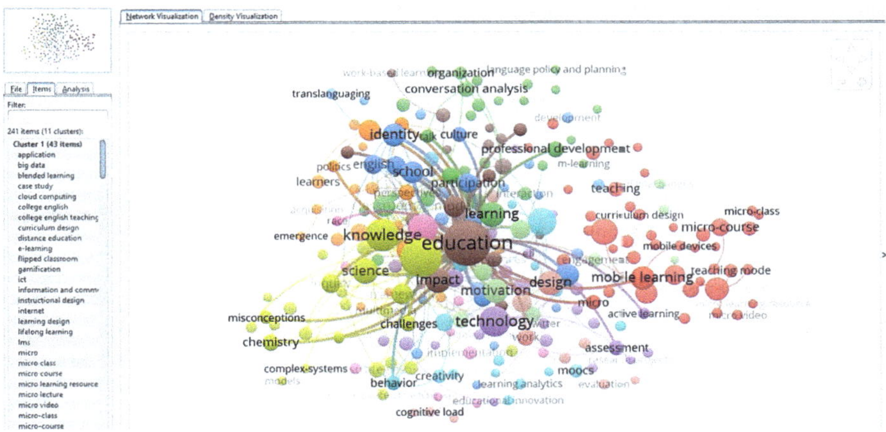

Fig. 2 Visualization of "total link strength" and "link strength" on the example of constructing a map of concepts according to the set W4 (minimum number of occurrences of keyword: 5). Source: Own research

To determine the main directions of research according to publications placed in different scientometric databases (groups of data sets W and S), we analyzed maps based on data from pairs of sets (W1, S1), (W2, S2), (W3, S3) and (W4, S4). In particular, in the field of educational sciences (W2, W4 and S2, S4), an analysis of thesauri shows that the main keywords include e-learning, education, learning systems & technology, information system, learning platforms, deep learning, machine learning, etc. However, the number, composition and capacity of clusters depend on various factors. The following are examples of VOSviewer-built maps and their interpretation. It should be noted that the interpretation of clusters is based on the grouping of keywords, but this distribution is quite conditional because both clusters and terms are interrelated. Moreover, the structure of clusters depends on the selected minimum number of occurrences of keywords for one data set (see Figs. 2 and 3) and the number of keywords on which the map is based for the different sets. For example, to build maps on data sets W4 and S4 according to the same algorithm, thesauri with 4639 and 1057 keywords, respectively, were generated. Accordingly, the frequency of use of certain terms in different publications is different, so, analyzing the terms with the minimum number of occurrences of keyword: 15, we obtained terminological maps with visualization, of which 40 meet the threshold of the 4639 keywords (Fig. 3) and 73 meet the threshold of the 10,057 keywords (Fig. 4), respectively.

An analysis of visualization of the maps built on one query, but from different scientometric databases (Figs. 3 and 4) is the basis for the assumption that the directions of microlearning research in the field of educational sciences, in general, do not depend on the scientometric base, where their results are presented, because the key terms in both samples are identical. A slightly larger number of keywords in set S4 with about the same number of articles in sets W4 and S4 may depend on the

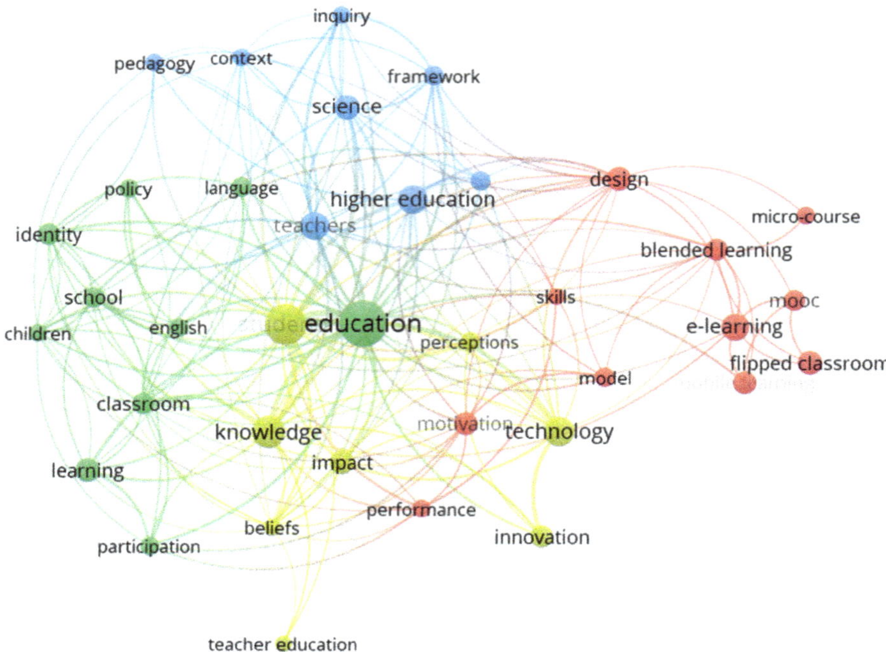

Fig. 3 Visualization of "total link strength" and "link strength" based on the example of constructing a map of concepts according to the set W4 (minimum number of occurrences of keyword: 15)

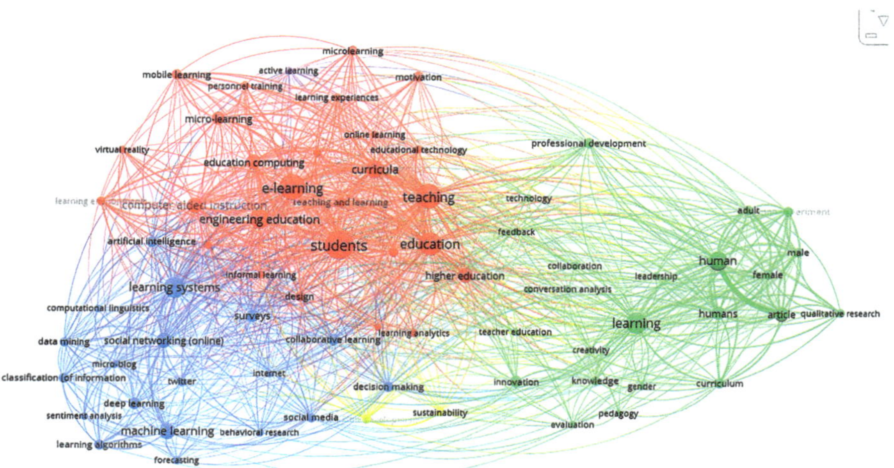

Fig. 4 Visualization of "total link strength" and "link strength" based on the example of constructing a map of concepts according to the set S4 (minimum number of occurrences of keyword: 15)

publisher's terms regarding the number of keywords in each article, the selection of thematic keywords, and so on. The analysis of the formed clusters is the basis for determining the main directions of research on a certain topic because we analyzed only keywords with a high frequency of use.

Despite the difference in the results of mapping data groups W4 and S4 (Figs. 3 and 4), we can identify (with some generalization) three main areas of research in the subject area of microlearning as an educational technology, which can be designated as:

– "Human and knowledge" (yellow cluster in Fig. 3 and green—Fig. 4);
– "Education and learning technology" (red, green, dark blue—Fig. 3, red—Fig. 4);
– "Learning system" (blue—Fig. 4).

It should be noted that the greater focus of publications from the Web of Science Core Collection (Fig. 3) on the study of methodological and psychological-pedagogical research (highlighted by separate clusters of teaching and research in higher education (blue cluster) and secondary (green cluster)) and learning research systems in publications indexed in Scopus (Fig. 4).

To determine the directions of interdisciplinary research in the subject area of microlearning, we compared thematic maps based on a single data set (as an example, consider the data set S3), with filtering according to the identified leading Research Areas (Table 1).

Based on the analysis of relevant visualizations (Figs. 4, 5, 6), we can confirm the assumption that the educational component is the least researched, as evidenced by both the smallest number of selected articles and the number of keywords: we obtained terminological maps with visualization, of which 73 meet the threshold of the 10,057 keywords (Fig. 4), 234 meet the threshold of the 15,382 keywords (Fig. 5) and 241 meet the threshold of the 16,345 keywords (Fig. 6) respectively.

Researchers in the field of Computer Science and Engineering, as related to the technical sciences and engineering, pay attention to ensuring the implementation of microlearning—in Table 5 and Fig. 6, the main clusters are identified, which can be conventionally designated:

– "Artificial Intelligence", which is a combination of red and green clusters (Figs. 5, 6) and partially blue (Fig. 6) and contains the concept of Machine learning, Deep learning (as a set). Machine-learning methods), Learning algorithms, in particular, based on neural networks;
– "Learning system" (Lilac cluster—Fig. 5 and partially red—Fig. 6);
– "Data processing" (yellow cluster—Fig. 5 and partially blue—Fig. 6);
– "Human" (blue cluster—Fig. 5 and Lilac—Fig. 6).

It should be noted that in contrast to the terminological map, which reflects the mapping of microlearning as an educational technology, where all key terms are distributed more or less evenly with a slight "reinforcement" of the terms "e-learning", "student", "teaching" (Fig. 4), in the maps that reflect the research of the technical

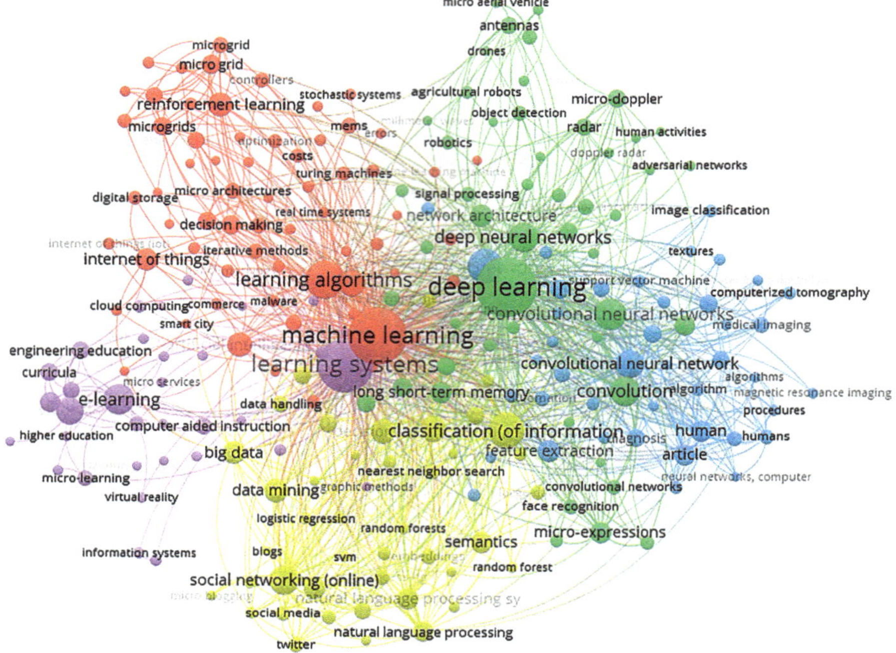

Fig. 5 Visualization of "total link strength" and "link strength" based on the example of constructing a map of concepts according to the set S3 with filtering by Computer Science Research Area (minimum number of occurrences of keyword: 15)

direction (Figs. 5, 6) in the centre of the analysis are the concepts of "machine learning", "deep learning", "learning system".

In general, the presence of clusters of the same name in terminological maps of publications from various Research Areas (Figs. 4, 5, 6), in particular, "Human" and "Learning system", as well as "complementary" categories "Education and learning technology" in the field of education, "Artificial Intelligence" & "Data processing"—in the field of technical sciences and "Network architecture" as a supplement to Engineering) can be interpreted as a comprehensive approach to research and the development of micro-learning as a promising area of modern e-education.

4 Conclusions

Micro-learning technologies have long been the subject of research mainly in the corporate sector and non-formal education. However, in the context of the COVID-19 pandemic and its possible consequences, when uncertainty remains high, the issue of changing the paradigm of education in higher education institutions is relevant. One of the areas is the creation of an improved micro-learning environment to

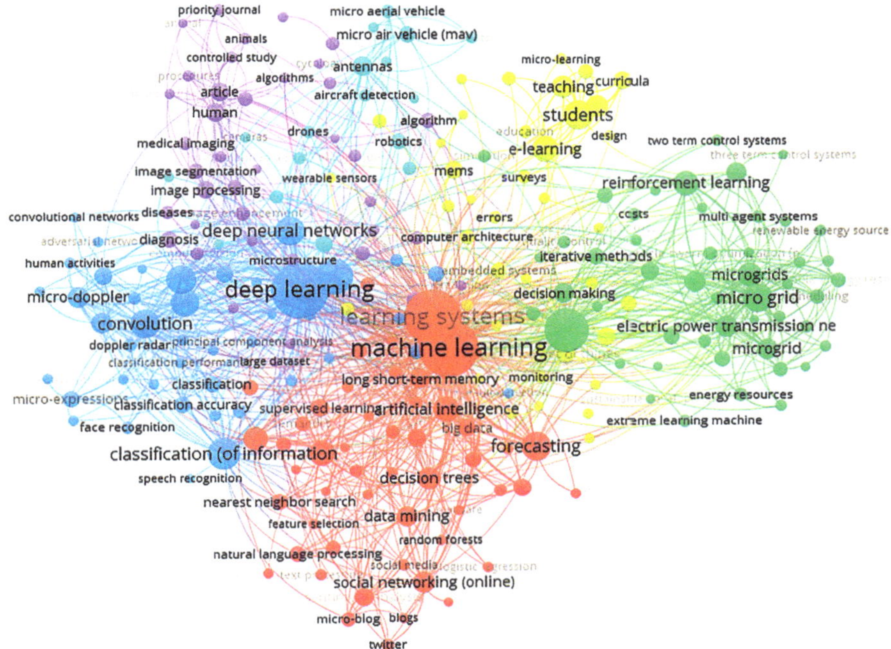

Fig. 6 Visualization of "total link strength" and "link strength" based on the example of constructing a map of concepts according to the set S3 with filtering by Engineering Research Area (minimum number of occurrences of keyword: 15)

Table 5 Symbols of clusters according to the defined Research Areas

Cluster colour	Research area	
	Computer science (Fig. 5)	Engineering (Fig. 6)
Red	Machine learning & learning algorithms	Machine learning & learning systems
Green	Deep learning	Learning algorithms & resources
Lilac	Learning system	Human & Research
Yellow	Classification of information & data processing	
Dark blue	Human & Convolutional neural network	Deep learning & classification of information
Blue		Network architecture

Source: Own Research

ensure the efficiency and effectiveness of teaching and learning, which is preceded by a scientific justification and analysis of the state of development of a particular subject area.

The study was conducted using the method of extensive search in electronic databases. The analysis covered scientific publications for the years 2010–2021, as presented in the abstract and citation databases Scopus and Web of Science Core Collection.

The results of the analysis of the formed samples by types of inquiries, years of publication, countries of origin of the authors, branches of research, as well as the openness of access are presented in the above tables and diagrams. Applied refinements (period, databases, key queries, search categories, etc.) limit its scope and facilitate processing, but somewhat narrow the analyzed area. In general, there is a tendency for researchers to support the open access initiative and, consequently, to expand the scientific and educational community to the results of research on a wide range of issues related to micro-learning.

As a result of bibliometric analysis and mapping, the growth of scientific interest in the problem of the effective implementation of microlearning in three main areas: Computer Science, Engineering and Education Research (Social Sciences), which indicates the consideration of microlearning as an interdisciplinary phenomenon.

For a qualitative study of the experience of microlearning, it is advisable to pay attention to the research of scientists from the United States and China, because they are the authors of approximately 20% of all publications in each of the defined sets of bibliometric data. At the same time, research on the application of micro-learning as an educational technology, i.e. with the narrowing of the field of research to educational (social) sciences, is more actively conducted in universities within the Czech Republic, Spain and Australia.

Based on an analysis of the visualizations of the terminological maps, the main directions of interdisciplinary research of microlearning are revealed, namely: "Human and knowledge", "Education and learning technology", "Learning system", "Data processing", "Artificial Intelligence". At the same time, the educational component is the least researched, i.e. technologies for the development and creation of channels for the delivery of micro-learning content attract more attention from Computer Science and Engineering researchers. Therefore, it is necessary to motivate teachers and experts in the field of Education Educational Research (Social Sciences) to conduct additional research and seek solutions to create a reliable model of implementation of micro-learning in educational institutions that will meet the expectations of teachers and students. We can distinguish the most important educational impact of the FITPED project—namely, new methodologies and modernized didactical approaches for IT topics as investigated by the project, were proposed and evaluated. Improved evaluation methods based on automation was used across the whole educational model (Drlik et al., 2019). Some important project results are presented in other chapters of the current book. The project has not only an IT area of implementation, but could develop in the several interdisciplinary fields.

References

Alqurashi, E. (2017). Microlearning: A pedagogical approach for technology integration [special issue]. *Turkish Online Journal of Educational Technology, 2017*, 942–947.

Aristovnik, A., Ravšelj, D., & Umek, L. (2020). A Bibliometric Analysis of COVID-19 across Science and Social Science Research Landscape. *Sustainability, 12(21), 9132. MDPI AG.* https://doi.org/10.3390/su12219132

Bannister, J., Neve, M., & Kolanko, C. (2020). Increased educational reach through a microlearning approach: Can higher participation translate to improved outcomes? *Journal of European Continuing Medical Education (CME), 9*, 1. https://doi.org/10.1080/21614083.2020.1834761

Buchem, I., & Hamelmann, H. (2010). Microlearning: A strategy for ongoing professional development. *eLearning Papers, 21*(7), 1–15.

Churbanova K. (2021). *Do you need to train your employees?* Think about this new online education format Retrieved from https://rb.ru/opinion/microlearning/

Creswell, J. W. (2014). *Research design: Qualitative, quantitative, and mixed methods approaches* (4th ed.). Sage.

Digital. (2021). *Global overview report*. Retrieved from https://datareportal.com/reports/digital-2021-global-overview-report

Drlik, M., Smyrnova-Trybulska, E. & Szczurek, A. (2019) New IT project. *University newspaper, 6*(266). Retrieved March 12–13, 2019, from http://gazeta.us.edu.pl/node/424333

EDUCAUSE. Horizon Report is a registered trademark of EDUCAUSE (2021). Retrieved from https://library.educause.edu/-/media/files/library/2021/4/2021hrteachinglearning.pdf?#page=12&la=en&hash=64CACBDA4DAC0F6158951941AD2A8952A9A81100

Fisch, C., & Block, J. (2018). Six tips for your (systematic) literature review in business and management research. *Management Review Quarterly., 68*, 103–106. https://doi.org/10.1007/s11301-018-0142-x

Gill, A.S., Irwin, D. S., Ng, R. Y. K, Towey, D., Wang T., & Zhang, Y. (2020) The future of teaching post-COVID-19: Microlearning in product design education. *2020 IEEE international conference on teaching, assessment, and learning for engineering (TALE)* (pp. 780–785) https://doi.org/10.1109/TALE48869.2020.9368322.

Leong, K., Sung, A., Au, D., & Blanchard, C. (2021). A review of the trend of microlearning. *Journal of Work-Applied Management, 13*(1), 88–102. https://doi.org/10.1108/JWAM-10-2020-0044

Pandurov M. (2021). *10 incredible microlearning trends shaping 2021*. Retrieved from https://markinstyle.co.uk/microlearning-trends/

Shemshack, A., & Spector, J. M. (2020). A systematic literature review of personalized learning terms. *Smart Learning Environment, 7*(33). https://doi.org/10.1186/s40561-020-00140-9

Smyrnova-Trubulska, E., Morze, N., & Kuzminska, O. (2019) Networking through scholarly communication: Case IRNet project. In E. Smyrnova-Trybulska, P. Kommers, N. Morze, J. Malach (Eds.), *Universities in the networked society. Cultural diversity and digital competences in learning communities. critical studies of education* (vol. 10). Springer.

Smyrnova-Trybulska, E., Morze, N., Kuzminska, O. & Kommers, P. (2017), Bibliometric science mapping as a popular trend: Chosen examples of visualisation of international research network results. In P. Kommers, T. Issa, P. Isaías, & A. Hol (Eds.), *Proceedings of the international conferences on educational technologies 2017* (ICEduTech 2017) Western Sydney University, Sydney, Australia 11–13 December, 2017 (pp. 3–11) ISBN: 978–989-8533-71-5.

Smyrnova-Trybulska, E., Morze, N., Kuzminska, O., & Kommers, P. (2018). Mapping and visualization: Selected examples of international research networks. *Journal of Information, Communication and Ethics in Society, 16*(4), 381–400.

Van Eck, N. J., & Waltman, L. (2010). Software survey: VOSviewer, a computer program for bibliometric mapping. *Scientometrics, 84*, 523–538. https://doi.org/10.1007/s11192-009-0146-3

Van Eck, N. J., Waltman, L., Dekker, R., & van den Berg, J. (2010) A comparison of two techniques for bibliometric mapping: Multidimensional scaling and VOS. *Journal of the American Society for Information Science and Technology, 61*(12), 2405–2416. https://doi.org/10.1002/asi.21421

Wang, T., Towey, D., Ng, R. Y., et al. (2021). Towards post-pandemic transformative teaching and learning. *Springer Nature: SN Computer Science, 2*(271). https://doi.org/10.1007/s42979-021-00663-z

Wormell, I. (2000). Bibliometric analysis of the welfare state topic. *Scientometrics, 43*(2), 203–236. https://doi.org/10.1023/A:1005696722014

Guidance for Introductory Programming Courses Creation Using Microlearning and Automated Assessment

Ján Skalka, Lubomir Benko, Martin Drlik, Michal Munk, and Peter Svec

1 Introduction

The challenges for changing the work process brought by the COVID-19 crisis are focused on flexibility and autonomy of employees, quality of working time, work intensity and workload, and the line between work and home activities (Eurofound, 2020). These changes have also accelerated the IT (information technologies) trends, where automation and the digitalisation of society bring many new tasks and requirements for employees. The need for staff with IT skills, programs and scripts understanding, and finally, the ability to write source code, has been fully demonstrated during the suppression of activities of everyday working life and their transfer to homework (Kogan et al., 2020; Gibson et al., 2020)

Universities have managed to adapt education to a virtual environment at various levels. The fast adaption was administered by those institutions that implemented the distance form of education in the past or had prepared sufficiently robust electronic support for education (Skalka et al., 2012, 2013; Saxena et al., 2021). The virtual learning environment (VLE) built within the FITPED project (ERASMUS + Program 2018, KA2, project number: 2018–1-SK01-KA203–046382 – Work-Based Learning in Future IT Professionals Education) enabled an effective and smooth transition from blended learning to complete online education. Today's e-learning is not only a tool for isolating students at home, but MOOCs are the best choice for educating large numbers of students with different levels of knowledge and skills.

VLE named Priscilla (Skalka & Drlik, 2018) is based on an educational framework (Skalka et al., 2021) combining primary microlearning activities with an automatic evaluation of programs using automated assessment (AA). It integrates the

---

J. Skalka (✉) · L. Benko · M. Drlik · M. Munk · P. Svec
Constantine the Philosopher University in Nitra, Nitra, Slovakia
e-mail: jskalka@ukf.sk; lbenko@ukf.sk; mdrlik@ukf.sk; mmunk@ukf.sk; psvec@ukf.sk

E. Smyrnova-Trybulska et al. (eds.), *Microlearning*,
https://doi.org/10.1007/978-3-031-13359-6_3

standards obtained by research carried out within international teams in recent years (Svec et al., 2017; Drlík et al., 2017). The environment is designed for optimal teaching of programming languages using adapted types of activities and user interface design. Within the school year 2020/2021, it was used by around 1500 users registered in more than 20 training courses that covered eight programming languages.

Mastering the first programming language is a very challenging task for every user (Vivian et al., 2014). At present, research is most often focused on predicting behaviour, educational failure/success, or user categorisation in introductory programming courses (Skalka & Drlik, 2020; Hawlitschek et al., 2020; Çetinkaya & Baykan, 2020). However, many authors point out that the primary prerequisite for mastering and thinking in a programming language is precisely prepared educational content (Berglund & Lister, 2010; Iqbal Malik & Coldwell-Neilson, 2017).

The preparation of the structure and content of the course using microlearning and AA has many aspects.

The article aims to define the rules of content creation based on the practical implementation and pilot use of the introductory course in programming in the Java programming language. The article describes the structure, content creation and results of the pilot use of the course to identify and generalise the principles of content creation for programming courses using microlearning, AA and providing immediate feedback to students.

The article has the following structure. The next chapter presents the complexity of teaching programming and the need to provide each student with their own way of advancing and achieving the educational goal. The third chapter presents the form and structure of the Java programming course, which is a pilot course for the use of the Pricilla system in teaching and which was used during the COVID pandemic period. This chapter also includes a description of the implementation of the course at CPU in Nitra. The discussion summarises the results of the pilot deployment and, based on the experience and feedback from students, generalises the principles of creating educational courses based on microlearning and AA.

2 The Complexity of the Programming Learning

Learning programming is a very complex activity. Student must understand and master the way of thinking, which is often different from the thinking to which he is accustomed in everyday life. During getting acquainted with "machine thinking," the student goes through several levels of understanding until he becomes an independent analyst and programmer in a specific programming language. Based on the summaries of areas of knowledge and skills domains (Winslow, 1996; Ganapathi et al., 2011; Castellanos et al., 2017), the following levels of students' ability to program were identified:

- Problem domain understanding (focused on problem description using natural language or metalanguage; the need to use commands of a programming language is not necessary):
  - understanding the definition of problems expressed in natural language,
  - understanding the goal of a solution expressed in natural language,
  - understanding the description of the solution in natural language,
  - problem transformation from natural language to a limited area of metalanguage (not in programming language yet),
  - solutions obtained from metalanguage transformation to the natural language;
  - discuss a problem, explain the solution procedures.
- Programming language domain understanding (focused on understanding syntax and semantic):
  - understanding commands of programming language and their use,
  - understanding programming language fundamentals (variable, input, output),
  - knowing parameters and syntax of fundamental commands,
  - understanding semantic of algorithmic structures (usually sequence, conditions, cycles),
  - knowledge to find suitable command need for the realisation of necessary activity.
- Transformation problem to the programming language and data structure domain:
  - understanding the concept of data structures,
  - knowledge of main data structures implemented in language and their use,
  - mental transformation of the problem to programming language design,
  - ability to use programming structures with a combination of data structures to solve the defined assignments,
  - selection of suitable problem-solving strategies.
- Source code understanding domain:
  - the ability to read foreign code,
  - verification of correctness and identification of errors in source code,
  - understanding boundary and unsolvable inputs,
  - manual testing and repairing code using checkpoint and output partial results.
- Subroutines using to make a program more understandable and more effective:
  - understanding why and how to divide the program into smaller parts,
  - understanding subroutines, parameters and types of parameters,
  - to make the first contact with the effectiveness of programs (not only) using subroutines.

- Use of development tools:
  - to use pre-compiler and help in the development environment,
  - understanding why and how to debug programs,
  - the ability to build applications,
  - the ability to program with a focus on performance and memory.
- Deep understanding (join of programming and problem-solving) domain:
  - experience of problem-solving application (optimisation, specialisation, abstraction),
  - good-practice adoption (design patterns, code writing, documentation building).
- Software development domain:
  - ability to select powerful and appropriate technology,
  - skills in the management of the team,
  - development planning and team performance calculating,
  - problem-solving skills building and using.

The presented complexity of the programming learning process is the reason for educational failures, student frustration and lack of motivation. Therefore, it is necessary to offer students different ways to achieve the goal.

The Matrix Taxonomy, presented in (Fuller et al., 2007), describes the framework for assessing learners' computer science and engineering capabilities. The taxonomy is based on the complexity of intrinsic characteristics of computer science and covers the above requirements of students' ability to program. The model reflects the fact that understanding the program and the ability to write a code independently are two semi-independent capabilities. Students who acquired the ability to read source code may not necessarily be able to write new programs. Likewise, the ability to write program code does not mean the ability to identify errors, debug programs and correct bugs. Visualising these facts takes the form of the two-dimensional matrix to represent the two separate ranges of competencies: the ability to understand and interpret an existing product (program code) and design and build a new program.

Different students use different "learning paths". Some students get the skills to read and debug code at first, and other students build skills in writing code instead before they skills to read or debug foreign ideas. Figure 1 presents different learning paths and mapped programming activities of various groups of students.

Building programming skills for university students in the "classic" way often encounters a barrier build by modern technologies. Currently, students reject passive time-consuming activities and prefer immediate testing, verification, and rapid application of acquired knowledge and skills.

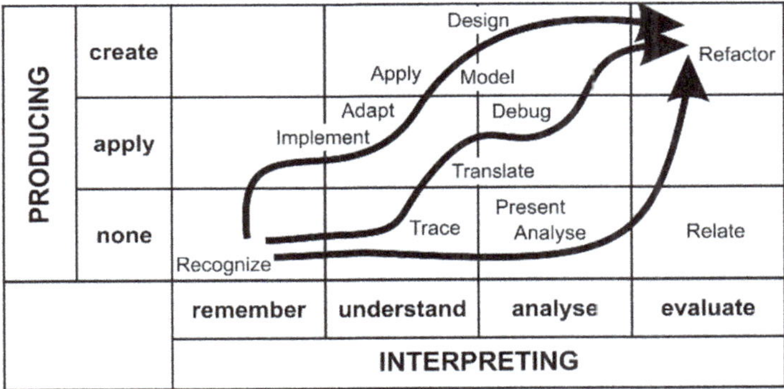

Fig. 1 Different learning paths of programming skills learning and building (Fuller et al., 2007)

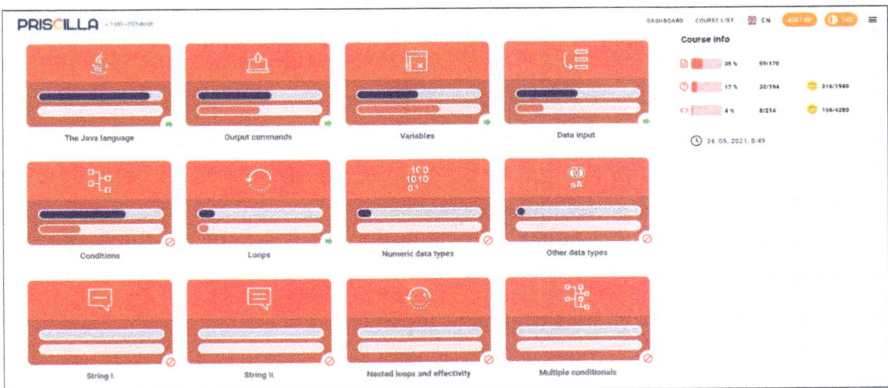

Fig. 2 Java course chapters in Priscilla system

3 Java Course in Priscilla

The Java programming language course is an introductory programming course for students of applied informatics at the University of Constantine the Philosopher in Nitra. Its full deployment in the Priscilla system was realised in the winter semester of 2020/2021.

Following the complexity of programming learning, the course structure was designed to gradually pass through the individual levels of skills and knowledge and deepen them in a spiral. The design of this structure is based on several years of experience and tuning of topics, their scope and examples published in (Capay et al., 2017; Skalka et al., 2019).

The course is divided into chapters, and then each chapter is divided into lessons. Every lesson contains 5–10 pairs of content micro-lessons and a control question or series of programs. A visual representation of the part of the course content is available in Fig. 2.

3.1 Course Components

The course components are defined based on the functionalities of the Priscilla system, which allows combining microlearning content, microlearning tasks and AA assignments. The content is built using the following types of micro-lessons:

- microlearning content,
- short answer or result of the program activity,
- selection of one correct answer from several options,
- multiple selections of multiple answers from multiple choices,
- filling the code in the empty field,
- supplement the code by choosing from the options (correct and incorrect),
- arrangement of code or lines/paragraphs of text.

The example of question/task answering is presented in Fig. 3.

Although the system allows the creation of program tasks evaluated by xUnit libraries, in the case of the introductory course, program assignments based on output control for a given series of inputs (I/O approach) will suffice.

The assignment consists of three main parts:

- description of the assignment with a precisely specified shape of input and output,
- preprepared code – in the introductory programs, it is advisable to insert comments defining the expected lines of code,
- test cases – defining the inputs for which the program will be tested and the expected outputs assigned to them.

A typical example of program assignment is presented in Fig. 4.

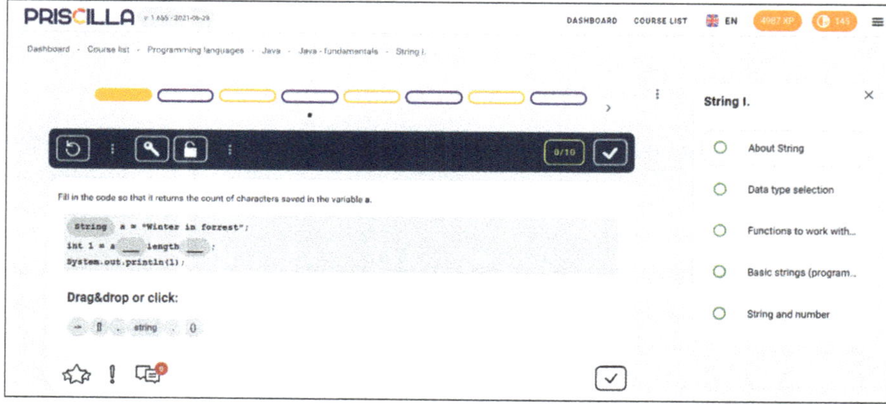

Fig. 3 Question type 6 – selection of missing code snippets

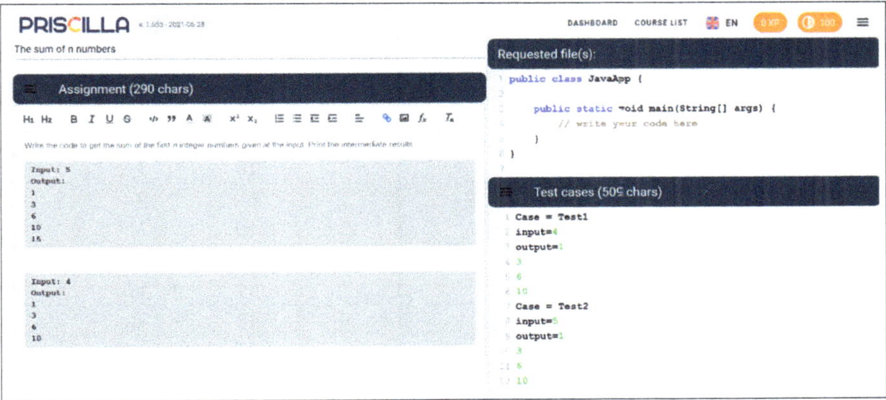

Fig. 4 Preparation of a program entry in the administrator interface

3.2 Course Structure

For some students, the course is the very first contact with programming. For this reason, it is necessary to start the course with an explanation of the concept of commands, variables, control structures and data types in the introductory parts. The second part is focused on the use of cycles and strings. The emphasis is placed on developing algorithmic and programming thinking, efficiency and debugging of code in this section. The course closes with multiple branches, arrays, random numbers, and working with files.

The detailed structure of the course with individual chapters and their scope is shown in Table 1.

After an introductory acquaintance with terminology and fundamental concepts, chapters focus on problem-solving/writing programs. The sum of tasks and programs achieves the principle of active study and minimises the passive activities of the student. Table 1 shows the gradual increase in the number of program assignments at the expense of microlearning tasks.

3.3 Course Students

The course is intended for students of the first year of the university study program of applied informatics. The pilot study population consists of 83 students aged 19–23 years of the first year of the study in the winter semester of 2020/2021 at Constantine the Philosopher University in Nitra (Slovakia).

Teaching during the pandemic period took place in the first 2 weeks in a face-to-face form, then moved to the virtual space. The task for the students was to complete the defined chapters within the week. Every chapter consists of micro-content and

Table 1 Java course structure – chapters and quantity of task types

Chapter name	Lessons	Microlessons		Programs
		Content	Task	
The Java language	2	10	10	0
Output commands	2	5	5	4
Variables	2	6	10	3
Data input	2	3	6	9
Conditions	3	8	10	3
Loops	5	14	15	12
Numeric data types	6	17	19	17
Other data types	4	13	18	4
String I.	5	18	20	4
String II.	5	10	10	22
Nested loops and effectivity	4	3	5	25
Multiple conditionals	2	5	5	11
Exceptions	2	6	6	4
Arrays	6	15	18	15
Array processing	4	6	6	23
2D arrays	4	13	14	16
Files	4	17	17	10
Summary	**62**	**169**	**194**	**182**

program code writing. Students obtained basic information through online lectures (usually 90 minutes per week), from which a video recording was made, and they could visit optional consultations. As part of practical exercises and seminars (approximately 90 + 90 minutes per week), students solved selected tasks with the tutor and discussed tasks that they could not solve independently within a week. The content of the presented course covered half of the semester (approx. 6 weeks).

After completing the course, a test aimed at verifying students' ability to write independent programs followed. The test contained four simple AA tasks that had to be solved in 100 minutes. The tasks were randomly generated from the prepared series. The examples of the assignment are presented in Fig. 5.

The test took place in a special mode. Due to the high risk of using unauthorised support materials and plagiarism, all students wrote the test simultaneously in 10 parallel virtual rooms. Because this form of ensuring objective evaluation was used for the first time, students had no experience with its violation. The distribution of test results approximately corresponded to the distribution in previous years. The test results and their distribution is presented in Fig. 6.

The evaluation of the whole course is a combination of:

- results of work in a virtual environment,
- success in tests (written twice during the semester),
- an exam test aimed at understanding the source code
- and an oral answer from the content of lectures.

1. Write a code that will calculate the volume and surface of a block given by three float values a, b, c. Do not round the result.
    - Equation for volume: a * b * b
    - Equation for surface: 2 * (a * b + a * c + b * c)
2. Write a code that will determine how many even and odd digits are contained in a given number.
3. Write a code that will determine how many of an array of 20 numbers (given from the input) are below average, above average and equal to the average.
4. Write a code that will save numbers into an array. The numbers are given from the input and are separated by commas. The numbers should be sorted and then written out to separate the numbers, and after the last number is a dot. After that, write out the minimum and maximum from the numbers.

Fig. 5 Examples of four test assignments in various levels of difficulty

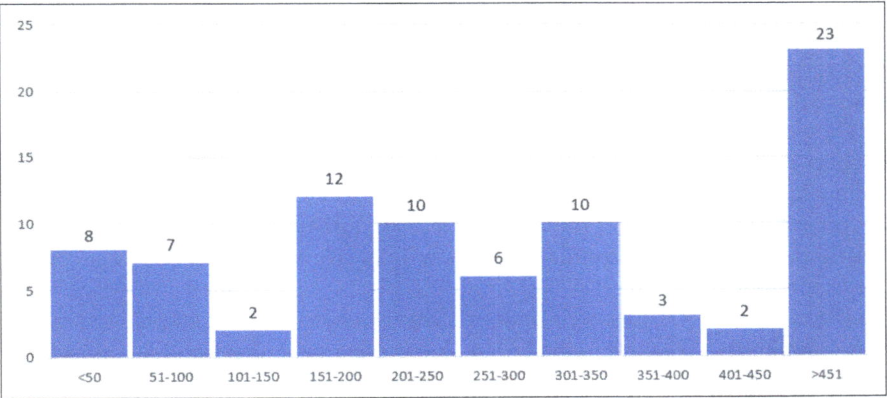

Fig. 6 Student test results after completing the course

The overall results of students who have taught in the Priscilla environment are available in Table 2.

4 Discussion and Conclusion

Table 2 shows the discrepancy between the student's results from the first test (Fig. 6) and the overall results from the subject. In this case, it is a consequence that the initial knowledge of programming was different at the beginning of the semester. Some students had the experience of programming at a high school (usually in Python); others encountered programming for the first time. However, some

Table 2 The structure of the comprehensive assessment of students

Grade	Count of student	The average number of points of micro-tasks	The average number of points of programs	The average number of the first test
A	10	81.6	78.8	99.2
B	11	78.4	79.2	87.7
C	10	90.6	66.3	74,9
D	6	80.1	60.2	44.8
E	16	88.5	58.1	42.1
Fx	30	93.9	41.5	28.9
Sum	**83**	**88.1**	**58.0**	**55.9**

students who started with considerable experience did not maintain the level of the first test. At the end of the semester, they received B, C, possibly D grades.

However, according to Table 2, differences in the average results of groups can be observed. While students with a final grade of A achieved a success rate of 99.2%, the success rate is 74.9% for a grade of C, and for Fx, only 28.9%.

It is interesting to investigate the achieved scores in micro-lessons and AA. In the case of micro-lessons, students with worse final grades show better results. In the case of AA, a declining success rate is seen together with a declining final grade.

On the one hand, a result confirms the correct design of the course – the student chooses his own path, which is easier for him. On the other hand, it can be seen that the choice of own way does not lead every time to successful management of the course, and this observation should be the goal of further research. It can be observed that students with better results chose more intensive creation of program code at the expense of micro-tasks.

The course is probably well built in terms of content, as its microlearning part was completed by students who failed to complete programming (as a university course) and that with more than 90% success.

A questionnaire focused on opinion findings of students was realised after the course pass. The majority of students expressed a positive opinion on the use of AA and microlearning in education. 77% of students were positive of the use of microlearning and 79% of the use of AA.

Free answers of students combined with the facts above make it possible to define and generalise the principles of creating programming courses using a microlearning approach (to become acquainted with the content) and automated assessment (for learning and practising programming as such).

The principles for content creation can therefore be formulated as follows:

Course

- The course must allow freedom of movement through the content – the aim of the course is not to test the student but to teach him. When a student needs it, he has to move to the position where the problem he is solving is explained.
- The course must allow a movement between lessons and chapters even if the student has not completed previous activities. The aim is not to delay and bore

the student in the education but to motivate him to progress at his own pace and based on his own decisions. The student can understand some parts of the content without going through the lessons and can skip them.

- The course must be sufficiently detailed for the weaker student to absorb the content to the extent necessary to write the programs. It requires enough microlearning tasks to practice elementary operations.
- The student must not be bored – the course aims to learn to program. Microlessons have to direct and prepare the student – the main tool for teaching programming is writing programs.
- The types of tasks and their difficulty must alternate. Different types can keep the student's attention. The various difficulty of the tasks motivates different kinds of students to progress.

Microlearning

- The micro-content must be truly micro-content. A long content lesson can only really be justified in rare cases.
- Microlearning requires the transmission of information and its immediate fixation through a micro-question. If possible, two micro-contents in a row should be avoided. It is more appropriate to insert between them a micro-question focused on repetition.
- Micro-questions must be formulated so that they can be answered within a maximum of tens of seconds.
- In the case of more demanding micro-topics, or topics that have greater variability, it is advisable to repeat a similar task with other values or aspects.
- Micro-questions prepare the student for programming – they must convey concepts, commands and programming thinking to him.
- If the micro-questions are focused on the gradual solving of the task, it is suitable to display the previous (already solved) content so that the student also perceives the context.
- For micro-questions, it is advisable to set the same score level. It is assumed that the student should go through all of them and not choose the highest-rated ones. Unnecessary micro-tasks do not belong in the course.
- You can prepare and use program building in micro-tasks. The creation of programs must be gradual – the student first selects the commands from the list, then completes the program by typing using the keyboard. After thoroughly mastering the chapter or lesson, writes the programs independently using AA.

Automated Assessment

- The programming assignment must be concise and unambiguous. The assignment should also include a precisely determined input and a precisely determined output.
- In the introductory tasks, when the student is acquainted with the language, it is desirable to have the individual steps of the algorithm/program in comments.

- Initially, it is necessary to formulate tasks at the level of programming language commands. Later, it is needed to force the student to solve problems in a word problems form. It should not be immediately clear from the assignment what the program should look like.
- In addition to the initial tasks, the assignments should not be formulated so that the result is a simple value selected from a small group of values, e.g. true/false, 1/0 etc. Students like cheating.
- Programming tasks should have different scores set – assigned based on the expected difficulty. Scores can be defined later based on the success of task solving or based on the average time spent solving a task.
- When defining inputs in test cases, it is necessary to think about the time and computational complexity of the used algorithm. The system aims to enable the current work of as many users as possible and not overwhelm the system with unnecessary complexity.

It can be assumed that respecting these principles will enable the effective creation of content and the broadest possible use of the created courses.

The results obtained from the application of microlearning principles in programming teaching can be generalized to provide sufficient support for creators of more general content.

Probably the most important element in creating the course architecture is deciding whether the student will be left free to move through the content or it will be more appropriate to force him to acquire knowledge in a directive way. Allowing free passage through the course is accepted positively by students – it is necessary to leave them the opportunity to choose a chapter regardless of the order.

Microlearning as a technology does not solve the problems of educational content. Technology can never compensate for improperly structured or poorly explained or described content. When creating the content, it is necessary to follow the didactic procedures – the micro-lesson must be short and the micro-question must focus on the essential fact of the previous micro-content. It is also necessary to gradually consolidate the older content by including questions verifying the understanding of the relationships or simply by repeating the previously acquired knowledge.

It is also appropriate to support the memorization of the content with a final or repetitive test enrolled in a larger unit of study. Repetition can be solved in the form of a series of questions without additional micro-content or the form of competition between students.

Acknowledgements This research was funded by European Commission under the ERASMUS+ Programme 2018, KA2, grant number: 2018-1-SK01-KA203-046382 "Work-Based Learning in Future IT Professionals Education", Ministry of Education of Slovakia, grant number 004UKF-2-1/2021 "Preparation and development of teaching courses in English with a focus on artificial intelligence in the form of blended-learning", and Ministry of Education of Slovakia, grant number: 2020/8148:34-A1101 "Support for the development of practical skills of UKF students in Nitra".

References

Berglund, A., & Lister, R. (2010). Introductory programming and the didactic triangle. *Conferences in research and practice in information technology series*, p. 103.

Capay, M., Skalka, J., & Drlik, M. (2017). Computer science learning activities based on experience. In *IEEE global engineering education conference, EDUCON*. Retrieved from https://doi.org/10.1109/EDUCON.2017.7943025.

Castellanos, H., Restrepo-Calle, F., González, F. A., & Echeverry, J. J. R. (2017). Understanding the relationships between self-regulated learning and students source code in a computer programming course. In *Proceedings – Frontiers in education conference, FIE* (Vol. 2017 October). Retrieved from https://doi.org/10.1109/FIE.2017.8190467.

Çetinkaya, A., & Baykan, Ö. K. (2020). Prediction of middle school students' programming talent using artificial neural networks. *Engineering Science and Technology, an International Journal, 23*(6). https://doi.org/10.1016/j.jestch.2020.07.005

Drlík, M., Švec, P., Kapusta, J., Munk, M., Noskova, T., Pavlova, T., et al. (2017). Identification of differences in university E-environment between selected EU and non-EU countries using knowledge mining methods: Project IRNet case study. *International Journal of Web Based Communities, 13*(2). https://doi.org/10.1504/IJWBC.2017.084416

Eurofound. (2020). *COVID-19 could permanently change teleworking in Europe*.

Fuller, U., Johnson, C. G., Ahoniemi, T., Cukierman, D., Hernán-Losada, I., Jackova, J., et al. (2007). Developing a computer science-specific learning taxonomy. *ACM SIGCSE Bulletin, 39*(4). https://doi.org/10.1145/1345375.1345438

Ganapathi, G., Lourdusamy, R., & Rajaram, V. (2011). Towards ontology development for teaching programming language. In *Proceedings of the world congress on engineering 2011, WCE 2011* (Vol. 3).

Gibson, A., Bardach, S. H., & Pope, N. D. (2020). COVID-19 and the digital divide: Will social workers help bridge the gap? *Journal of Gerontological Social Work*. https://doi.org/10.1080/01634372.2020.1772438

Hawlitschek, A., Köppen, V., Dietrich, A., & Zug, S. (2020). Drop-out in programming courses – Prediction and prevention. *Journal of Applied Research in Higher Education, 12*(1). https://doi.org/10.1108/JARHE-02-2019-0035

Iqbal Malik, S., & Coldwell-Neilson, J. (2017). Impact of a new teaching and learning approach in an introductory programming course. *Journal of Educational Computing Research, 55*(6). https://doi.org/10.1177/0735633116685852

Kogan, M., Klein, S. E., Hannon, C. P., & Nolte, M. T. (2020). Orthopaedic education during the COVID-19 pandemic. *The Journal of the American Academy of Orthopaedic Surgeons*. https://doi.org/10.5435/JAAOS-D-20-00292

Saxena, C., Baber, H., & Kumar, P. (2021). Examining the moderating effect of perceived benefits of maintaining social distance on E-learning quality during COVID-19 pandemic. *Journal of Educational Technology Systems, 49*(4). https://doi.org/10.1177/0047239520977798

Skalka, J., & Drlik, M. (2018). Priscilla – Proposal of system architecture for programming learning and teaching environment. *IEEE international conference on application of information and communication technologies*. Retrieved from https://publons.com/publon/27387754/

Skalka, J., & Drlik, M. (2020). Automated assessment and microlearning units as predictors of at-risk students and students' outcomes in the introductory programming courses. *Applied Sciences (Switzerland), 10*(13). https://doi.org/10.3390/app10134566

Skalka, J., Drlik, M., & Svec, P. (2012). E-learning courses quality evaluation framework as part of quality assurance in higher education. *2012 15th international conference on interactive collaborative learning (ICL)*. Retrieved from http://gateway.webofknowledge.com/gateway/Gateway.cgi?GWVersion=2&SrcAuth=ORCID&SrcApp=OrcidOrg&DestLinkType=FullRecord&DestApp=WOS_CPL&KeyUT=WOS:000335746300143&KeyUID=WOS:000335746300143

Skalka, J., Drlik, M., & Svec, P. (2013). Knowledge discovery from university information systems for purposes of quality assurance implementation. In *IEEE global engineering education conference, EDUCON*. Retrieved from https://doi.org/10.1109/EduCon.2013.6530165.

Skalka, J., Drlik, M., & Obonya, J. (2019). Automated assessment in learning and teaching programming languages using virtual learning environment. *Proceedings of ieee global engineering education conference (EDUCON2017)*. Retrieved from https://doi.org/10.1109/EDUCON.2019.8725127.

Skalka, J., Drlik, M., Benko, L., Kapusta, J., Del Pino, J. C. R., Smyrnova-Trybulska, E., et al. (2021). Conceptual framework for programming skills development based on microlearning and automated source code evaluation in virtual learning environment. *Sustainability (Switzerland), 13*(6). https://doi.org/10.3390/su13063293

Svec, P., Drlik, M., Noskova, T., Pavlova, T., Yakovleva, O., & Munk, M. (2017). Analysis of university E-environment in selected European countries – IRNet case study. *Green Energy and Technology*. https://doi.org/10.1007/978-3-319-57070-9_17

Vivian, R., Falkner, K., & Szabo, C. (2014). Can everybody learn to code? Computer science community perceptions about learning the fundamentals of programming. In *ACM international conference proceeding series* (Vol. 2014-November). Retrieved from https://doi.org/10.1145/2674683.2674695.

Winslow, L. E. (1996). Programming pedagogy – A psychological overview. *SIGCSE Bulletin (Association for computing machinery, special interest group on computer science education)*. Retrieved from https://doi.org/10.1145/234867.234872.

Learning by Designing, Imagination and Programming

Piet Kommers

Preface We as members of the FITPED project team asked ourselves: What directions of innovation look promising in terms of 'perceived needs' and 'meeting endemic values'. From a pure scientific point of view, operationalizing "Quality of Learning" is one of the hardest nuts to be cracked; Once listing all relevant dimensions of learning processes and outcomes, there is no end. Similar to listing qualities in fashion, gastronomy, music, every new trend in socio-economic era, brings its own new desires and ideologies. The list of quantifiers for qualities of learning: the speed of, easiness for the student and the teacher, endurance of what is learnt, the depth of it, its flexibility, its authenticity, its pedagogical soundness, self-efficacy and … indeed, the students' capacities to become a successful programmer. For those ICT teachers who admit that student autonomy is key in future societies, there might still be hurdles before arriving at confirmation on how to nurture entrepreneurship: "Are there dependencies between pure knowledge, craftmanship and programming skills?" And also: "To what extent is the programming skill a generic one?" Taking gamification as major source for acquiring a programmer's mindset, is a bold statement. Gamification pretends to be "catalytical" to the ongoing evolution of Higher Education and its fan out for socio–/economical evolutions nowadays; Kommers (2021).

Gamification seems to be a strong trigger for changing the school- and course culture in ICT education. Are the traditional teacher-student roles in conflict with the specific didactics as we ought to prefer in computer science? We think not; a large part of the algorithmic mindset relies on the apprentice's eagerness to learn from unexpected situations and persons who can demonstrate competencies that may lead to solutions for unexpected problems. However, this very 'transfer-paradigm' (from teacher to student), though very much needed, is not enough as

P. Kommers (✉)
University of Twente, Enschede, The Netherlands

E. Smyrnova-Trybulska et al. (eds.), *Microlearning*,
https://doi.org/10.1007/978-3-031-13359-6_4

students in a receptive attitude are slow and even averse from 'changing themselves'. The classical teaching-learning paradigm is that students are supposed to adapt in order to comply with the assessment criteria. In order to create a life-long ICT-savvy learner it is more the 'willingness to change oneself', in order to grow along dimensions that were not foreseen by experts so far. Good examples are the growing battles against viruses, fake news, fake identities, big data etc. In this sense computer sciences are more than adapting your competences; it is developing a sharp eye for 'what is needed by others' rather than obeying your superordinate. A good programmer does not just follow what his/her customers want now. It is a matter of narrating to your potential customer in order to create his/her need of tomorrow. Here is where gamification and constructivist learning come in: It helps Higher Educational students to open additional mindsets. The real job for FITPED now is to find effective design rationales on how to weave gamification in existing computer science curricula. Rather than delivering hard-core recipes, we claim that ICT trainers need to go through a set of experiences how gaming opens additional genres for our mentor roles in entrepreneurial stages of FITPED.

1 Introduction

Creative didactics is the core target for future ICT curricula in this FITPED project. As will be elaborated further in this book, student-oriented learning is as multi-facetted as programming itself. There are many avenues for innovating ICT curricula that have not been fully exploited yet: 1. Gamification, 2. Playing, 3. Collaborative Learning, 4. Storytelling and 5. Simulations are just the most obvious ones. However also Mobile Learning, Virtual Reality and the many more techno-driven innovations to come are essentially promising candidates for the future of ICT curricula. In order to make programming more effective, efficient and sustainable we need a strong foundation for its embedding in the actual educational situations and further consolidation. Seen the recent scientific literature and good practice examples, this envelope is PBL (Problem-Based Learning): The method to place the apprentice at the very core of his/her learning process; (s)he (re)gains full ownership of the start of a life-long learning process. For the sake of innovative ICT skills it means that apprentices who typically have a less favorable earlier school experience, they need to be encouraged by being welcomed and empowered through a student-centered pedagogy. Problem-Based Learning should not be confused by Project-Based Learning. The essence of the PBL approach is to learn about a subject through the experience of solving open-ended problems found in trigger material; prototypical questions that orient the learner towards understanding what PBL questions ideally are. The PBL process does not focus on problem solving with a defined solution, but it allows for the development of other desirable skills and attributes. This includes knowledge acquisition, enhanced group collaboration and communication. As overall recommendation: Motivate ICT trainers to see the elegance and sustainability of PBL; (Smyrnova-Trybulska et al., 2017). It is a powerful paradigm before adopting and integrating the new ICT-based tools as presented before. Main driver behind the integration of PBL in ICT is that it fits very well with the type of motivation of young apprentices "to make a difference" and "find a job" or "start a company". More in general, we see a recent policy towards preparing ICT students for "Smart Jobs"; (Issa et al., 2017). It preludes a more active learning approach and ready for the post-industrial era where men and machine face new complementary skills and autonomous life-long learning. This inherent trend not only holds for including ICT skills; it is a much more intricate shift from technical-, via communicative- to conceptual skills. According to "Balance-Careers" the Top-Five conceptual skills are: Analysis, Communication, Creative Thinking, Leadership and Problem-Solving. According to "Business-Directory," conceptual skills can be delineated as: The ability to think creatively about, analyse and understand complicated and abstract ideas. Using a well-developed conceptual skill set, top level business managers need to be able to look at their company as a holistic entity, to see the interrelationships between its divisions, and to understand how the firm fits into and affects its overall environment. Until very recently these 'conceptual skills' were supposed to belong to the repertoire of corporate leaders and top managers. Now we see that very rapidly these skills are seen as essential for labour force throughout the enterprise pyramid.

2 Cognitive Hexagon

Before going into details on how the didactics in 'learning to programming' needs to be developed further, it might be good to present the 'cognitive hexagon' by Valera Mariscal. Its six ingredients show a wider context of disciplines then we generally accept (Fig. 1).

1. At the top is philosophy. Its role is not only to reify the traditional desire towards Ph.D. certification. It is the deep trust that true knowledge on learning can only be harvested if we owe the discipline to think about all transitions between the involved concepts. For instance, if we value the process of 'understanding' rather than acquiring knowledge and skills, it is inevitable that we concern all super- and sub-ordinate concepts and processes around the phenomenon of 'understanding'.
2. Going clockwise we meet Mariscal's (2014) mentioning of 'linguistics'. Not only to stress the need for De Saussure's or Chomskian attention for structuralism of transformable generative syntaxis. The need for linguistics in learning goes deeper. It is the acknowledgement that language, consciousness, and knowledge go hand in hand; they need each other and finally it is hard to pin down the three in its contrast to the other two. Lev Vygotsky (1986) is maybe the most renown pioneer who questioned maybe the most essential question in his book "Thought and Language". For instance, Vygotsky's attention for 'private language' has been inextricably linked to the question in how far pre-

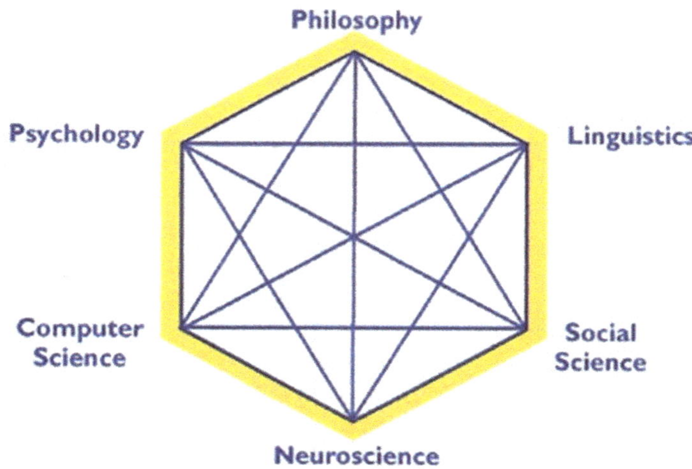

Fig. 1 the 'cognitive hexagon' by Valera Mariscal

communicative language is needed before youngsters can sense the root of one's existential roots? As we come closer to the need for reflection and metacognitive awareness, it will be clear that linguistics is a much deeper need than just sharing ideas amongst tutor and tutee.

3. Social science gained momentum in the sixties as human processes need an idiosyncratic stand, based upon the cognitive duality that we typically call "the phenomenological" stand towards understanding human development. Typical for social science is its in-depth need for multi-variate constellations rather than the two or three parameters that we meet in for instance physics. Social sciences are not only the aggregation of adding individual disciplines like psychology, pedagogy, sociology etc.; it is rather an epitome that alerts us for the needed uniqueness of cases as we look to persons and unique situations.
4. Neuroscience conquers more and more attention from educationalists. It alerts teachers and student coaches to be keen on the neural substrate of the human mind, memory, and processes like 'self-regulation' and 'consolidation' as it now manifests to be crucial for semantic integration during the slow-wave sleep. Until 10 years ago it was generally understood that sleep is vital for new learning. Since few years we now know what happens if (even without being awakened) one's slow wave sleep is interfered with a subtle sound. Its effect is monstruous and will lead to psychotic problems. We recently discovered that during the slow wave sleep, the spread of neurotransmitters goes from the hip-

pocampus to the cortex, where the electric patterns from the experiences of the day before becoming 'consolidated' into chemical structures so that it is ready for being reconciled with earlier prior experiences and ready for future new information.

5. Computer science, and the term 'information science' might even fit better in this context, has already been proven a wide set of learning theoretical orthogonalities that would never had emerged from psychology or pedagogy. For instance, Wiener's coining of 'cybernetics' has been the trigger to frame the teaching/learning process as a progressive targeting of 'hitting' the right learning 'goals'. Gordon Pask can be seen as one of the most influential cyber protagonists who formalized the learning/teaching dialogue a discursive process where students were supposed to 'teach back' to the tutor in order to provoke a new diagnostics and complementary instructional intervention.
6. Finally, but not least is 'psychology' as catalyst for innovating teaching/learning processes. Most characteristic is its attempts to find underlying mechanisms in the learning processes. Behaviourism, cognitivism, and later neural modelling; they all show attempts to formalize the wide plethora of types of learning and the even more wide scale of individual characteristics in one's fully unique reflections and deriving meaning from earlier experiences (Fig. 2).

In summary: even the widest circle of disciplines brings limited views on how to arrange a better learning. It seems that there is no hope to reduce learning models to the formal categories as we have nowadays. Similar to food, fashion, art and lifestyles, learning will show new varieties the coming decades.

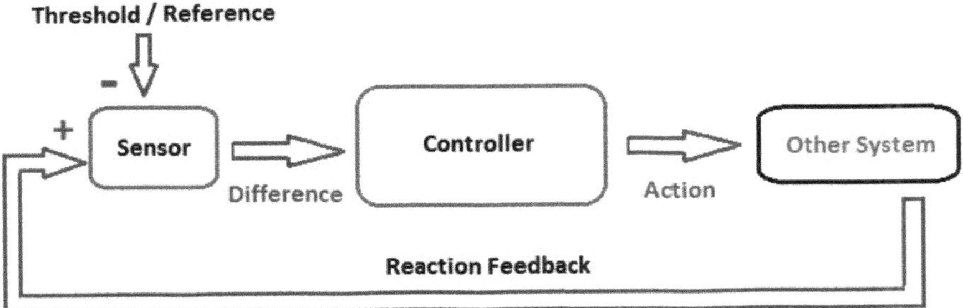

A Cybernetic Loop

Fig. 2 Wiener's Cybernetic control loop

3 Five Dimensions for Innovative Didactics

At the outset of the wide spectrum of didactic rationales and methodologies we see the next five dimensions that have generally been recognized as the most prominent ones (Fig. 3).

1. The first one is the most undisputed one: The attempts to make students active learners. Active learning implies that the teaching/learning process is no loner limited to sending and receiving; The student is considered to regain ownership of his/her own learning processes and thus becomes a co-designer of the didactic situation.
2. It leads to the more articulate second dimension towards constructivist learning. In its most radical interpretation, it is the apprehension that during the learning process the actual formation of concepts and understanding is one of 'reverse engineering': Though all of the concepts to be learnt are ready for 'taking away' it is not enough to see, hear, feel and taste the ideas. Before understanding the full meaning and impact of a concept, the learner needs to 're'-build a concept from its primitives and through applying it in various contexts.
3. The third dimension is the trend towards 'cooperative' rather than 'soloistic' learning. At least it is hard to see that from the pragmatic side we claim that job performance is teamwork for 90% of the cases, while we still defend its stages of learning, training, and maturation as an individualistic process. By accepting the full collaborative paradigm, we need to accept that learning processes not only need to be orchestrated as collectivistic ones; also, its testing and accreditation need to be in the full collaborative context.

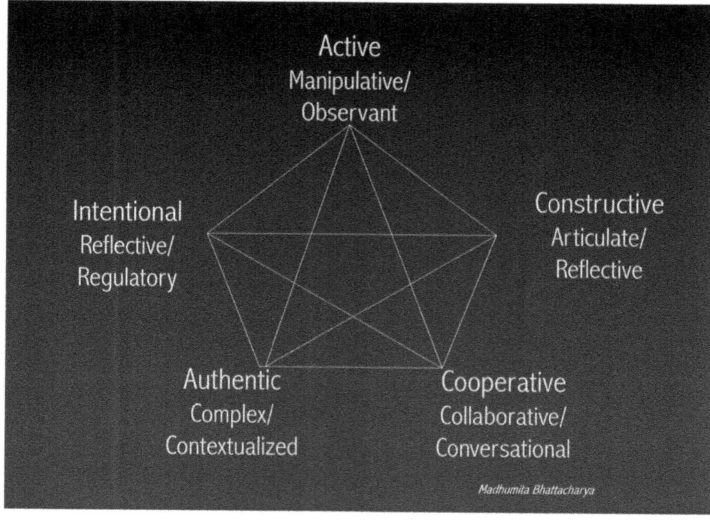

Fig. 3 The five most prominent innovative dimensions for future didactics

4. The authentic learning paradigm is the plead for students' unique personal traits like incidental prior knowledge, idiosyncratic passions, hobbies etc. This alternates to the overall view that learning in curricular contexts needs to focus on the commonalities rather than its differential elements.
5. Intentional learning is the recommendation to teachers to embed instruction in holistic real-world actualities; What keeps students busy before entering the lecture hall is no longer seen as 'noise' or as 'distraction'. It is the real cognitive basis where next formal education needs to be built upon.

In case of 'learning programming skills' it is of vital importance that both content and method of didactic innovation needs to be mapped back to at least one of these five essentials. Too often, educational novelties carry away teachers' full attention, without promoting the awareness that students are not that impressed by 'new' tools and methods like for instance 'learning by simulations', 'gamification' or '3D virtual worlds'. In case of teaching programming skills, it is important that the 'skill' element does not 'supplant' the awakening of meaningful intuition and understanding. Especially the ingredient of 'conceptual reconstructions' in combination with reflection and the promotion of imagination, are vital in order to improve the essence of the learning process.

4 Learning by Designing

The notion that 'programming skills and experiences' are vital for making learning more 'active' and 'generic', has been coined by Seymour Papert who created the LOGO system for educational purposes; Papert, 1980. At that time the ultimate term was 'constructivism'. Based upon students learning algorithmic thinking, the implication was that the inevitable way of learning primitives like Boolean expressions, control variables for iterations, etc. was to let some-one build and explore its behaviour in a wider context. In this way, Papert's idea on constructivist learning in his book 'Mind Storms' started a Copernican swivel in thinking on conceptual learning, where exploration, imagination and 'playing' were the key ingredients. The FitPed project builds upon the essential understanding that students in Higher Education need at least one curricular strand that allows them to explore consciousness and metacognition in order to become better learners

4.1 Gaming by Playing for Learning

Before exploring the potential of Gaming and Storytelling it is useful to provide two main reasons for our searching in the next directions. The first is that, complementary to our day-to-day classroom efforts for converting students into better learners, the main question is to make educational systems better by rephrasing Kenneth

Dunn (Kaufman et al., 1997): "If students don't learn the way we teach the, let's teach them the way they learn". The second one is the notion that programming competencies face moving targets; Progressing from procedural to declarative to object-oriented to functional programming. The third direction is that employees face more and more demands for strategic thinking. Though the term "conceptual skills" may suggest that it belongs to high level managers, there is a growing understanding that for a large class of jobs conceptual thinking is needed in order to promote problem solving and creative approaches. This trend goes together with the growing need for knowledge- rather than industrial workers. Conceptual skills are the next step after we mastered factual and procedural knowledge. Both knowledge and skills are consolidations after good practice has found an optimum; As our surrounding world evolves, new ICT skills need to be identified: Its goal is to prevent a group of youngsters to become obsolete. We hope to illustrate that gamification, storytelling and many more are indispensable in this continuous process.

Definition Gamification is the application of game-design elements and game principles in non-game contexts (Werbach, 2014). The main reason for defining gamification as a process is that it provides a scale for gamification and not an absolute category. Gamification commonly employs game design elements to improve user engagement, organizational productivity, flow, learning, employee recruitment and evaluation, physical exercise, traffic violations, voter apathy, and more. Werbach and Hunter (2015) identified five game dynamics used in gamification:

- **Constraints** are about balancing limitations and freedom for a player as well as integrating forced trade-offs in the design of a gamified solution.
- **Emotions** aim to produce enduring player engagement and appear during an activity.
- **Narrative** is represented for a player through either an explicit or implicit storyline having its own consistent inner logic and following a certain context.
- **Progression** reports the player's growth and development when navigating through a game and the possibilities to do so.
- **Relationships** consider the social interactions of players in a game which can create feelings of camaraderie, status and altruism.

Jayalath and Esichaikul (2016) provide a model in which the dynamics, mechanics and Element are combined (see Fig. 1). This provides teachers and researchers with a framework to design engaging learning environments. Just using an element does not necessarily create an engaging gamification environment. For instance, providing points as in grading tests would not be considered an engaging gamification environment for most students as they a used to this. Creating teams to compete in an engaging set of problems to be solved and keeping a leaderboard scoring system might be challenging and create intensive team cooperation (Fig. 4).

A number of studies on gamification show that it has positive effects on individuals in terms of cognitive flexibility, changing role perspectives, etc. However, individual and contextual differences exist. Gamification can improve an individual's ability to comprehend digital content and understand a certain area of study such as

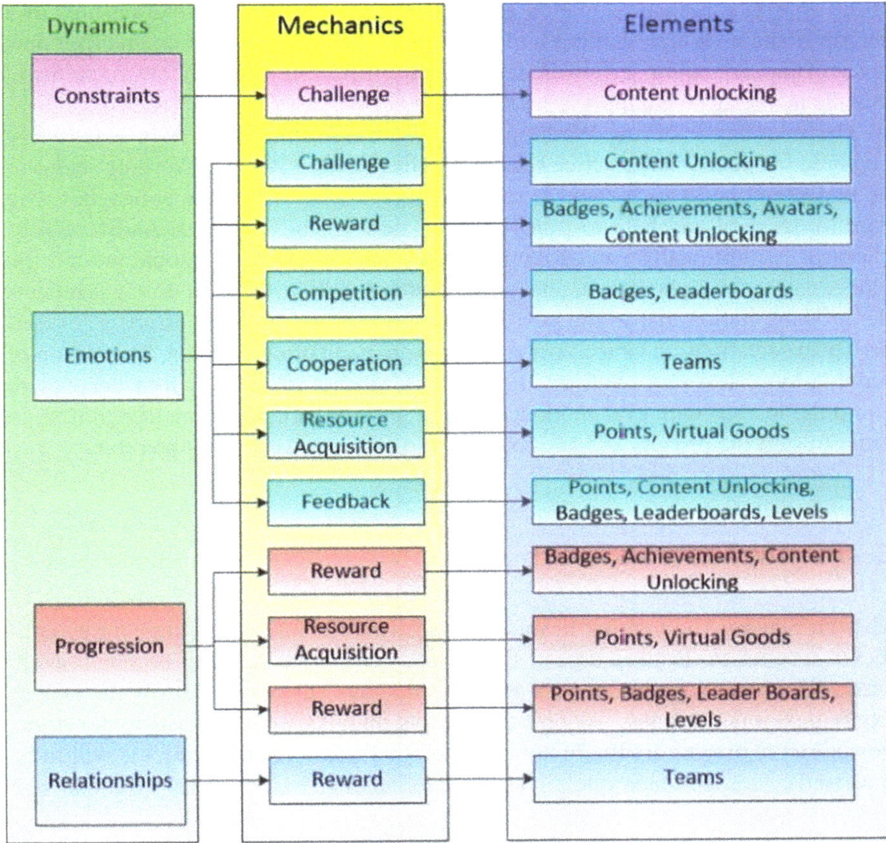

Fig. 4 Linkage Diagram of game dynamics, mechanics and elements. From: Jayalath and Esichaikul (2016)

music. Research into the use of gaming for learning shows that gamification penetrates all sectors of life where awareness, latent ambitions and mental growth are at stake. As such, gaming may not only increase the effectiveness of traditional learning goals like memorization and skill routinization; It may help learners to refresh their concept of what learning is about. In its deepest sense, learning can be seen as one's developing willingness to change him/herself; (Kommers et al., 2004).

The contrast between single- versus double-loop learning is that single-loop learning can be compared with a thermostat that learns to switch-off the heating when a certain temperature is reached, whereas double-loop learning occurs when a device (or a person) learns to monitor a wide set of parameters and becomes keen on which of them are the best first-order predictors for anticipation when heating or cooling is needed. Games as we typically know for increasing speed and precision have already proven its value for learning. Its overall metaphor is "beat your peer student or your own score in the past". Double-loop learning games place the learner at the core of a realistic situation and ask to discover 'hidden' relationships in a certain domain. Where gaming aims at winning, playing aims at conquering new levels of understanding, self-awareness and self-efficacy. In terms of Constructionism, it is the learner who attempts to become his/her own coach (Figs. 5 and 6).

The relations Learning-Working and Playing-Working have been extensively explored in educational practice before. The intersection Playing-Working seems to be underexploited yet. Its goal is to make apprentices better new colleagues who dare to question and help to transform into new business models. As Steve Jobs claimed: "Traditionally we, as Apple, scout and hire the best people around the globe, pay them highest fees, and subsequently tell them what to do..."; It reflects the growing notion that in the post-industrial era, working is the efforts to exceed earlier expectations and survive in an ever more competitive market. The notion of 'double-loop' learning confirms the manifold efforts in the last four decades to equip the learner with ever more autonomy, self-regulation, and metacognition, in order to start the process of a life-long learning attitude as early as possible.

5 Playing Versus Gaming

Though playing and gaming have a completely different source, they have sentiments in common. Both emerge in situations when no real urgences or threats are at stake. So typically, between work and worshipping. The play is simply the lack of explicit external agendas; whereas the gaming allows external merits to penetrate. For instance, playing football may have no other goal than enjoying the ball to be traversed and experience one's body to be challenged in mastering the ball that

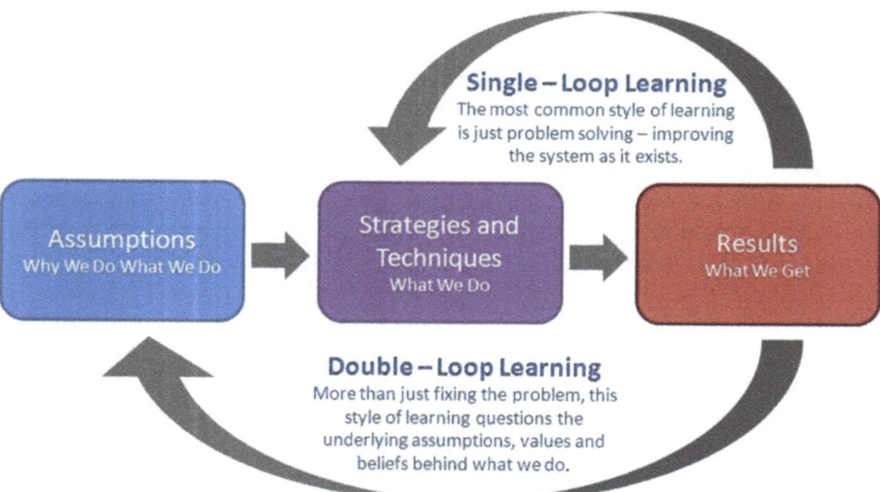

Fig. 5 Double-loop learning by Argyris (2005)

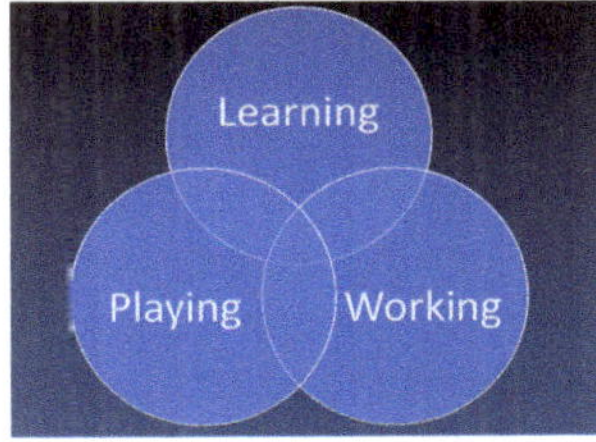

Fig. 6 Learning, playing, working as dynamics for double-loop learning (Bonanno & Kommers, 2008)

Fig. 7 Children's Games is an oil-on-panel by Flemish Renaissance artist Pieter Bruegel the Elder, painted in 1560. It is currently held and exhibited at the Museum in Vienna

shows unpredictable reactions initially. The 'game' of playing football starts from the playground where youngsters centre around two favourite players and pretend to 'win'. At the top level of the football game, the playing has evaporated: No risk taking, no search for additional challenges. One could say that at the top level of the gaming pyramid the goal is to 'bypass' the playing. The reward is much higher than the excitement of joining the match. Therefore, in the field of learning and education, the playing has a more direct role compared to competition and 'winning' (Fig. 7).

Pieter Breughel pictured a densely compiled set of plays that are typically invented by youngster at the very spot of 'feeling released' from pressure and being observed. Though the picture resonates an encyclopaedic collection of plays, it helps the spectator to admire the intrinsic motivation, the variety, and the improvisation of all types. Studies still lack a systematic characterization of how children learn from these plays and how they build new plays on earlier experiences. In the framework of the FitPed project, we can just say that playing in its purest form, offers an antagonism to the formal learning where grading and pass/fail decisions are at stake. Seen the attempts of didacticizing 'programming skills', there has been a high affinity for the exploratory- and experiential nature that helps novices to find out the power of 'new' control- and data structures. Constructivism as propagated by Seymour Papert has conquered its role among the many formalistic approaches where syntax- and correctness proofing have taken over the regime. From a pedagogical point of view, Breughel's playground has the undertone of 'sense making': It is the actual moment of improvisation and excitement that keeps hum development going. Quite important for situations where the learner has only little affinity with 'writing code'. The Construit! Project[1] has formulated a more exact underpinning of why playing is a needed ingredient in the formation of creative procedural solutions for applications where the computer can soon exceed the human performance like in recursive and np-complete problems that fight the 'complexity wall'.

6 Why Play-Based Learning? Methodologies and Approach

Play-based learning as research topic has been presented as method for pre-school learning mainly. In this O1 an effort is made to position the playing-working combination as new prospect for VET. In the triangle learning-playing-working the phase of learning is traditionally seen as mitigation between work and play, in which play is unnecessarily seen as 'leisure time', 'divertissement' and 'digression'. The essence of playing is the immediacy between actual interest, affordance and try-out. There is no other agenda than "follow your interest" and "see how far you can go". So, though the improvisation and impulsiveness may look as "unfocussed" and "senseless", the optimal sense-making occurs in the playing attitude as it completely absorbs the person. In terms of the net learning (understanding a complex of variables through experiencing direct- and indirect side effects of an earlier intervention) one can say that playing is one of the very few activities with a minimal of cognitive overload; no prescriptive agenda, no extrinsic motivations and a one-to-one match between cognitive repertoire and intuitive horizon. Just like virtual and vicarious allow the learning to take freedom and fully focus on the proximate zone of achievement, so is a situation of playing the de-facto match between momentary intention, imagination and cognitive operation. It is now a matter of finding complementary arrangements for ICT teachers to convey such a process and find adequate scenarios for progressively integrating its learning outcomes in meaningful segments of the job performance. As a summary we may state that gamification is meant to regulate people's natural desires for socializing, learning, mastery, competition, achievement, status, self-expression, altruism, or closure. It provides incentives for players to master relevant tasks. Typical rewards include credit points, badges, play levels and tokenized recognition by the other players.

[1] The CONSTRUIT! project introduces new principles and tools that enable educators and learners to collaborate in creating 'construals'—live interactive resources that capture personal understandings of a phenomenon. Tools developed are more expressive and powerful than conventional programming tools, but yet accessible for everyone. http://construit.org/

7 Gamification of Learning: Principles and Mechanisms for Engagement

Gamification of learning is a much broader process than finding appropriate game templates and integrate them in curricular and instructional contexts. One of the recent efforts has been to classify better what element of gaming would contribute to the learning process. The prefix "serious" has been chosen to narrow the spectrum of diverse gaming genres. Critics came along that gaming for the gamer is always a serious matter. At the other side game ambassadors claim that an explicit serious connotation may squeeze out the attraction of game-experience soon.

1. One of the drivers of game-based learning is Engagement; Learners feel immersed and sometimes even obsessed while playing a virtual reality where a certain number of performance parameters are continuously measured and displayed.
2. The second driver is Flow; Its effects increase the learners' strength of experience, concentration, and endurance.

In particular for VET, gamification in learning has the extra effect of "Breaking the Yoke of Seriousness"; As "Work" is inextricably bound to serious business, the novice might easily get too much infatuated with "avoiding mistakes" so that "risk avoidance" easily emerges and hampers mindset for learning and understanding. Avatars in Gamified Instruction.

Characters or its representatives (Personas) allow the audience / student to identify with the teacher's exposition. The most compact guideline for the introduction of characters can be found in film-script guidelines. Crucial in establishing characters are the features of what we call 'a personality'. Let the listener immediately know who (s)he is via expose of (trans)actions and contrast with the other players on stage. Make clear that (s)he is going to play a decisive role in the coming adventure. Typically, the listener should be able to identify with the main character, but at some essential point there needs to be ambiguity: 'strange' behavior that cannot be explained or could not be recognized before. Overwhelm the listener very soon with typical bloopers ('big mistakes') by the main character. Keep your instruction compact so that the main line can easily be remembered. Insert looking back and forth as mental perspective; The listener is supposed to 'create' his/her own interpretation. In case of more abstract concepts in the knowledge domain, elaborations are needed; encourage the listener to interweave prior and final understanding and keep this discrepancy until the very end of the lesson.

8 Procedural and Spatial Imagination for Programming

Both gamification and narrative discourse for learning can be seen in the many simulation programs that have been integrated in various levels from early regular unto the highest levels in corporate and civil training in everyday life already. Since computers became multimedia (Multi Modal), its potential contribution to let people explore almost any context, inclusively 3D spatial environments with stereopsis for surgical training, kinematic and proprioceptive sensations for vehicle control and haptic experience for training manipulation feedback. The instructional context and the apprentice's prior knowledge and skills is decisive for what is actually learnt from a simulation model. The underlying photo of an expert surgeon who calibrates a haptic device before the students start working with it; (Kommers et al., 2004). A typical phenomenon is that after few hours of practicing, the novice will perform better than the expert. This is the moment that the students need to go to the more realistic context so that many more parameters like the total constitution of the patient, the smell, heart functioning etc. should be taken into account (Fig. 8).

As many competences imply social interaction and teamwork, also a large proportion of didactic simulations demand collaborative tasks. The Teams-Games-Tournament format (Ke and Grabowski, 2007) originally defined by Bob Slavin (1977), prescribes an overall sequence of cooperative- and competitive group work. Skills progress through simulations have been described by Luursema et al. (2008). Its conclusion is that stereopsis only makes a positive difference in case the novice has a limited capacity in spatial imagination (Figs. 9 and 10).

Monitoring pathways of skills: One critical factor in the success of learning with simulations is the overview of students' partial successes/failures in the targeted skill domain. The underlying diagrams allow trainers to quickly analyze novices' learning performances. It is an example on how e-tools allow the human factor to survive and even excel, compared to the f2f classroom situation (Figs. 11, 12, 13).

The study by revealed that though virtual reality is one of the prime candidates in vitalizing learning by its realism and direct appeal to the students' natural

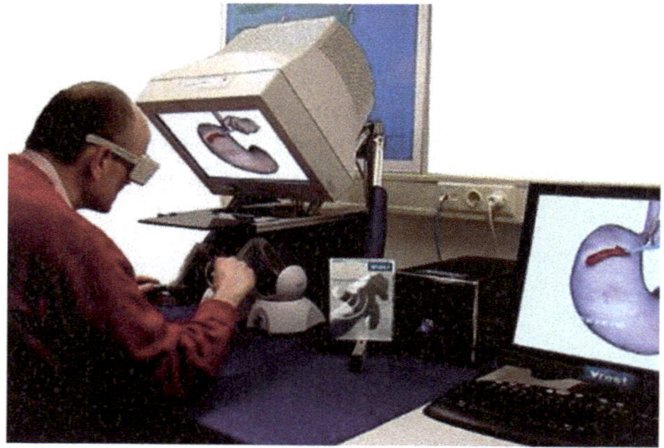

Fig. 8 Dr. Bob Geelkerken calibrating the haptic feedback that corresponds with palpating a virtual patient's stomach

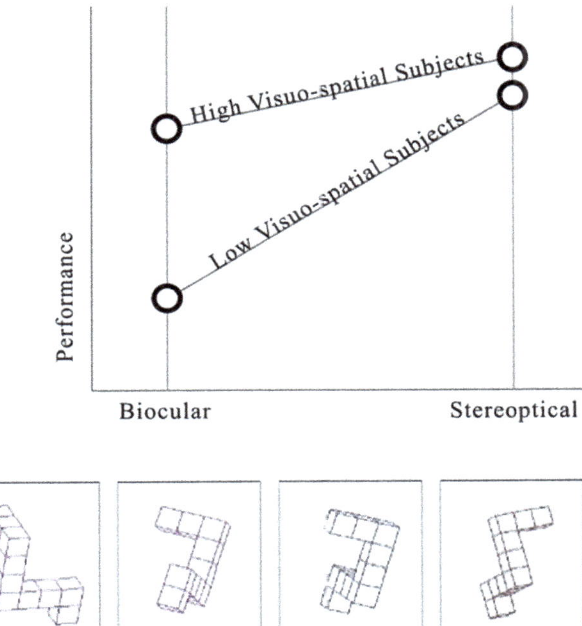

Fig. 9 Luursema's finding that the added value of the heavier 3D stereoptic goggles emerges more in case of a weaker visual imagination

Fig. 10 Pretest: (visuo-spatial ability) Mental rotation test

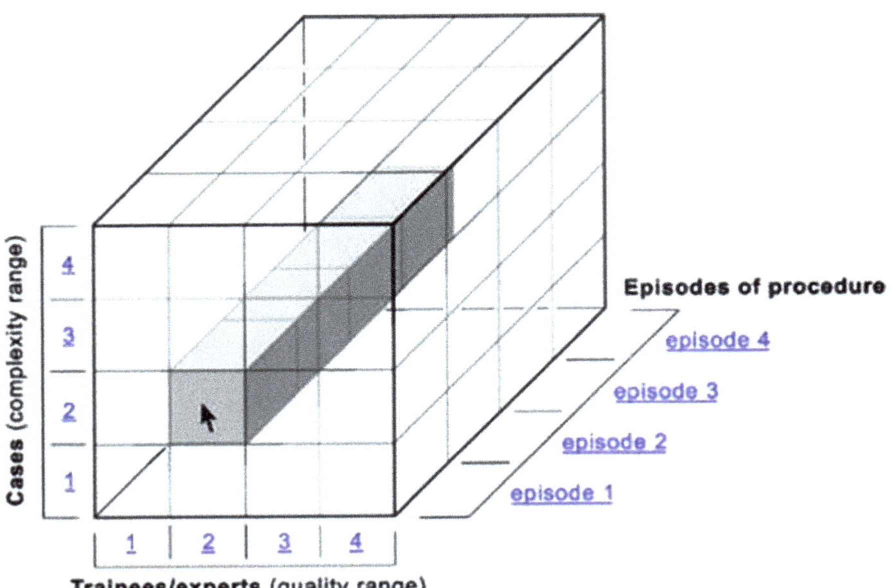

Fig. 11 Selecting a trainee/patient intervention history

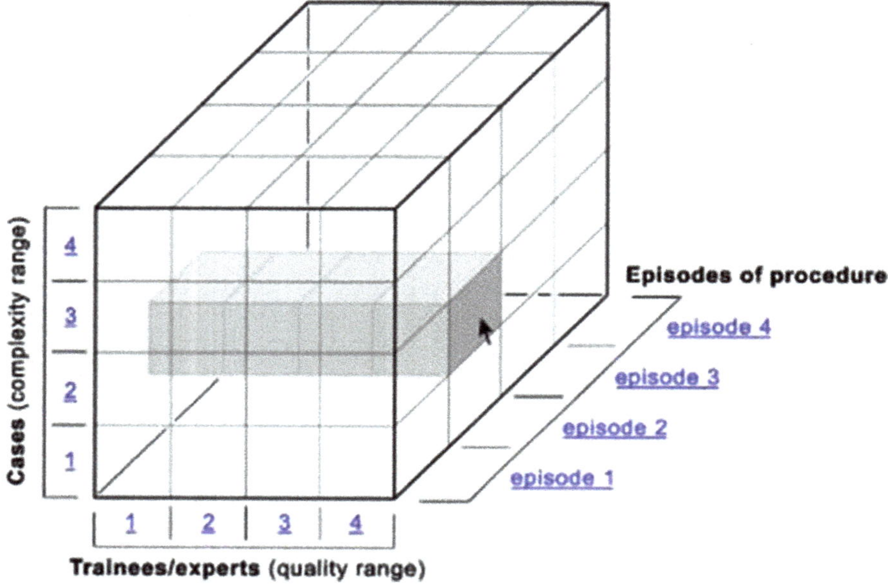

Fig. 12 Selecting a particular intervention episode across all trainees for one particular patient

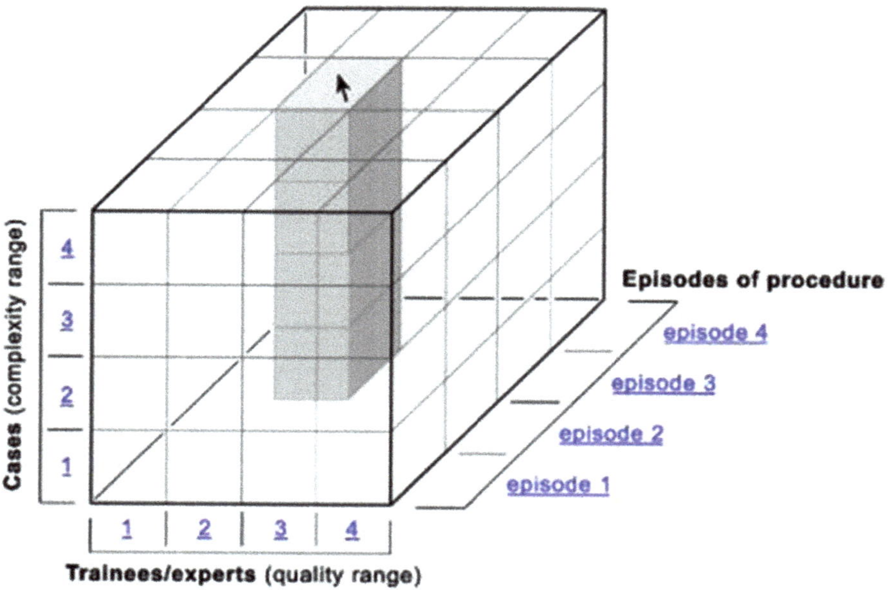

Fig. 13 Selecting a particular intervention episode across all patients for one particular trainee

affordance to act upon urgencies rather than to "know" what experts are saying; VR in itself is not enough to make the learning more effective. Obviously, the realism in VR cannot exceed the real situation itself. As the experiences with Link Trainers for airplane pilots has shown, we know that the simulation can be more effective, once it elicits the novice to go into critically complex situations; exactly those situations that we never hope to meet in reality. The added value is not just that the learner's reflexes are trained to survive in the panic of preciously decisive seconds. The value is also that learners can best understand the fundaments of complex mechanisms when they are forced to work on the edge of what is a success versus a failure. Training through real-patient interventions are not allowed to approach this area. That is why the VR-based medical intervention is an even better preparation to the first clinical steps compared to witnessing dozens of impeccable operations performed by the master. For clarifying the potential value of simulations in ICT, few examples maybe be helpful: One of the programs used in secondary education in The Netherlands is a simulation environment called SIMQUEST in which teachers can create their own simulations to use in their lessons. The program is free and available in Dutch and English. Although the example is from physics it can be used in any area that employs numeric equations (Fig. 14).

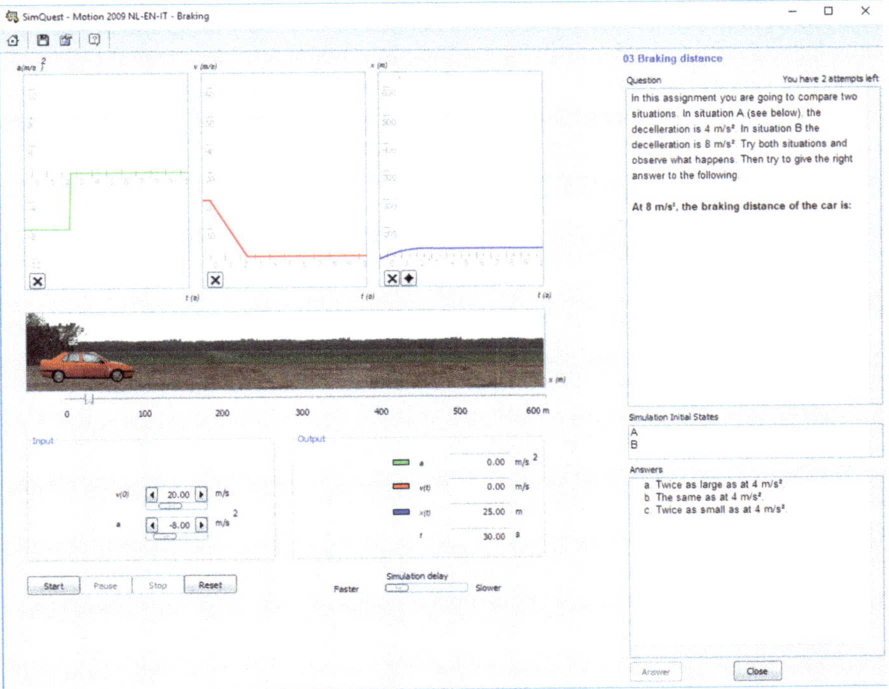

Fig. 14 The SIMQUEST environment for the students

Advantages of simulations:

- Safety; E.g. flight simulator, nuclear power plant or operating cranes
- In most cases cheaper than real-life
- More accessible than real-life; You can take it home
- Platform for discovery learning; Students can manipulate and observe (intrinsic feedback)
- Learning as (guided) discovery
- Student controls the learning environment
- Does research to foster knowledge just like a researcher
- Constructs knowledge in his/her personal way
- Skills should be more flexible and retained longer
- Fostering of research skills

9 Lego Serious Play

"… The LEGO® SERIOUS PLAY® Method is a facilitated meeting, communication and problem-solving process in which participants are led through a series of questions, probing deeper and deeper into the subject. Each participant builds his or her own 3D LEGO® model in response to the facilitator's questions using specially selected LEGO® elements. These 3D models serve as a basis for group discussion, knowledge sharing, problem solving and decision making…" Its method is the collaborative process in which each of the participants have a decisive role. The group process needs to be moderated by a trained LEGO® SERIOUS PLAY® facilitator. As conditions for applying Lego Serious Play its web-site mentions:

- The subject is complex and multifaceted and there is a need to grasp the bigger picture, find connections and explore options and potential solutions
- It is important to reach decisions which everyone commits to and honors after the meeting even though he or she does not agree 100%
- Asking each team member or participant the same question results in substantially different answers
- Everyone in the group has an interest or stake in what is on the agenda
- It is important that everyone participates in the discussions and contributes with his or her knowledge and opinions
- You want to increase team understanding and at the same time avoid frustration
- You want to use the time efficiently
- There are no obvious answers
- You would like to gain new learning, insights and new ways of thinking
- You want to deal with tough and complex issues in a constructive atmosphere

- It is vital that participants speak their true feelings without intimidating anyone or being intimidated
- You have a situation in which a few members tend to dominate the discussions and you want to break that routine without offending anyone
- You have a group which feels meetings tend to be a waste of time
- You want to create a level playing field for discussion
- Your meetings or learning events tend to focus more on the messengers than on the messages
- You want to avoid excuses or lack of initiative after the meeting
- There's a risk, participants feel they were not heard or involved in the decision
- You want to ensure that all participants share a common understanding and frame of reference

Its "Creative Commons License Deed" declaration can be found here. The web-site mentions that the LEGO Group after 2010 no longer offers certification programs in the LEGO® SERIOUS PLAY® method, nor does it have a direct association with the end-client. As preliminary conclusion we may say that Lego Serious Play is an elegant demonstrator method to let trainers and students experience the difference between gaming and playing. Gaming is to let its members compete in a limited set of skills and performance qualities, while playing is a broader exploration method for letting its members discover a certain design/creation domain and eliciting one's latent intuition in that field.

10 Contexts for Simulations

Simulations have been developed in industrial projects in order to prepare better for the unforeseen complexity during calamities. Its main effect was that engineers and decision makers became better prepared compared to those who just concentrated on formal models with a high degree of precision. As simulations became easier to emulate more complex realities, education has gathered more than only interest and got more and more convinced that a reduced reality had advantages for gaining understanding compared to the situation with full reality and scale. Simulation has even become a metaphor for education at large: If the real setting cannot absorb novices' presence and contributions, it is needed to build a reduced version of a particular enterprise. Not only to increase safety and flexibility for the time of learning, also for breaking-out when no urgent maintenance or trouble shooting was needed. For example, Hewlett-Packard's inkjet cartridge filling factory in Dublin had a mini factory where employees could exercise in fault-finding so that they reached a shorter downtime in case of failure. In other words: Simulations have a wide potential scale of functions. Its use for learning purposes can be focused on tackling renown problems like flight pilots who need to practice emergency landings that they would never voluntarily undertake in reality. But also, simulations allow novices to explore and experiment configurations in order to develop a better What-If thinking for the cases that fresh reasoning is needed in a future break-down.

11 Minecraft for Schools: MinecraftEdu

A New York City school teacher has crafted a version of Minecraft for schools called MinecraftEdu. Given the sandbox game's simple premise—a pixelated world of blocks that users manipulate with tools—plus the ability to add customizable maps, educators can drop students into a world of ancient cultures, Chemistry, English, and more. MinecraftEdu creator Joel Levin, who teaches second-grade computer classes at Columbia Grammar and Preparatory School in New York City and runs a Minecraft club for high schoolers, has been incorporating Minecraft into his classes for the past 2 years.

12 Storytelling: Didactic Genre for Initial Programming Skills

Before any computational- and even procedural thinking emerges, learners need to develop episodic reflections, based upon facts, dependencies, and agents as we know from literary theories. Hypertext has brought us the beauty of decontextualization, however at the same time it demanded the price of losing chronology and situational coherence. This is the main reason the teachers' expositions again tend to build upon storytelling. Also for the stage of natural language preceding formal assertions like clauses and declarative logic, the storylines need to be developed in students' meta-cognitive awareness.

13 Integral Justification of Innovative Learning Paradigms

The reader may ask him/herself to what extent the various innovative approaches bring better formats for learning and teaching? The summative answer is complicated as learning is a multi-facetted process and has a wide spectrum of positive side effects to be included. So indeed, we still need more wide and intense studies on the precise effects of Gamification, Playification, Collaborative Learning, Narration and Simulations. What are recent understandings that may help you to trust the added values of active learning methods that make the learner as a codesigner / co-owner of his/her learning process.

14 Conclusions

Game-oriented learning can only be adopted and effectively integrated if an overall pedagogical framework has been articulated. Problem-Based Learning seems the best candidate as it places the learner at the very core of the life-long learning process. Scaffolding (and subsequent fading) is seen as a safe way to make learners less dependent from the teacher and institutional guidance. The same is true for the initial and further (in-service) training of ICT teachers. The choice of "narration" is a clever choice to let existing ICT trainers build upon their prior traditions and reflexes; (Kommers & Simmerling, 2015). At the same time, they need an appropriate didactic framework that allows all the new-coming ICT tools to be integrated by the learners themselves. For the moment it is gamification and simulations. In the near future it will be a wealth of MOOCs, Big Data applications, Learning Analytics, Artificial Intelligence, etc. The chosen didactic framework is Problem-Based Learning with an ever-stronger focus on the existential factors of the learner with his/her unique talents.

References

Argyris, C. (2005). Double-loop learning in organizations: A theory of action perspective. In Smith, G. Ken, & M. A. Hitt (Eds.), *Great minds in management: The process of theory development* (pp. 261–279). Oxford University Press. ISBN 0199276811. OCLC 60418039. January, 2008.

Bonanno, P., & Kommers, P. A. M. (2008). Exploring the influence of gender and gaming competence on attitudes towards using instructional games. *British Journal of Educational Technology*. https://doi.org/10.1111/j.1467-8535.2007.00732.x

Issa, T., Kommers, P. A. M., Issa, T., Isaías, P. & Issa, T. B. 2017. *Smart technology applications in business environments*. IGI Global, p. XX–XXV, 429p.

Jayalath, J. & Esichaikul, V. (2016). *Gamification-embedded eLearning courses for the learner success of competency-based education: Case of technical and vocational education and training*. Downloaded from http://hdl.handle.net/11599/2540.

Kaufman, D., Sutow, E., & Dunn, K. (1997). Three approaches to cooperative learning in higher education. In The *canadian journal of higher education; La revue Canadienne d'enseignement supérieur*. Vol. XXVII, Nos. 2,3, pp. 37–66.

Ke, F., & Grabowski, B. (2007). Gameplaying for maths learning: Cooperative or not? *British Journal of Educational Technology, 38*(2), 249–259. https://doi.org/10.1111/j.1467-8535.2006.00593.x

Kommers, P.A.M.; TEXTVISION, conceptual representation beyond the HYPERTEXT metaphor. European Journal of Psychology of Education. Vol. 3, No. 2 (June 1988), pp. 201–216.

Kommers, P. A. M. (2021). *Sources for a better education; lessons from research and best practices*. Springer.

Kommers, P. A. M., & Simmerling, M. (2015). Editorial special issue on the future of lifelong learning MOOCs, e-learning platforms and web communities. *International Journal of Continuing Engineering Education and Life-Long Learning, 25*(2), 135–137.

Kommers, P. A. M., Luursema, J. M., Rodel, S., Geelkerken, B., & Kunst, E. (2004). Virtual reality for training medical skills. *International Journal of Continuing Engineering Education and Life-Long Learning, 14*(1/2), 142–166.

Luursema, Jan-Maarten, Willem B. Verwey, A.M. Kommers, Jan-Henk Annema. The role of stereopsis in virtual anatomical learning. In: Interacting with computers, 20, 4–5, 2008, 455–460, https://doi.org/10.1016/j.intcom.2008.04.003.

Mariscal, V. (2014). Looking Inside the Black Box Albert Bandura "Social Cognitive Theory" "self-efficacy" Solomon Ash "Conformity" Heiner, Weiner "Attribution Theory" Martin Seligman "Positive Psychology" Richard M. Ryan, Edward L.Deci "Self-determination Theory" Mihály Csíkszentmihályi "Flow" Donald Broadbent "Selective Attention" "Short-Term Memory" Jerome Bruner "scaffolding" Jean Piaget "cognitive development".

Papert, S. (1980). *Mindstorms: Children, computers, and powerful ideas*. Harvester Press.

Slavin, R. E. (1977). *Student learning team techniques: Narrowing the achievement gap between the races (Report No. 228)*. Center for Social Organization of Schools, The Johns Hopkins University.

Smyrnova-Trybulska, E., Morze, N., Pavlova, T., Kommers, P. A. M., & Sekret, I. V. (2017). Using effective and adequate IT tools for developing teachers' skills. *International Journal of Continuing Engineering Education and Life-Long Learning, 27*(3), 219–245.

Vygotsky, L. (1986). *Thought and language*. MIT Press.

Werbach, K. (2014). (re) defining gamification: A process approach. In *Persuasive technology* (pp. 266–272). Springer International Publishing.

Werbach, K., and Hunter, D. (2015). The Gamification toolkit: Dynamics, mechanics, and components for the win. Wharton.

Micro-learning in Improving Professional Competences of Programmers: Pilot Studies

Anna Stolińska, Wojciech Baran, Jozef Kapusta, and Katarzyna Wójcik

1 Introduction

Programming skills are recognized by the European Commission as one of the key competencies, included both in the Digital Education Action Plan 2021–2027 (2021) and in the conclusions of the European Council formulated in December 2017 for all throughout life. The Heads of State and Government stated that programming is one of the key competences (Developing Key Competences, 2021). The ability to program is not only associated with the possibility of professional development (preparation for the profession of a programmer) but is also believed to offer the possibility of the general development of problem-solving skills in various areas of life (Martín-Ramos et al., 2017) and the growth of creativity and collaboration. The programming ability is also needed for many jobs, because currently more than 90% of professional occupations nowadays require digital competences, including programming (Coding – the 21st century skill, 2021). The rapid development of ICT and new technologies puts pressure on not only educating young people in programming but also enabling working people to acquire programming skills (Katane & Katans, 2018). The demand for programmers exists not only in Europe but also around the world. For example, on the official website of the United States government, you can read that: *Employment of software developers, quality assurance analysts, and testers is projected to grow 22 percent from 2019 to 2029,*

A. Stolińska (✉)
Department of Computer Science, College of Economics and Computer Science, Kraków, Poland
e-mail: astolinska@wsei.edu.pl

W. Baran · J. Kapusta · K. Wójcik
Pedagogical University of Krakow, Institute of Computer Science, Kraków, Poland
e-mail: wojciech.baran@up.krakow.pl; jozef.kapusta@up.krakow.pl; katarzyna.wojcik@up.krakow.pl

E. Smyrnova-Trybulska et al. (eds.), *Microlearning*,
https://doi.org/10.1007/978-3-031-13359-6_5

much faster than the average for all occupations. These workers will be needed to respond to an increased demand for computer software (Software Developers, 2021).

The growing demand for programmers has highlighted the problems related to coding education, in particular a talent shortage as the education system is slow to react to new demands (Coding – the 21st century skill, 2021). Moreover, learning to program is perceived as difficult. There are many problems in teaching programming that researchers write about (Tsai, 2019; Shefer et al., 2018, Ouahbi et al., 2015; Basawapatna, 2016). Many students have difficulty mastering abstract programming concepts such as conditionals and loops, syntax problems of different languages, and constantly applying what they learn to new and unknown problems (Butler & Morgan, 2007). It turns out that students devote a great deal of time learning syntax and semantics while searching for solutions to problems seems to be marginalized (Andrzejewska et al., 2016). These and other problems show that teaching programming requires effort, learner involvement, and individualization in the learning process. Isong (2014) proposes a departure from traditional methods of teaching programming based on a lecture, demonstration with instruction. The researcher believes that teachers must make more use of ICT-supported learning environments. Programming teaching methods should promote the active participation and involvement of students. The answer to these problems may be, inter alia, proposing micro-learning courses. This concept is in line with the theory of Baumgartner (2013), who argues that professional knowledge is irreducible, complex, uncertain, instable, and unique. The characteristics of professional knowledge assume that we live in an inherently turbulent environment, with undefined problem situations that are "not in the book" and it is micro-learning that can provide an appropriate learning environment to support creative problem solving and inventing new things. Micro-lessons can provide knowledge quickly, inspire to create simple and effective solutions, and at the same time present content that is easily accessible, also from mobile devices (Hug, 2006). Moreover, micro-learning is closer to the already natural learning methods of young people as it is adapted to their attention span (Jaokar, 2007).

Micro-content is available through various platforms, one of the most popular is Youtube (Moghavvemi et al., 2018). It seems, however, that a very good proposal is to create generally available micro-lection courses, prepared by specialists, so that the knowledge provided is reliable and factually correct, and at the same time well thought out in terms of its structure. In our opinion, these requirements are met by the courses on the Priscilla platform, developed under the Erasmus+ Capacity Building in the Field of Higher Education project's No. 2018-1-SK01-KA203-046382 "Work-based learning in future it professionals education".

To summarize these facts, there is still no answer to the question of how professional programmers assess the effectiveness of learning programming with the use of micro-learning.

2 Background

Learning to program begins more and more in primary school (Serafini, 2011; Fatourou et al., 2018) and continues through the stages of education. A report by European Schoolnet (2018), a network of 33 European ministries of education based in Brussels, a non-profit organization that strives to innovate teaching and learning, shows that more and more ministries of education are analyzing the issues of teaching programming and looking for answers to questions how to define life-long learning in the field of programming, how to design the programming science so that it influences the development of students' skills in the twenty-first century.

However, preparation for the profession of programmer requires specialized training in vocational education at the secondary or universities level. The specific education programs and scopes vary by country, but the overall framework for programming education is very similar (Robins et al., 2003). Teaching strategies, programming languages, or supporting tools such as the integrated development environment, IDE, also differ slightly (Pears et al., 2007). In the case of programming languages, their choice is determined not only by didactic reasons, but also by the labor market. The popularity ranking dictates the trends to which schools and universities adapt. This fact was emphasized by Cass (2020), who published research on the popularity of programming languages.

Learning to program is considered difficult, and difficulties (although different) are experienced by both students and teachers – both for students and teachers. Hence, various teaching concepts arise in order to adapt them to the needs, abilities and preferences of students. Recently, there has also been a limited amount of research into adult programming education (Begel & Simon, 2008; Chilana et al., 2016; Dorn & Guzdial, 2010; Ericson et al., 2016). And yet the change of profession, retraining, is part of today's professional careers. Interesting research on programming learning by older adults was conducted in 2017. Using an online survey of 504 respondents aged 60–85, coming from 52 different countries, it was found that older adults were motivated to learn to keep their mind healthy as they got older, make up for lost opportunities in their youth, make up contact with younger family members and improve career prospects (Guo, 2017).

Programming courses are also generally considered challenging, and often have the highest dropout rates. It is generally accepted that it takes about 10 years of experience to turn a novice into a proficient programmer (Robins et al., 2003). It is also not easy to become a programmer just after learning on your own. More and more people are learning programming on their own, and a lot of people who learned independently apply for a job. But in this case, a little discipline and motivation are not enough – it is very important to know where to get knowledge and good practices from.

In learning programming, you can use various sources and teaching aids. The most popular are:

1. Tutorials and documentation – this is the first source worth consulting. By familiarizing yourself with these materials, it should be possible to quickly determine which language suits the learner best.
2. Books and e-books – it can be said that learning from books is not the most convenient form of learning, because it does not provide practical learning, but rather focuses on theory. It is inconvenient to rewrite multi-page code.
3. Programming blogs – in this case, there is a risk of acquiring bad habits or even incorrect knowledge. However, they are often a source of novelty in a given programming language.
4. Development community support – e.g. on StackOverflow.
5. Video courses are an increasingly popular method, thanks to which you can learn programming both from the theoretical and practical side. The available courses can be paid or free.
6. Bootcamps – they involve learning with a teacher (mentor) who orders tasks to be performed, helps to solve them, shows sources that can be used. Bootcamps allow you to gain extensive knowledge, the training is intensive, focused on practical knowledge. The material covers not only the basics of programming, but also the science of technology that will be useful in the future work of a programmer. Bootcamps are most often held online, although there are also those where classes are held in a lecture hall. Classes last from several months to even a year. Such classes require a lot of systematic work, you need to devote several hours a day to learning (Tu et al., 2018).

These methods can be supplemented by online micro-learning interactive courses. The method is based on getting to know theoretical knowledge and then solving short tasks that are checked by the system. The courses are adapted to various levels of advancement, they are flexible, and you can learn at your own pace, at any time convenient for you (Zhang & Ren, 2011). It should be noted, however, that there is research indicating that microlearning courses can be useful in teaching programming. Skalka i Drlik (2018) described conceptual framework of microlearning-based training for improving programming skills. Researchers have addressed the topic of teaching programming using microlearnig, but it is difficult to find references in the literature to studies that discuss the issue of improving the competencies of adults (working professionals).

3 Research Design

In order to determine to what extent IT specialists (professional programmers) acquired, acquire or would like to acquire programming skills with the use of the micro-learning type of teaching method, a survey was conducted with the use of an Internet questionnaire (CAWI). The survey questionnaire consisted of several questions and was structured in such a way that the respondents answered only those questions that were related to their situation. This non-linear questionnaire consisted of single- and multiple-answer questions, and the 7-point Likert scale was used in most of the questions about the ratings, opinions of the respondents. The link to the survey was posted on polish websites: on LinkedIn, Facebook and sent to 4 IT companies. Data was collected for 4 days. 50 people took part in the study, of which 35 were men (70%), 12 women (24%), and 3 people (6%) refused to provide information about their gender.

In the study participated programmers that use various languages, as shown in Fig. 1. The most popular language turned out to be JavaScript, in which 27 respondents (54%) program, as well as PHP and Java (17 [34%] and 16 [32%] participants, respectively. research).

Basic statistics on age and seniority (the measure used was a year) are presented in Table 1.

Most of the respondents are young people (Mean = 26.8 years, SD = 4.7), with a short work experience (Mean = 3.8 years, SD = 4.02). 11 people (22%) are employed as Full Stack Developer, 9 (18%) – Software Engineer, 7 (14%) – Back-end Developer, 5 people (10%) – Front-end Developer. 23 people (46%) described their level of professional experience as a medium developer / regular developer, 19 people (38%) as a junior developer, 7 people (14%) – a senior developer. 26 respondents (52%) work in a large company employing over 250 people, 13 (26%) in a small company (10–50 employees), 8 (16%) in a medium company (51–250 employees).

The main research problem concerned the way in which people working as programmers improve their coding skills. Finding an answer to this question required the formulation of detailed research questions, among which they were included:

1. How did IT specialists acquire the programming skills (competences)?
2. How many programmers declare improving their programming competences during their professional career?
3. What forms of training do professional programmers use?

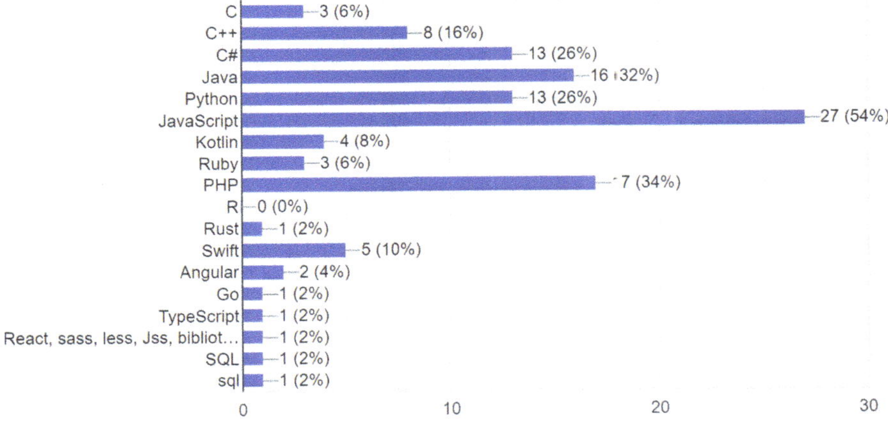

Fig. 1 Programming languages dominating in the respondents' current tasks/professional projects

Table 1 Age and work experience in the profession of a programmer

Age		Number of years of professional experience as a programmer	
Mean	26.79	Mean	3.83
Standard deviation	4.66	Standard deviation	4.02
Median	25.00	Median	3.00
Dominant	25.00	Dominant	4.00
Kurtosis	4.92	Kurtosis	10.62
Skewness	2.03	Skewness	2.84
Range	23.00	Range	23.00
Minimum	22.00	Minimum	0.00
Maximum	45.00	Maximum	23.00
Trust level (95.0%)	1.32	Trust level (95.0%)	1.14

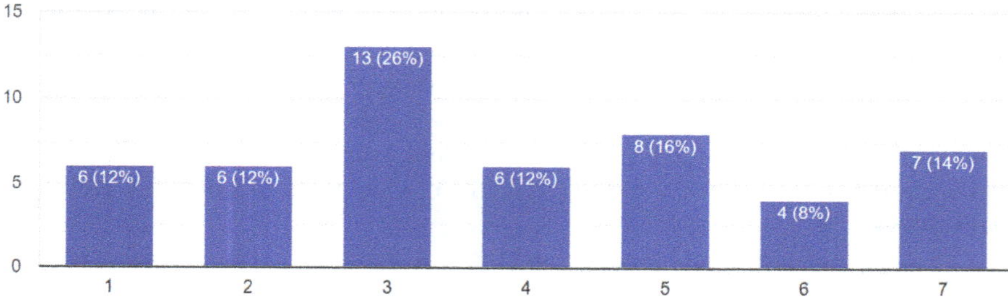

Fig. 2 Assessment of the preparation obtained during studies to work in the profession of a programmer

1. How many developers are using a learning method called micro-learning?
2. To what extent is it used by micro-learning programmers as a method of learning / improving competences?

4. What is the interest of programmers in using micro-learning in improving their professional competences?

4 Results

4.1 How Did IT Specialists Acquire the Programming Skills (Competences)?

The vast majority of the respondents, ie 46 people (92%) graduated in computer science, the others in related fields of study, only two people indicated that they did not study the field of computer science. The respondents indicated on a scale from 1 to 7, where 1 means very poorly to 7 (very good), how they assess the preparation obtained during their studies to work as a programmer. The results are shown in Fig. 2.

The respondents assessed their preparation for work in the profession of programmer at the level M = 3.5 (SD = 1.9).

4.2 *How Many Programmers Declare Improving their Programming Competences During their Professional Career?*

As many as 98% of the respondents (49 people) declared improving their programming skills during their professional career.

4.3 *What Forms of Training Do Professional Programmers Use?*

The respondents supplemented their knowledge and skills in programming in various ways. 44 people (88%) learned using the content (lectures) posted on various websites, e.g. Youtube, 39 (78%) from books and magazines, 22 (44%) participated in stationary training courses, 8 people (16%) attended bootcamps. Currently, while working, most of them declare that they independently find knowledge / skills while implementing projects and solving problems (41 people, 83.7%), many still use YouTube (39 people, 79.6%) or learn from books, trade magazines (22, i.e. 44.9% of respondents).

4.3.1 How Many Developers Are Using a Learning Method Called Micro-learning?

Most of the respondents (37 people, 74%) declared that they use micro-learning. The frequency of using this teaching method varies – 8 (21.6%) people indicated the option "very often, almost every day", 12 people (32.4%) – "often, several times a week", the option "sometimes, what at most a few times a month" was indicated by 10 people (27%), rarely (several times a year) – 7 people (18.9%). People who declared that they do not use micro-learning, as the reason for this state of affairs stated that they have not experienced this type of course (11 people), 2 people said that they do not like learning this way – they prefer longer materials, exactly describing a given issue, problem, another two people said that programming is coding – you can't learn something just by reading or watching.

4.3.2 To What Extent Is It Used by Micro-learning Programmers as a Method of Learning/Improving Competences?

The vast majority of respondents who declared to learn using the micro-learning method, at the same time indicated that they learned this method of programming (33 people, 89.2%). Below are the respondents' opinions on micro-learning in programming teaching, with each rating related to a given statement being formulated on a scale from 1 to 7, where 1 meant: completely disagree and 7: completely agree (Table 2).

4.4 What Is the Interest of Programmers in Using Micro-learning in Improving their Professional Competences?

The respondents rated their interest in micro-learning courses on a scale from 1 to 7, where 1 meant no interest, 7 – high interest. The average interest in micro-learning courses was M = 5.5 (SD = 1.87). A value below 4 was indicated by 8 people, of which 3 declared a total lack of interest in micro-learning in the field of programming.

Table 2 Assessment of micro-learning in learning programming

Learning with the use of micro-learning is:	Efficient (you can learn a lot)	Convenient (you can study anywhere. anytime)	Fast (small bits of knowledge can be mastered quickly)	Flexible (you can only choose what you need at the moment)	Common (many people I know learn this way)
Average	5.51	5.78	5.68	5.92	4.68
Standard deviation	1.43	1.78	1.67	1.46	1.94
Median	6	7	6	7	5
Dominant	7	7	7	7	7
Kurtosis	−0.43	0.02	1.01	0.75	−1.28
Skewness	−0.64	−1.21	−1.31	−1.32	−0.23
Range	5	5	6	5	6
Minimum	2	2	1	2	1
Maximum	7	7	7	7	7
Trust level (95.0%)	0.48	0.59	0.56	0.49	0.65

5 Discussion

Most of the time, programmers who were at the beginning of their professional career took part in the study. It is not surprising, therefore that research indicates a high activity of IT specialists in the field of improving programming skills. The use of various forms and methods of training has been confirmed, while the frequency of using textbooks and trade magazines seems to be quite high compared to participation in bootcamps or stationary courses.

6 Conclusion

The research confirmed that the set of micro-learning courses prepared as part of the "Work-based learning in future it professionals education" project can and should also be made available to professional programmers who want to improve their skills in other languages, or to improve those already possessed. It also seems advisable to build a community of programmers around the Priscilla platform, who would enrich its content with tasks, mini-problems that would strongly relate to projects implemented at work.

Pilot studies also allow for the formulation of certain conclusions that should be taken into account during subsequent, already relevant studies. You need to diagnose what specific knowledge programmers are looking for and from what specific materials (where are they made available? Are they peer-reviewed?) They learn as part of professional development.

References

Andrzejewska, M., Stolińska, A., Błasiak, W., Peczkowski, P., Rosiek, R., Rożek, B., Sajka, M., & Wcisło, D. (2016). Eye-tracking verification of the strategy used to analyse algorithms expressed in a flowchart and pseudocode. *Interactive Learning Environments, 24*(8), 1981–1995. https://doi.org/10.1080/10494820.2015.1073746

Basawapatna, A. (2016). Alexander meets Michotte: A simulation tool based on pattern programming and phenomenology. *Journal of Educational Technology & Society, 19*(1), 277–291.

Baumgartner, P. (2013). Educational dimensions of microlearning – Towards a taxonomy for microlearning. In P. A. Bruck & M. Sedlaczek (Eds.), *Designing microlearning experiences – Building up knowledge in organisations and companies*. Innsbruck University Press.

Begel, A., & Simon B. (2008). Struggles of new college graduates in their first software development job. In *Proceedings of the 39th SIGCSE technical symposium on computer science education (SIGCSE '08)* (pp. 226–230). New York: ACM. https://doi.org/10.1145/1352135.1352218.

Butler, M., & Morgan, M. (2007). Learning challenges faced by novice programming students studying high level and low feedback concepts. In *Proceedings of ASCILITE – Australian Society for Computers in Learning in Tertiary Education, annual conference 2007* (pp. 99–107). Retrieved 15 July 2021 from https://www.learntechlib.org/p/46043/

Cass, S. (2020). The top programming languages: Our latest rankings put Python on top-again – [careers]. *IEEE Spectrum, 57*(8), 22–22. https://doi.org/10.1109/mspec.2020.9150550

Chilana, P. K., Singh, R., & Guo, P. J. (2016). Understanding conversational programmers: A perspective from the software industry. In *Proceedings of the 2016 CHI conference on human factors in computing systems (CHI '16)* (pp. 1462–1472). New York: ACM. https://doi.org/10.1145/2858036.2858323

Coding – The 21st century skill. European Commission. Retrieved 1 July 2021 from https://ec.europa.eu/digital-single-market/en/coding-21st-century-skill

Developing key competences for all throughout life. European Commission. Retrieved 1 July 2021 from https://ec.europa.eu/education/sites/default/files/document-library-docs/factsheet-key-competences-lifelong-learning_en.pdf

Digital education action plan. European Commission. Retrieved 1 July 2021 from https://ec.europa.eu/education/education-in-the-eu/digital-education-action-plan_en

Dorn, B., & Guzdial, M. (2010). Learning on the job: Characterizing the programming knowledge and learning strategies of web designers. In *Proceedings of the SIGCHI conference on human factors in computing systems (CHI'10)* (pp. 703–712). New York: ACM. https://doi.org/10.1145/1753326.1753430

Ericson, B. J., Rogers, K., Parker, M., Morrison, B., & Guzdial M. (2016). Identifying design principles for CS teacher Ebooks through design-based research. In *Proceedings of the 2016 ACM conference on international computing education research (ICER'16)* (pp. 191–200). New York: ACM. https://doi.org/10.1145/2960310.2960335

European Schoolnet's 2018 annual report. European Schoolnet. Retrieved 2 June 2021 from http://www.eun.org/documents/411753/817341/activity-report_2018_online_FINAL.pdf

Fatourou, E., Zygouris, N. C., Loukopoulos, T., & Stamoulis, G. I. (2018). Teaching concurrent programming concepts using scratch in primary school: Methodology and evaluation. *International Journal of Engineering Pedagogy, 8*(4), 89–105. https://doi.org/10.3991/ijep.v8i4.8216

Guo, P. J. (2017). Older adults learning computer programming: Motivations, frustrations, and design opportunities. In *Proceedings of the 2017 CHI conference on human factors in computing systems*, May 2017 (pp. 7070–7083). https://doi.org/10.1145/3025453.3025945

Hug, T. (2006). Microlearning: A new pedagogical challenge (introductory note). In T. Hug, M. Lindner, & P. A. Bruck (Eds.), *Microlearning: Emerging concepts, practices and technologies after E-learning, Proceedings of microlearning conference 2005: Learning & Working in New Media*. Innsbruck University Press.

Isong, B. (2014). A methodology for teaching computer programming: First year students' perspective. *International Journal of Modern Education and Computer Science, 6*, 15–21. https://doi.org/10.5815/IJMECS.2014.09.03

Jaokar, A. (2007). Mobile Web 2.0, micro-learning, intertwingularity, and mobile widgets. *Educational Technology, 47*(6), 43–45.

Katane, I., & Katans, E. (2018). Environmental contexts of programmer's professional self-development through learning: Ecological and synergetic approach. In *Proceedings of the 17th International Scientific Conference "Engineering for Rural Development"*, Jelgava, Latvia, May 23–25 2018. https://doi.org/10.22616/ERDEV2018.17.N057

Martín-Ramos, P., Lopes, M. J., da Silva, M. M. L., Gomes, P. E. B., da Silva, P. S. P., Domingues, J. P. P., & Silva, M. R. (2017). First exposure to Arduino through peer-coaching: Impact on students' attitudes towards programming. *Computers in Human Behavior, 76*, 51–58. https://doi.org/10.1016/j.chb.2017.07.007

Moghavvemi, S., Sulaiman, A., Jaafar, N. I., & Kasem, N. (2018). Social media as a complementary learning tool for teaching and learning: The case of Youtube. *The International Journal of Management Education, 16*(1), 37–42.

Ouahbi, I., Kaddari, F., Darhmaoui, H., Elachqar, A., & Lahmine, S. (2015). Learning basic programming concepts by creating games with Scratch programming environment. *Procedia – Social and Behavioral Sciences, 191*, 1479–1482. https://doi.org/10.1016/j.sbspro.2015.04.224

Pears, A., Seidman, S., Malmi, L., Mannila, L., Adams, E., Bennedsen, J., Devlin, M., & Paterson, J. (2007). A survey of literature on the teaching of introductory programming. *ACM SIGCSE Bulletin, 39*(4), 204–223.

Robins, A., Rountree, J., & Rountree, N. (2003). Learning and teaching programming: A review and discussion. *Computer Science Education, 13*, 137–172. https://doi.org/10.1076/csed.13.2.137.14200

Serafini, G. (2011). Teaching programming at primary schools: Visions, experiences, and long-term research prospects. In *Proceedings of the 5th international conference on informatics in schools: Situation, evolution and perspectives*. Berlin, Heidelberg: Springer-Verlag.

Shefer, O. P., Nosova, L. S., & Lebedeva, T. N. (2018). A modern methodology for teaching programming at a university. *Scientific and Technical Information Processing, 45*(2), 81–86. https://doi.org/10.3103/S0147688218020077

Skalka, J., & Drlik, M. (2018). Conceptual framework of microlearning-based training mobile application for improving programming skills. In M. Auer & T. Tsiatsos (Eds.), *Interactive Mobile communication technologies and learning. IMCL 2017* (Advances in intelligent systems and computing) (Vol. 725, pp. 213–224). https://doi.org/10.1007/978-3-319-75175-7_22

Software developers, quality assurance analysts, and testers, U.S. Bureau of Labor Statistics. Retrieved 1 July 2021 from https://www.bls.gov/ooh/computer-and-information-technology/software-developers.htm

Tsai, C.-Y. (2019). Improving students' understanding of basic programming concepts through visual programming language: The role of self-efficacy. *Computers in Human Behavior, 95*, 224–232. https://doi.org/10.1016/j.chb.2018.11.038

Tu, Y-C., Dobbie, G., Warren, I., Meads, A., & Grout, C. (2018). An experience report on a boot-camp style programming course. In *Proceedings of the 49th ACM technical symposium on computer science education*, February 2018 (pp. 509–514). https://doi.org/10.1145/3159450.3159541.

Zhang, X., & Ren, L. (2011). Design for application of micro learning to informal training in enterprise. In *2nd international conference on artificial intelligence, management science and electronic commerce (AIMSEC)* (pp. 2024–2027). https://doi.org/10.1109/AIMSEC.2011.6011235.

Teaching and Learning Activities Based on the Priscilla Tool

Beata Zielosko, Małgorzata Przybyła-Kasperek, Kornel Chromiński, Arkadiusz Nowakowski, and Eugenia Smyrnova-Trybulska

1 Introduction

Both online and blended learning poses many challenges regarding the methods of working with students, their activation in the learning process, and the selection of tools to support students and teachers. The chapter describes selected collaborative learning strategies and tutoring methods as important elements in the process of personalized education. An example of a tool supporting the work of both students and teachers is the Priscilla educational platform developed under the FITPED project.

2 Background

The topic of introducing innovative methods, tools and forms to the educational process is very important and actual, in particular in e-learning and blended learning processes and environments. The Covid-19 pandemic, with the accompanying lock-downs and the global transformation of the educational process to online education proved that in times of crises we do not have an alternative to online education and because of this, this mode of teaching and learning should be permanently improved and increased in quality.

B. Zielosko · M. Przybyła-Kasperek · K. Chromiński · A. Nowakowski
University of Silesia in Katowice, Katowice, Poland
e-mail: beata.zielosko@us.edu.pl; malgorzata.przybyla-kasperek@us.edu.pl; kornel.chrominski@us.edu.pl; arkadiusz.nowakowski@us.edu.pl

E. Smyrnova-Trybulska (✉)
Department of Humanistic Education, University of Silesia in Katowice, Katowice, Poland
e-mail: esmyrnova@us.edu.pl

E. Smyrnova-Trybulska et al. (eds.), *Microlearning*,
https://doi.org/10.1007/978-3-031-13359-6_6

From a different perspective, in the framework of the FITPED project (www.fitped.eu), the new educational "model is focused on minimizing the number of students with problems in learning" (Drlik et al., 2019, p. 12). The researchers and partners of the project stressed that increasing the level of knowledge obtained by students in the introductory courses focused on the development of programming skills need for increasing the level of of knowledge of highly specialized IT skills, as well as for training students for LLL. As a conclusion, they stressed, „the features of work-based learning, active learning, collaborative and problem-based learning approaches will be used during this process" (Drlik et al., 2019, p. 12).

Skalka et al. (2021) described the design of the framework from a peda-gogical point of view. Authors emphasize that Bloom's taxonomy is applied to all phases of the process of building knowledge and skills, from a programmer start-ing from zero experience to a professional ready to develop applications in practice within the context of microlearning too, and described the students' shift across the stages, according to Bloom's taxonomy from top to bottom.

There are various definitions of *microlearning*. For example, Theo Hug proposed it thusly: "The term *microlearning* has been used since the beginning of the twenty-first **century** mainly in the context of e-Learning. Commonly it stands for an abbreviated manner of expression for all sorts of short-time learning activities with microcontent." (Hug, 2012). The author also stressed:

> The term is used in many different ways. The spectrum of implicit or explicit definitions ranges from (1) unspecified forms of webspeak about learning by means of digital media and (2) ideological concepts of how learning processes ought to be organized according to the fast-moving world of technology to (3) differentiated conceptualizations of learning processes as related to micro-perspectives in the context of learning, education, and training. (Hug, 2012)

Aldosemani stressed that, "the development of new skills and knowledge requires a variety of teaching methods and learning strategies" (2019). "Students' opinion overviewed through an outline of the various phases of microteaching, implementation aspects, and microteaching content and activities used in this teaching method." (Aldosemani, 2019).

Other researchers "explore[s] [the] current understanding of microlearning as an effective model for professional development. From a theoretical perspective, the authors explore the rationale for microlearning by considering the literature on competency-based education (CBE) and microcredentialing." The authors "argue that microlearning can be a powerful model if the design is appropriate" (Zhang & West, 2020).

Experts Lee et al. (2021) conducted the "formative research to study the mobile microcourse's learning efficacy, defined as effectiveness, efficiency, and appeal… The results indicate that learners of this mobile microcourse had an increase in knowledge, more certainty in decisions about practical applications, and an increase in confidence in performing skills."

In conclusion, the authors stressed that "automated feedback, timed gamified exercises, and interactive real-world content indicate room for improvement to enhance effective learning" (Lee et al., 2021).

Another study (Jahnke et al., 2020) underlines that the results of their research "show a set of 15 principles regarding technical issues, pedagogical usability of micro-content interaction and sequenced instructional flow."

In a further part of the article, some learning strategies and methods using, in particular, Priscilla platform within the framework FITPED project will be presented and analysed.

3 Collaborative Learning Strategies

Collaborative learning is the instructional use of small groups of students, so they can work together to maximize their own and each other's learning activities (Jonhson & Jonhson, 2013). It is an educational approach to enhance the learning process of students through their work together, as a group. There are a lot of benefits of collaborative learning, among them, we can distinguish developing social interaction skills, leadership skills and/or oral communication skills (De Hei et al., 2016). It is clear that this strategy of learning supports an active learning environment and beyond knowledge allows one to acquire and develop skills that are very important nowadays. Below are shortly described popular collaborative learning strategies such as Problem-based learning (PBL), Jigsaw, Role-playing, STAD&TGT, and Peer tutoring.

3.1 *Problem-Based Learning (PBL)*

PBL is an active way of learning in which students learn about a subject by working in groups to solve real problems. The main goals of the PBL system are orderliness of knowledge (often from various fields) so that it can be used in practice, development of learning skills of students and increasing their motivation to acquire knowledge. It is a method that by assumption makes the student search for solutions by themselves.

The idea behind this strategy can be presented in the form of the following steps (Problem-Based Learning, 2021):

1. Discussion in a group of students the problem that should relate to real situations. This step can be considered as a preparation stage. The teacher should define the time frame and the form in which the solution will be presented.
2. Problem analysis. In the framework of this stage, roles must be assigned to the group. Then the group discusses the directions to solve the problem, as well as possible tasks. It should be identified what the group already knows and what are the potential solutions.
3. Analyzing the results of the brainstorming session. After establishing goals and objectives, students discuss their plans and who is responsible for which activi-

ties (e.g. research, experimentation, literature, interviews, etc.). They also need to formulate learning goals for knowledge that is still lacking.
4. Solution. In this stage, **students** study and follow pre-assigned tasks to solve a problem, combining individual and group work.
5. Discussing the results. Students **summarize** the solution and turn it into a form that can be presented to others. Druing this stage, they can identify new concepts and knowledge acquired during the process of solving a problem.

3.2 Jigsaw

The jigsaw classroom is a research-based cooperative learning technique invented and developed in the early 1970s by E. Aronson and his students at the University of Texas and the University of California. This strategy can be used in different courses where students have to learn a certain part of the material, which can be divided into coherent fragments.

The idea is like in a jigsaw puzzle, where each piece (each student) is essential for the completion and understanding of the final result. The basic principle of the jigsaw method is that each member of the group should become an expert who significantly contributes to the achievements of the entire team. Everyone is important because the results of all depend on his work, each student must use the knowledge acquired by other students and has to help everyone else. This strategy can be presented in the following steps (The Jigsaw classroom, 2021):

1. Dividing students into jigsaw groups, each group contains five to six students.
2. The teacher should divide the content of the lesson into five to six segments, (for example, SQL language contains instructions that can be related to: (i) definition and modification of the table structure (CREATE, ALTER), (ii) selecting data with different conditions (SELECT WHERE), (iii) selecting data with aggregating functions and grouping (GROUP, HAVING), (iv) updating and deleting data (UPDATE, DELETE), (v) granting and revoking permissions (GRANT, REVOKE). Each student from the group has been assigned one segment to learn.
3. Creation of temporary "expert groups". Each such group contains one student from each jigsaw group. Such students have been assigned to learn the same segment of material. Expert groups organize their knowledge relative to the given batch of material, clarify doubts and think about the best method of teaching other members of their jigsaw group.
4. Bringing the students back into their jigsaw groups. Each student presents his segment of material to the group. Each group member should master all the material.
5. At the end of the session, the teacher can give a quiz related to the considered subject. Questions can be prepared by the teacher or by the students (for example, in expert groups—for each batch of material).

The Jigsaw strategy supported by the Priscilla platform (Skalka & Drlik, 2018) was used during database course provided at the University of Silesia. The considered topics were: database modeling and SQL realised in a form of blended learning. Students registered in the Priscilla platform were assigned to the groups created by the teacher. In case of database modeling, the scope of the material has been divided as follows: creating entity relationship diagrams including entities, attributes, relationship between entities, Barker notation, and creating a database implementation diagram, including the primary key, foreign key, rules for transforming a conceptual model into a relational model. The first possibility of verification of knowledge in this area of material was solving short test questions available on the Priscilla platform. The second possibility of analyzing and verification of knowledge involved the creation of entity relationship diagrams and the transformation to the relational model for a given problem description was solving in the form face-to-face. In the case of the SQL language, both the acquisition of knowledge and the execution of commands took place using the functionalities available on the Priscilla platform.

3.3 *STAD & TGT*

Student Teams-Achievement Division (STAD) is a learning strategy where students work together to learn and they are responsible for the learning process of themselves and their teammates. To test the learning process, students take individual quizzes.

The STAD method consists of the following steps:

1. The teacher presents the material (a lesson).
2. Students work in teams of four to five to make sure that all team members have mastered the material.
3. The quiz on the lesson is taken individually by all students.
4. Students are assigned individual improvement scores.
5. The points (scores) are then summed up to form team scores and teams are recognized for the highest scores.

Teams-Games-Tournament (TGT) is based on the same teams work as in STAD but quizzes are replaced with weekly tournaments where students compete with members of other teams to contribute points to their team score. Tournaments are played at a "tournament table" (three students) against other players with a similar score from the previous week. The winner at each tournament table wins points for their team. Similar to STAD, teams are recognized for the highest score.

TGT is appropriate for the same types of objectives as STAD. There are many studies on STAD and TGT which have shown the positive effects on using these methods in learning math, science, arts, and other subjects (Slavin, 2010).

3.4 Role-Playing

Role-playing is an active pedagogical approach where students engage in relevant scenarios in order to gain cognitive and behavioural understanding. They may "act out" imaginary characters or, in some instances, play themselves. Additionally, scenarios may be contemporary or historical (Golwitzer, 2018). This strategy of activating students during the learning process can be used in different disciplines, such as medicine, history, engineering, geography, international relations and many others. Researchers noted that role-playing can help students make more explicit connections between content, which can lead to the ability to apply knowledge in different contexts. Role-playing allows students to practice skills such as negotiating, making decisions, expressing their opinions and emotions, and communication, and leads to developing students' interests through experience. When a teacher decides to use the role-playing strategy in the class, the following issues should be considered:

1. Getting to know the problem/issue, which should be complex with multiple perspectives and opinions. Roles can be performed by individual students, in pairs, or groups.
2. Developing characters with sufficient detail. Students should receive information pertaining to background, goals, and expectations of their character (for example, an aggressive client).
3. Providing assessment or reflection and discussion about the interactions, such as alternative ways of dealing with the situation.

3.5 Peer-Tutoring

Peer tutoring is generally described as a specific form of collaborative learning in which the tutor (for example an experienced student) offers help and support to one or more tutees (students). There is a wide variation of how peer tutoring can be applied in practice, for example, peer tutoring with small or large groups, same-age or cross-age, online or face-to-face. In the next section, tutoring is described in more detail.

3.6 Tutoring

Tutoring is a very popular method of organizing individual learning. In many publications (Alegre Ansuategui & Moliner Miravet, 2017; Mohamed & Lamia, 2018), we can find arguments that this form of individual support brings very positive effects. It is aimed not only at the achievement/skills, such as learning a specific programming language but also at the general development of the tutti/student. A good organization of the tutoring process is very important. Initial arrangements should be made and the rules of the meetings should be written down. It is also extremely important to set a goal, which should be demanding, but not exceeding the possibilities of the tutti. In this section, the meaning of tutoring and the difference between mentoring, coaching and tutoring will be described. Guidance will be given on how to plan meetings and some selected tutorial tools will be discussed.

4 Differences and Similarities Between Tutoring, Mentoring and Coaching

Tutoring is a method of individual care for the tutti/student, an innovative method of developing creativity and independent thinking. Organized in this way, the teaching process is not only focused on achieving a specific goal, but also on the internal development of tutti—among others, the skills of independence, responsibility, constructive and critical thinking skills, self-discipline can be improved.

Traditional teaching methods are based on mentoring, i.e. an expert in the field/mentor knows, knows how to achieve the specified goal and passes this knowledge to the student. The student is rather passive in such a process, he should listen and take knowledge from the mentor. Tutoring follows completely different rules. The tutor knows, but he does not pass it on. It allows the tutor to independently choose how to achieve the goal. However, he supports the student in this way, by asking questions, he can indicate a wrong direction, but never imposes his opinion.

Coaching is also a modern technique for supporting individual development and achieving goals. A coach is a person who does not have knowledge in a given field, does not know the way to the goal, but is able to support and motivate in achieving the intended goals. The main tool for achieving goals in both tutoring and coaching is the ability to ask appropriate questions and use motivational techniques. Both methods are aimed at supporting the student, not leading or imposing the teacher's will. However, the main difference here is knowledge, the tutor has the knowledge, while the coach does not.

5 First Meeting—Setting Goals and Rules for Meetings

The tutoring process should consist of a minimum six meetings. The first meeting is very important and should be devoted to setting out the rules according to which the entire process will be organized. Such a set of rules should be written in the form of a contract and signed by both sides—the tuti and the tutor. Among these principles, issues such as confidentiality should be addressed. Tutoring meetings should be confidential, honest, friendly and devoted entirely to the tuti. In addition, the tutti has to ensure that they are ready to develop or change, and there is space between where the tutti is now and where they are going to be. It is also very important to define such basics as the time, form and place of meetings, punctuality and what will happen when an absence is not reported. The goal of the tutoring meetings should also be specified and described in the contract. This target may change, in this case, the contract must be renegotiated.

6 Selected Tutorial Tools

In this section, selected basic tools that could be applied during tutorial meetings will be discussed. A tutor circle can be used in the initial phase of tutoring meetings to explore the goals of the tutti in a given area of life. A values table can be used to make the tutti aware of what values are actually the most important for them and to check whether a given tutti and the tutor can work together—similar values are crucial for them. A matrix of questions is helpful in systematizing and making aware what could happen in case the goal will be achieved or not. It is a motivating tool. The SMART card is a tool that could be helpful in determining the path to the goal, i. e. what tasks must be performed, what steps should be taken to achieve the goal and how to recognize that the goal has been achieved.

6.1 *Tutor Circle*

A tutor circle is actually many circles with a common centre and different radius that have been divided into parts, Fig. 1. Each part in the tutor circle will reflect one area: competencies, skills, priorities, problems, opportunities or other aspects. This will be determined by the tutti. The tutti fills the part of the circle by giving the degree of a goal's achievement (in some scale e.g. from one to four). Such activities

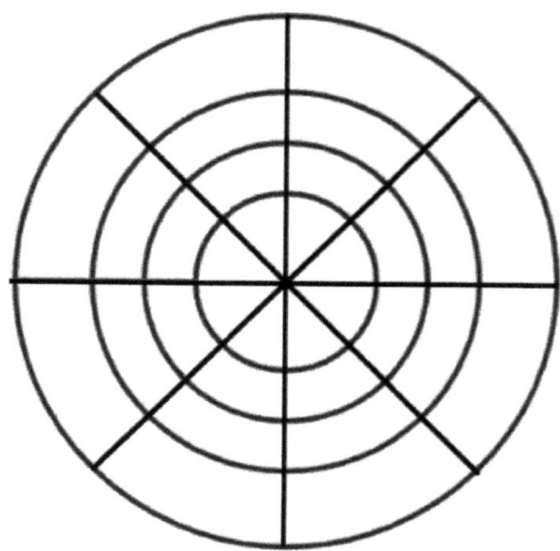

Fig. 1 Tutor circle. Source: Prepared by Małgorzata Przybyła-Kasperek

help the tutti be aware at what stage of achieving the goal they are currently located and in which particular areas they should work harder. Of course, the tutor should support the tutor with constructive questions, for example: Which area do you want to focus on first? Why?, What can you do to be satisfied with the results of this work?

6.2 *Values Table*

The table of values is helpful in determining the set of basic values that are the most important for the tutor. Firstly, this activity will determine the elements and areas which the tutti will not sacrifice in order to achieve the goal (it may be, for example, time spent with the family). The second important application of the values table is to check if the tutor and the tutti have a similar set of values. If there are fundamental differences, there is a high probability that good cooperation between such people will not be possible.

In order to apply this tool, we prepare a table containing different values. There should be a lot of values, e.g. 70. Among other things, there can be authenticity, safety, patience, curiosity, sensitivity, gentleness, pride, stability, flexibility, efficiency, enthusiasm, dignity, close relation, harmony, honour, consequence, creativity, loyalty, wisdom, love, hope, perfection. Then we ask the tutor to cross out the ten least important values, features from the table. Then we ask once again to cross out the next 20 least important values. We repeat these steps until the last five, the most important, values remain in the table. This tool not only allows one to learn about these most important features for a given person but also establishes a certain hierarchy of values.

6.3 *Matrix of Questions*

As was mentioned previously, the essence of tutoring is to support and motivate the tutti by, among other things, asking the right questions. The questions in different areas should be asked in order to analyze all possible scenarios. The matrix of questions can be helpful in this. It is presented in Fig. 2. The tutti should answer questions in each cell of the matrix, and then the consequences of various situations should be analyzed together.

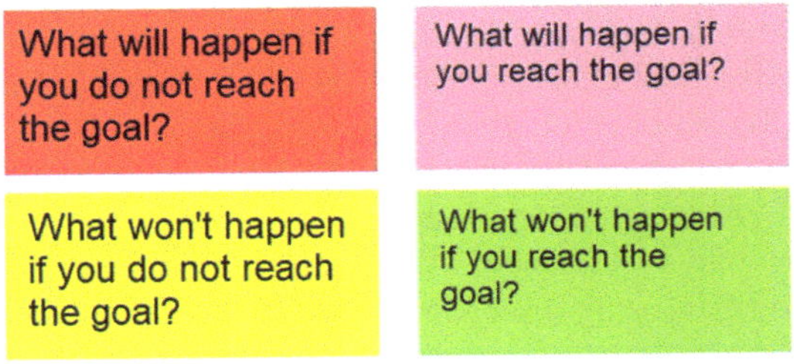

Fig. 2 Matrix of questions. Source: Prepared by Małgorzata Przybyła-Kasperek

6.4 SMART Card

A SMART card is a tool that helps to learn about the characteristics of the goal. A deeper understanding of the goal affects its specificity and deetermines what steps should be taken to achieve it. In the SMART card, five rows are given, in each, there is one of the goal's characteristics: Specific, Measurable, Ambitious, Realistic, Timely. In the appropriate rows questions that will help the tutti to define the goal are presented. Examples of questions in each characteristic are given below:

S—What exactly do you want to achieve?
M—How will you know when you will achieve this goal?
A—Why is it important?
R—What resources do you need for this?
T—When do you want to end the activities?

Of course, the tutor gives additional questions as appropriate and helps summarize the entire activity.

Teaching in accordance with the principle of tutoring can be carried out using the PRISCILLA application (Skalka & Drlik, 2018). The goal will be, for example, to learn one of the programming languages. PRISCILLA is a tool that allows the student to learn independently, acquire knowledge during microlessons and practise skills in tasks. The tutor should help to define the goal as well as motivate and accompany the student on their way to achieving the goal.

The PRISCILLA application was used during tutoring classes in the project "Masters of didactics—Tutoring for the best students" that was realized at the University of Silesia in Katowice. Students who participated in the program learned programming languages, such as Python, using the PRISCILLA application. In this process, students were supported by a tutor who helped in setting sub-goals and milestones in the learning process. Additionally, gamification elements available in the PRISCILLA application were used. This tool was very motivating for students and was a helpful tool to evaluate the learning progress. Overall, project's participants positively assessed the PRISCILLA application and used it with pleasure.

7 Automated Programming Assignment Based on Priscilla

In the tutoring of programming languages, we can distinguish two learning ways: rote learning and understanding (Mayer, 1981). In general, both methods perform well in learning problem-solving, yet, concerning teaching programming languages, it is essential to use techniques that foster understanding. The PRISCILLA platform (Skalka & Drlik, 2018) allows teaching the former as microlessons and the latter as an automated programming assignment.

Automated programming assignment is a type of exercise/assignment that employs a student to write small programs that are run on a server automatically and verified using premade test cases. This approach is very similar to unit testing, a method of software testing that tests an individual unit of source code to determine whether it is fit for use. Nevertheless, in terms of teaching, test cases should be prepared not only for verifying the code itself but also to show students flaws in their works alongside descriptive messages, which lead students to the correct solution. As in unit testing, a single automated programming assignment can be defined as three elements: arrange, act, and assert. The first element, "arrange", means all input data from test cases and preconditions like loading external libraries and variables definitions. "Act" is a student's work, but sometimes regarding the expected output, the form of the solution must be provided (e.g. a function with a specific name). The last element, "assert", is the verification of a student program result against expected values that sometimes includes data transformation. To enhance the above description, verify the below example from a PHP course.

Task description: *Assume you have the array $arr with numerical keys; print the keys (comma-separated) that values containing the value: 3.*

Example (a part of the description):

```
input : [1,2,3,3,5]
output: 2,3
The content of an assignment file:
<?php
// your array, do not remove this line
$arr = json_decode(trim(fgets(STDIN)),true);
// write your code here
```

The expected file includes the input transformation as test cases are written in plain text. Finally, after code verifying, a student receives points calculated based on the number of passed test cases.

Using automated unit testing in teaching programming languages is efficient. Barriocanal et al. report that all students who used unit testing in their assignments improved their code quality in the experiment (Barriocanal et al., 2002). However, for some cases like web-development programming languages, an automated programming assignment requires additional work as tutors need to prepare a mockup of the environment, e.g. a browser for testing DOM API in JavaScript. These bothersome cases can extend the time of creating teaching materials and introduce confusing assumptions.

7.1 A Modern Approach to Learning programming Languages on the Priscila Platform

Learning one of the programming languages is one of the basic skills that an IT specialist must have nowadays. The ability to create your own programs is also useful in many other professions. Nowadays, there are many opportunities to learn the programming language of your choice by yourself, from video tutorials to interactive platforms. One example of a platform that allows interactive learning of programming languages is the Priscila platform. Within the platform, it is possible to learn several programming languages, including Java, C++ and Python.

By learning through the Priscila platform, the learner has the opportunity to learn the syntax, commands and how to develop software in an accessible way, without having to install the development environment on their computer.

Learning particular issues in programming languages is based on three stages, as presented in the Fig. 3. In carrying out each topic, the learner is first introduced to the problem in the form of a theoretical introduction with examples. In the next step, the learner can verify the acquired knowledge by taking a test. The final stage of each topic is a set of programming exercises covering the discussed issue. The implementation of programming exercises takes place through the website of the platform.

Learning programming languages using Priscila platforms begins with introducing the basics of a given language, and then in the next steps, expanding the knowledge of the learner more and more, up to advanced programming (see Fig. 4). After reading a topic and practical exercises performed by confirming that the learner comprehends the material, they have the opportunity to move to the next question. For each well-solved task, the learner receives additional points, which can be exchanged for hints about tasks, which additionally allows them to better understand the problem.

Programming exercises are designed in such a way as to best teach the learner to use the aspects of a given programming language discussed in a given topic. For the implementation of programming exercises, the platform user is not required to have a programming environment installed locally on their computer. The entire code written as part of the exercise is entered directly on the platform's website. Each task has a description of the problem to be solved, as well as an example input and expected output for the program. After writing the program code, the user can run it directly from the Priscila platform, as an example, the Python programming task is shown in Fig. 5. After running the code written by the user, test cases checking the correctness of the written solution are evaluated, and the user is informed about the result of this check.

Each task from the administrative side that creates the course, apart from the content of the task itself, also contains a solution that the platform user can display

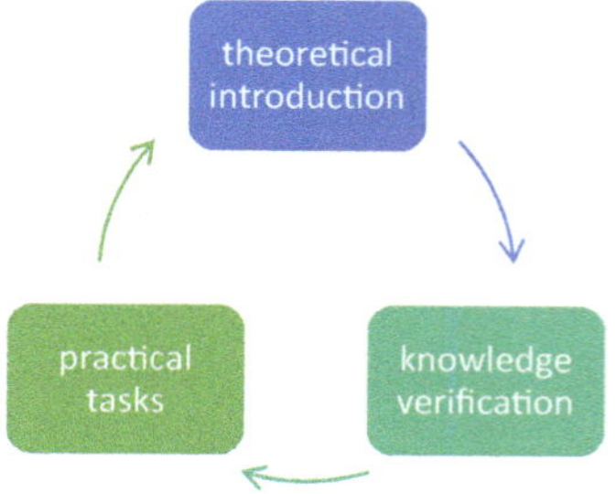

Fig. 3 The stages of teaching particular issues of programming languages on the Priscila platform. Source: Prepared by Kornel Chromiński

Fig. 4 the stages of introducing topics from programming languages. Source: Prepared by Kornel Chromiński

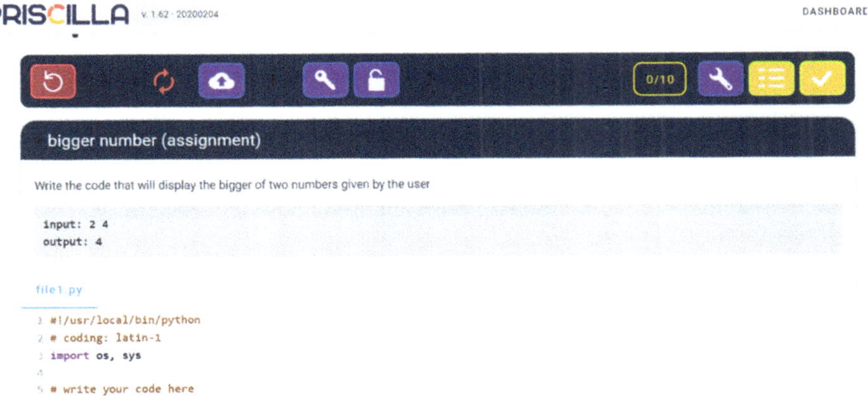

Fig. 5 Examples of programming tasks in Python language. Source: https://priscilla.fitped.eu/courses/3

if they have a problem with solving a given task, and a set of test cases containing sample inputs for the program and expected outputs (see Fig. 6).

This modern approach to learning programming languages allows a student to learn independently and verify their progress. The issues discussed in the framework of learning programming languages are divided into small blocks so as not to provide too much knowledge at one time, and to focus on practical tasks confirming the learning of a given part of the material. For example, for the Python language, the course is divided into 39 main thematic blocks, each block consists of several sub-topics, as well as practice questions and programming tasks. The Python course includes a total of 270 test questions and 225 programming tasks adapted in the best way to the presented topic.

The Priscila platform can also be a great tool to support the teacher in the process of teaching programming languages. As part of the platform, it is possible to create class groups and assign students to them, and to track their progress in the implementation of the course. It allows also to provide discussions on a given topic among students as well as modertate discussion by a teacher. Thanks to information about tasks solved by students and scored points, the teacher can follow the students' activity and progress. The implemented on the platform gamification module ensures the integration of elements of competitiveness and motivations for

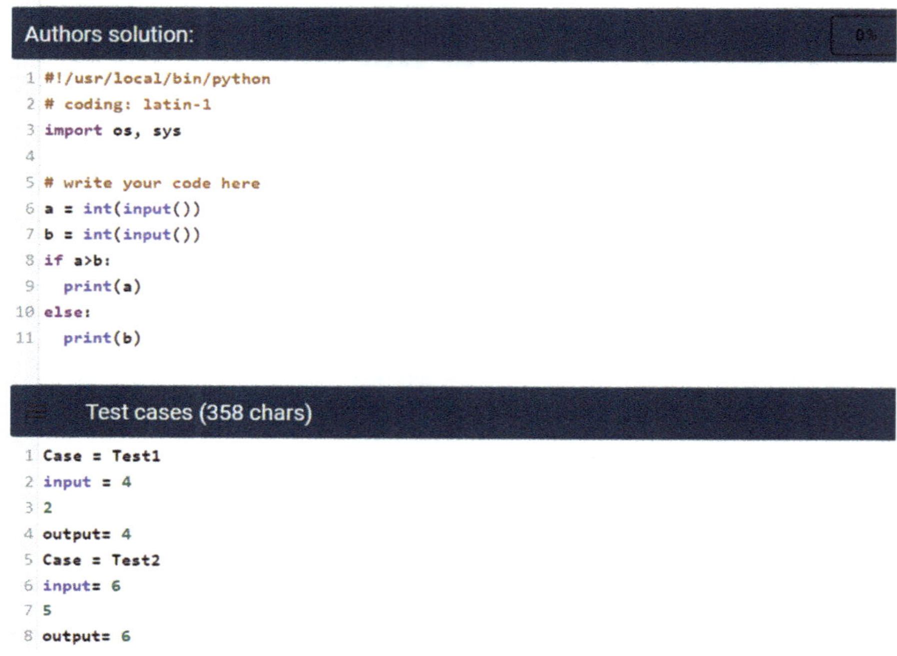

Fig. 6 Author's solution and a list of test cases for a programming task. Source: https://priscilla.fitped.eu/courses/3

surname	name	score (1860)	%	score (960/900)	Basic terminolo... (60/0)
		1190	91.7/34.4%	880/310	60/0
		60	06.3/00.0%	60/0	60/0
		908	62.3/34.4%	598/310	48/0
		900	70.8/24.4%	680/220	60/0

Fig. 7 Summary of students' activity within the class group. Source: https://priscilla.fitped.eu/courses/3

achieving goals. Based on the observation of students' work results, the teacher can apply an individual approach, assigning students tasks with various levels of difficulty adapted to their needs and skills. Thanks to the possibility of working in a group, the teacher can also use the chosen technique of colaborative learning, e.g. jigsaw, by dividing the group of students into smaller teams.

Self-learning or supporting the process of learning programming languages using Priscila platforms allows a student to master a given programming language in an easy and accessible way.

8 Conclusions

Blended learning is one of the modern teaching methods that combine face-to-face learning and online learning. In the framework of FITPED project, a platform named Priscilla was created. It can be used as a platform, for e-learning classes concentrated around programming languages. This chapter describes how an automated programming assignments were created and a case study for using Priscilla in the e-learning process for Python and how other programming languages were implemented.

Acknowledgements This research was funded by European Commission under the ERASMUS+ Programme 2018, KA2, grant number: 2018-1-SK01-KA203-046382 "Work-Based Learning in Future IT Professionals Education".

References

Aldosemani, T. I. (2019). Microlearning for macro-outcomes: Students' perceptions of telegram as a microlearning tool. In T. Väljataga & M. Laanpere (Eds.), *Digital turn in schools—Research, policy, practice. Lecture notes in educational technology*. Springer. https://doi.org/10.1007/978-981-13-7361-9_13

Alegre Ansuategui, F. J., & Moliner Miravet, L. (2017). Emotional and cognitive effects of peer tutoring among secondary school mathematics students. *International Journal of Mathematical Education in Science and Technology, 48*(8), 1185–1205.

Barriocanal, E. G., Urbán, M. Á. S., Cuevas, I. A., & Pérez, P. D. (2002). An experience in integrating automated unit testing practices in an introductory programming course. *ACM SIGCSE Bulletin, 34*(4), 125–128.

De Hei, M. S. A., Strijbos, J.-W., Sjoer, E., & Admiraal, W. (2016). Thematic review of approaches to design group learning. *Educational Research Review., 18*, 33–45. https://doi.org/10.1016/j.edurev.2016.01.001

Drlik, M., Smyrnova-Trybulska, E., & Szczurek, A. (2019). Nowy projekt IT. *Gazeta Uniwersytecka [New IT project. University of Silesia Magazine]. 6* (266) marzec 2019. Retrieved 12–13, from http://gazeta.us.edu.pl/node/424333

Golwitzer, B. (2018). *Role-play*. Retrieved from http://www.teachingtoolbox.us/role-play/

Hug, T. (2012). Microlearning. In N. M. Seel (Ed.), *Encyclopedia of the sciences of learning edition*. Springer. https://doi.org/10.1007/978-1-4419-1428-6_1583

Jahnke, I., Lee, Y. M., Pham, M., et al. (2020). Unpacking the inherent design principles of mobile microlearning. *Technology, Knowledge and Learning, 25*, 585–619. https://doi.org/10.1007/s10758-019-09413-w

Jonhson, D. H., & Jonhson, F. P. (2013). *Joining together: Group theory and group skills*. Wilfrid Laurier University.

Lee, Y. M., Jahnke, I., & Austin, L. (2021). Mobile microlearning design and effects on learning efficacy and learner experience. *Educational Technology Research and Development, 69*, 885–915. https://doi.org/10.1007/s11423-020-09931-w

Mayer, R. E. (1981). The psychology of how novices learn computer programming. *ACM Computing Surveys (CSUR), 13*(1), 121–141.

Mohamed, H., & Lamia, M. (2018). Implementing flipped classroom that used an intelligent tutoring system into learning process. *Computers & Education, 124*, 62–76.

Problem-Based Learning. (2021). *Problem-based learning*. Retrieved from Maastricht University. https://www.maastrichtuniversity.nl/education/why-um/problem-based-learning

Skalka, J., & Drlik, M. (2018) Priscilla—Proposal of system architecture for programming learning and teaching environment. In *Proceedings of the 2018 IEEE 12th international conference on application of information and communication technologies (AICT)*, 17–19 Oct 2018.

Skalka, J., Drlik, M., Benko, L., Kapusta, J., Rodríguez del Pino, J. C., Smyrnova-Trybulska, E., Stolinska, A., Svec, P., & Turcinek, P. (2021). Conceptual framework for programming skills development based on microlearning and automated source code evaluation in virtual learning environment. *Sustainability, 13*, 3293. https://doi.org/10.3390/su13063293

Slavin, R. E. (2010). Co-operative learning: What makes group-work work? In R. E. Slavin (Ed.), *The nature of learning using research to inspire practice*.

The Jigsaw Classroom. (2021). Retrieved from https://www.jigsaw.org/#overview

Zhang, J., & West, R. E. (2020). Designing microlearning instruction for professional development through a competency based approach. *TechTrends, 64*, 310–318. https://doi.org/10.1007/s11528-019-00449-4

Priscilla Evaluation Pilot Study: A Rasch Measurement Analysis

Elspeth McKay, Keven Asquith, and Eugenia Smyrnova-Trybulska

1 Introduction

In the digital society the e-learning and microlearning is becoming more and more popular. This innovation could become more effective both for students and teachers.

The term microlearning describes learning in small amounts ("micro"). The microlearning module is small in size, focused and is easily digestible. Most often, it is three to five minutes long with short chunks of information focused on a specific topic or task. Learners no longer need to sit in long and boring seminars, lectures or presentations. Now they can find time to study in their busy schedule. Features of microlearning are: • *Conciseness:* • *Focus:* • *Autonomy:.* • *Variety:* • *Interactivity:* • *Flexibility:* (Mikhailov, 2018) as well as *Time, Content; Curriculum; Form; Process; Mediality; Learning type* (Hug, 2005, p. 4).

A good example of a tool and environment supporting the work of both students and teachers is the Priscilla educational platform based on microlearning and microcources developed under the auspices of the FITPED project (www.fitped.eu).

E. McKay · K. Asquith
Cogniware.com.au, Melbourne, VIC, Australia
e-mail: e.mckay@cogniware.com.au

E. Smyrnova-Trybulska (✉)
Department of Humanistic Education, University of Silesia in Katowice, Katowice, Poland
e-mail: esmyrnova@us.edu.pl

E. Smyrnova-Trybulska et al. (eds.), *Microlearning*,
https://doi.org/10.1007/978-3-031-13359-6_7

2 Background

The research study authors were involved in teaching the programming courses for their IT students and using microlearning for increasing the effectiveness of their learning and teaching. This work has already been reported showing important results relating to "the final four datasets that were analysed to confirm the suitability of automated assessment of the microlearning units as predictors of at-risk students and students" outcomes in the introductory programming courses (Skalka & Drlik, 2020). In another research study, an international team of authors describe their research proposing a conceptual framework focused on the comprehensive training of future programmers using microlearning and automatic evaluation of source codes to achieve immediate feedback for students (Skalka et al., 2021).

The study, conducted by Draxler (2020) researched the environment-triggered microlearning and stressed that "in ubiquitous (micro)learning, any place is a potential learning environment, be it a couch at home or a noisy place in public" (Draxler, 2020, p. 1).

"One such innovation gaining traction is Microlearning, which offers learning opportunities through small bursts of training materials that learners can comprehend in a short time, according to their preferred schedule and location" (Gill et al., 2020, p. 780). The research "explored the potential of Microlearningwithin design education and how it can be implemented into the Product Design Manufacture programme at University of Nottingham Ningbo China to support teaching instruction and enhance the student learning experience post-COVID-19. (Gill et al., 2020, p. 780).

Other research devoted "the context-sensitive microlearning of foreign language vocabulary on a mobile device" (Beaudin et al., 2007, p. 55). "Phrases were presented on average 57 times an hour; this intense interaction was found to be acceptable even after extended use" (Beaudin et al., 2007, p. 55).

Authors Javorcik and Polasek (2019) in their research analysed the various "forms of eLearning: mobile learning, blended learning, adaptive eLearning or eLearning with gamification elements." They stressed that "the term microLearning had also becoming established" and also emphasized that "the greatest advantage of microLearning was that it is not dependent on the technology that the student was using" (p. 254). Researchers described the study "in order to be able to determine the potential of microLearning, pilot microLearning courses had been created, which were then compared with existing eLearning courses" (p. 254).

3 Research Design

This chapter represents the results of a pilot-study involving 26-programming student participants. The online questionnaire design used a five-level Likert-scale (1, 2, 3, 4, and 5) by Eugenia Smyrnova-Trybulska and conducted by Irena Polak in framework programming classes). According to the following criteria, the questionnaire's instructions were to rate the Priscilla environment values on a scale from 1 to 5, where one meant negative, and five meant positive. There were three groups of test-items identified as (1) Substantive value; (2) Didactic value; and (3) Technical value (see Appendix). These groups also identified 'required' participation.

An educational researcher's key focus is to design reliable test instruments for measuring performance outcomes in particular settings. In this sense, the reliability property (or behaviour) of the set of attitudinal aspects of the Priscilla programming environment, describe how consistent or error-free the measurements were (Mulyani et al., 2020; Frisbie, 1988). Such test-measurement results can show whether the agreement-levels achieved represent whether or not, these agreements occurred and whether the Priscilla environment attributes were useful for that particular set of participants. It is helpful to understand participant reactions to the questionnaire-items. For instance: consistently low agreement levels across the cohort may indicate the need for remedial instructional strategies (for particular participants). Or where questionnaire-items were not showing much agreement among others, requiring additional Priscilla strategy-solving activities suggestions to stretch those participants cognitively.

It is equally important to ascertain the testing instrument has (knowledge) construct validity to represent the expected Priscilla knowledge/trait experienced by the higher education community involved in this study. In this case, the researcher needs to understand the anticipated scope of the Priscilla knowledge and skill development trajectory in so far as checking the intent of the questionnaire test-items with established experts in the field, and that the test results on a particular test reflect the expected results on another relevant test. Validity can, however, mean different things, based upon the supporting evidence. Therefore, it is essential to understand the need to establish the Likert-level characteristics' interpretation of the questionnaire's rationale.

4 Results

The results of the questionnaire were analysed using the RUMM2030 Prof software application. This unidimensional psychometric Rasch measurement tool developed at the University of Western Australia (RUMM-2030, 2015), presents an opportunity for conjoint measurement of participant ability and latent trait (knowledge constructs) on the same linear scale divided into equal intervals along the scale (Andrich, 2011). An essential feature of a Rasch analysis is to ensure that the data fit the model. Other measurement models follow the item response theory (IRT), where the researchers search for a model to fit the data.

5 Data Analysis

The first step of the analysis was a manual (or visual) check of the data-file. The left-hand table below shows the 26-participants' IDs (marked as 1–26 in the left-hand column) and the remaining columns represent their Likert-score for each questionnaire/test-item across the row. The scored-outcomes for participant-6 revealed all fives (meaning complete agreement with all Priscilla questionnaire/test-items) and participant-17 mostly ones (indicating lack of agreement). These scored-outcomes stand out as being anomalous and require further review in the analysis. The remaining participants showed some variance in consensus across the questionnaire/test-items. The analysis needed to determine participants' overall agreement level to the Priscilla questionnaire/test-items, and whether individual test-item responses had expected outcomes, or had anomalous distributions. The right-hand table below displays some of the initial Rasch measurement analysis design, with 998-iterations resulting in 72 of the 105-parameters converging to a reliable outcome.

```
1  544445545544534433553535555b
2  455545444554324454433444455a
3  233435334533323355555154455a
4  223445555554544522452415555a
5  445555445545435545333545555a
6  555555555555555555555555555a
7  544444444544444443344433455b
8  554545343535553354551453455a
9  445554444545434544544433455a
10 444454444444444445331334 55a
11 444544444225444411552224 55b
12 422545444344444435553423 55a
13 434424233442434444444443355b
14 555555553555535555531535 55b
15 333445444523552444555253455a
16 555555555445545455455555 55b
17 243344111111111111111111 11a
18 221125122522222233314431 25a
19 233355545554524443455451455a
20 554455453555453454553551555b
21 444343442132323433411432 15b
22 533455444555452553345551255a
23 544445554554534444445545 55b
24 555555555555535545553525 55a
25 554555555555543443455443455a
26 555555555555555511531535 55b
```

```
** PERSON  FACTORIAL  DESIGN
Person Factors              None entered

** ESTIMATION  DETAILS
Item Converge Limit         0.00010
Iterations [Items]          998 [only 72 parameters converged]
Iterations [Persons]        3
Lowest score                1
Highest score               130
Person Converge Limit       0.01000
Person Estimation           Weighted Maximum Likelihood method
Extreme Pers Criterion      0.220

** PARAMETERISATION
PC's requested              Location, Spread, Skewness and Kurtosis
Thresholds                  131: Unequal across the 27 items
```

5.1 Person-Item Interaction

The proverb that a picture speaks a thousand words communicates the initial research results. The starting point is to examine the questionnaire/test results in terms of the individual participant/person Likert agreement-scores relative to each participant's agreement-score and each questionnaire-item's behaviour relative to each questionnaire-item on a common unidimensional scale, shown in the Person-Item Location Distribution below (Fig. 1). Summary statistics identify the unidimensional Rasch logit-scale location and fit residual statistics. There were 26-questionnaire participants. Overall, there were 27-items: 26-questionnaire items, each using a five-level Likert-scale, and one free textual questionnaire input response.

The threshold distribution for participants (red boxes above the Logit scale, Fig. 1) shows a skewed distribution with a mean value of 3.323 and a standard deviation of 1.348.

The questionnaire/test-item distribution is shown in blue boxes under the logit scale (Fig. 1) and indicates a much lower mean (0.000) relative to the person distribution on the same scale.

The summary statistics table from RUMM2030 indicates the participant distribution has a positive skewness of 1.118 (to the right of the mean) and a large Kurtosis of 5.477. Cronbach's Alpha Coefficient is 0.947 and the Rasch measurement Person Separation Index is 0.927, both indicating a good correlation to the model's expected values. The fit residual mean is only 0.074.

The questionnaire/test item distribution has a Std Dev of 2.542. The tail skewed to the left, with Skewness of −1.228 and a Kurtosis 1.489 indicating a broader distribution than the participants. The fit residual: mean is larger than for the participants at 0.423.

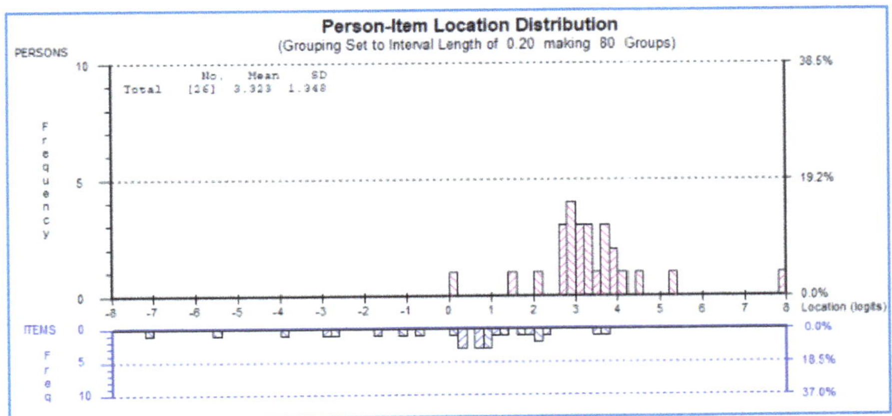

Fig. 1 Person-item location distribution – Full data set

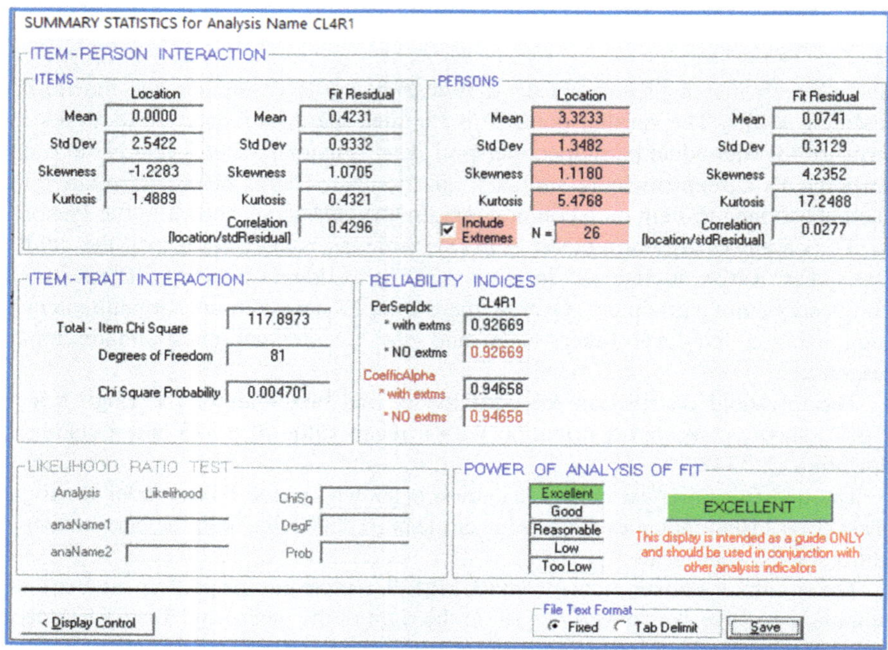

However, as identified in the data file's visual check, some participants and questionnaire/test-items may need further review. The data-file is redisplayed in the spreadsheet below to review questionnaire/test-items' ability to discriminate a range of responses. The response distribution for each test-item is colour-coded to identify the range of the 26-participants answers. Item-27 was a free text entry item, and therefore needs to be analysed separately to this Likert-scale analysis. Items-25 and 26, indicate that almost all participants answered the item at '5,' and consequently revealed they have a limited scored-value in discriminating response distribution. Test-items-6 and 10, also have a limited range of responses (again a large majority answered the test-item at '5') and needs further review.

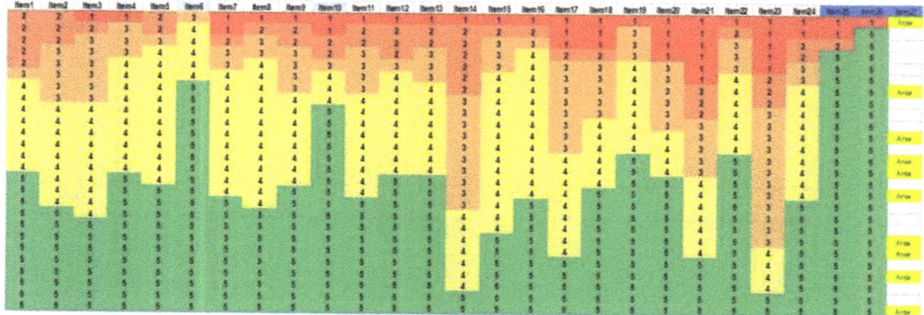

The Rasch measurement item characteristic curve (ICC) was used to evaluate which of the above four test-items (6, 10, 25 and 26) should be removed from the analysis. The ICC identifies class intervals that show an item's relative ability to discriminate among adjoining knowledge constructs (traits) along a linear scale. Rather than compare individual participant scores against the expected model curve, the Rasch measurement model divides the sample into classes, in this case, quartiles. So it determines the mean logit score of each 25% of the participant sample (1.929, 2.900, 3.240 and 4.031). As you will see in the expected value plots for individual questions, these red marks on the person logit scale do not change. However, the group's observed value (the black dot within the plot) does vary for each question. Figure 2 shows the ICC for questions 25 and 26. The model's estimated distribution demonstrates that the expected value of five was reached before most of the class interval means. Therefore the item does not discriminate between classes and should be removed from the analysis.

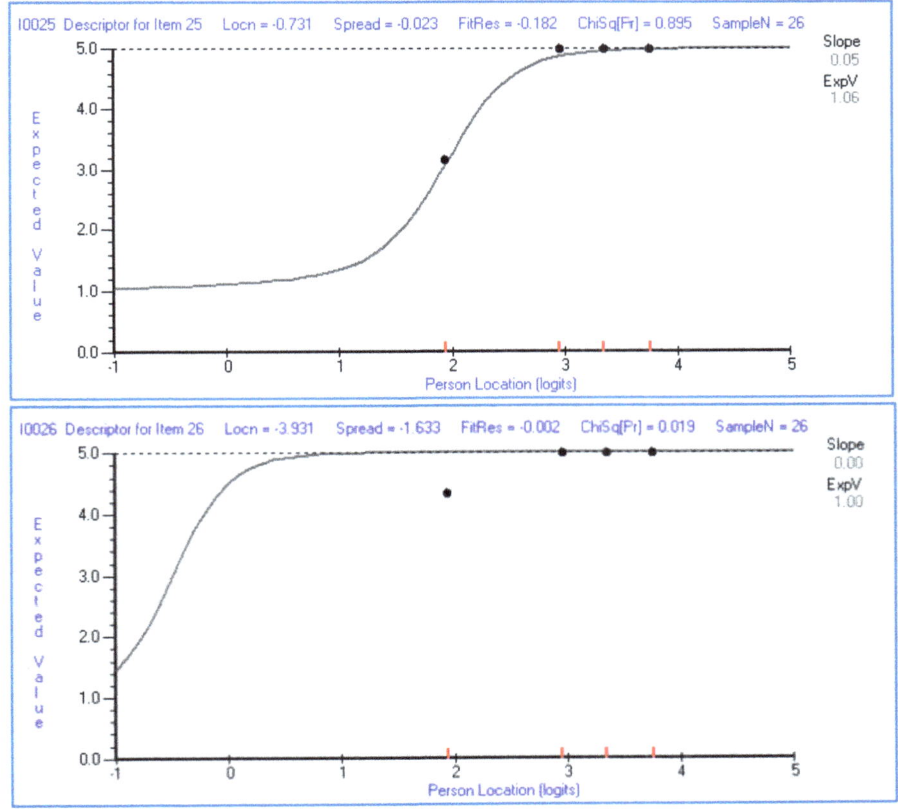

Fig. 2 ICC for items 25 and 26

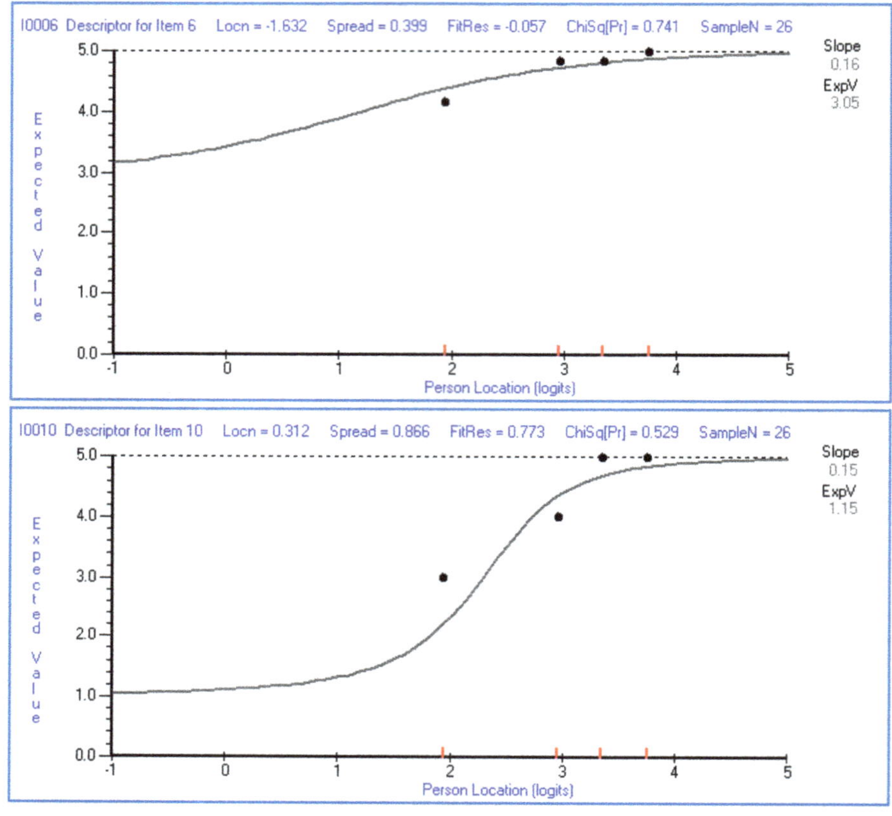

Fig. 3 ICC for items 6 and 10

Conversely, the ICC for items-6 and 10 shows response discrimination and therefore should be retained in the analysis.

The RUMM2030 analysis was then repeated, with items 25, 26 and 27 removed. Figure 4 displays the Person-Item Location distribution with the three-items removed. The Person distribution mean has increased slightly to a value of 3.405 (from initial 3.323) and the standard deviation is 1.829 (previously 1.348). The Skewness to the right has risen to 3.009 (1.118) and Kurtosis increased to over 13 (previously 5.477).

The Fig. 4 distribution plot clearly illustrates the outlier participant with a score of over 11. Participant-6 identified as answering '5' to every test-item. This extreme (participant) was skewing the distribution and was also removed from the analysis.

Figure 5 illustrates the Person-Item location distribution and summary statistics with the extremes removed from the analysis (now a sample of 25). Note that RUMM2030 did not remove participant-17 (answers mostly '1') as their overall score did not fall outside the extreme criteria.

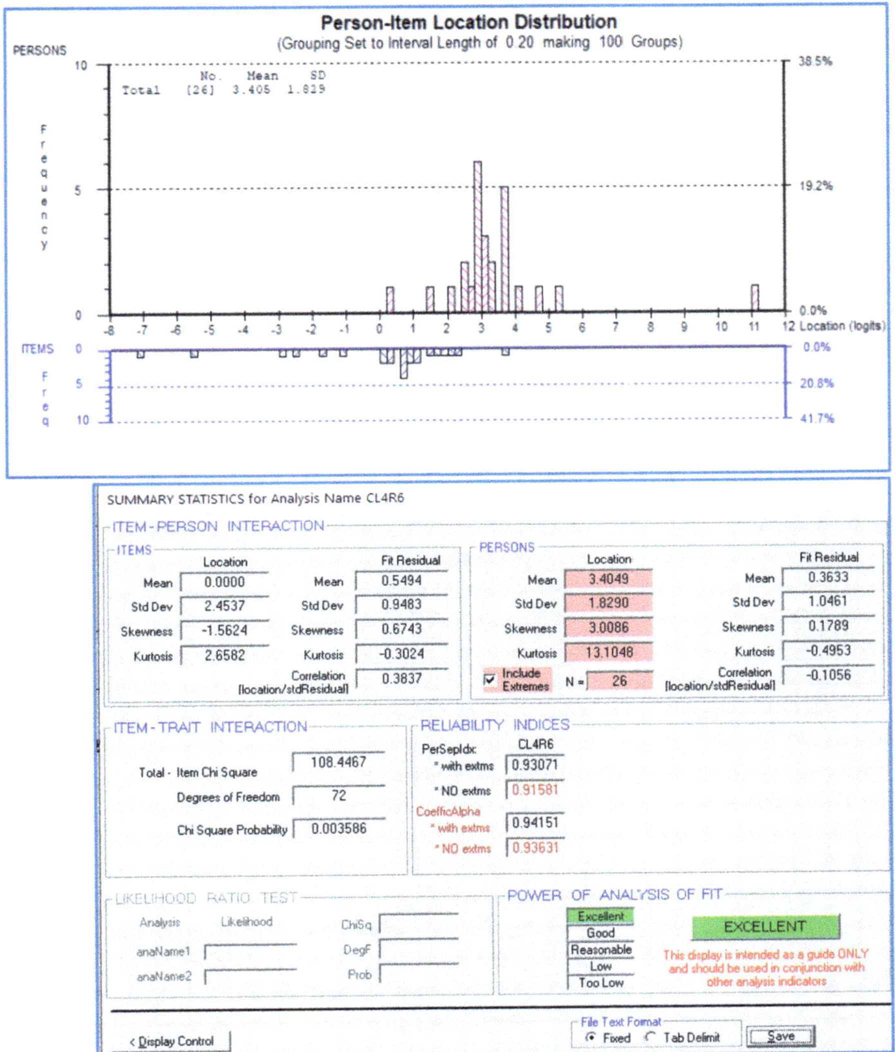

Fig. 4 Person-item location distribution and summary statistics – With 3-items removed

The participant mean value has reduced to 3.097, almost 10% lower than the analysis with all participants (3.405) and the standard deviation has reduced to 0.967 (from 1.829). With the extreme removed, the participant results are nearing a normal distribution with a slight Skewness to the left of −0.533, and the Kurtosis has reduced to 2.498.

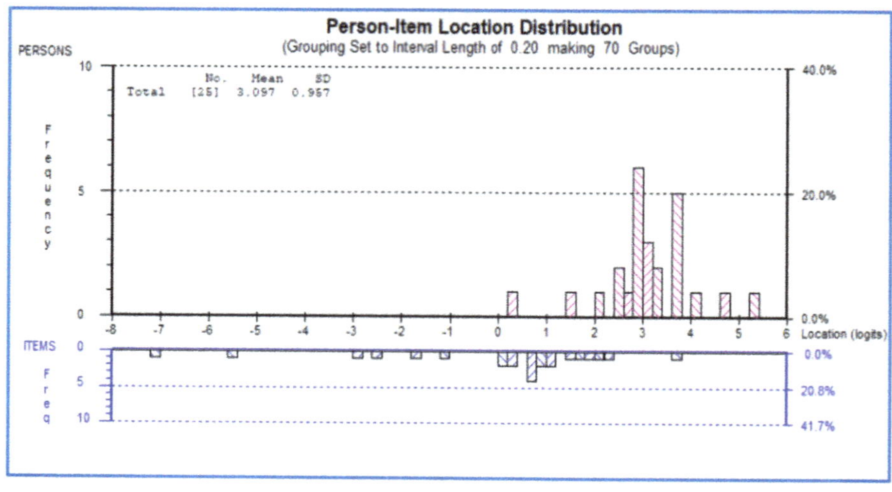

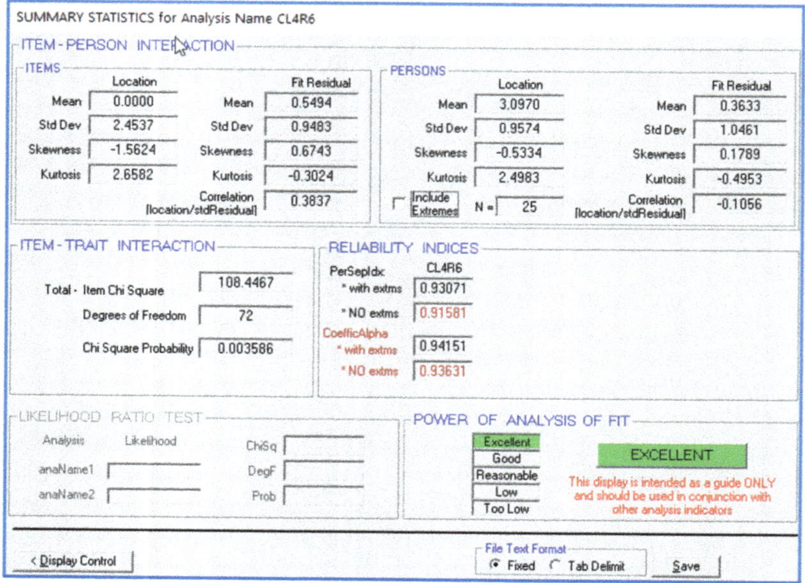

Fig. 5 Person-item location distribution – Extreme participant removed

Cronbach's Alpha Coefficient is 0.936, and the Rasch model Person Separation Index is 0.916, both still indicating a good correlation to the model's expected values. The fit residual mean is only 0.363. Although this person-item threshold distribution map reveals a power of analysis fit as excellent, it should be noted that the display is intended as a guide only and should be used in conjunction with other analysis indicators (RUMM-2030, 2015).

The questionnaire item distribution, shown in blue histogram under the logit scale (shown earlier in Fig. 1), retains the mean of 0.000, while the Standard Deviation (SD) is 2.454 (the initial run-1 SD was 2.542). Similarly, there is an only minor variation in Skewness and Kurtosis between the initial analysis and the final analysis (with three questions and one participant removed).

Figure 6, an expanded version of the earlier person-item location distribution map, illustrates the different Likert-scaled agreement-levels for each question. The agreement levels generally progress upwards on the Logit scale from a 1-meaning a 'negative' attitude towards Priscilla and a 5-meaning a 'positive' response. Item-19 is highlighted to demonstrate the normal progression up the logit-scale. However, not all questions will follow this regular progression. It should be noted that the third level of the question often has a higher logit-value than level-4 of that same question, which may indicate participants selecting the midpoint of the Likert-scale if they were not sure of their response.

Individual Item Analysis

As previously mentioned, the questionnaire had 27-questions that grouped into three categories:

1. Substantive value (items 1–6)
2. Didactic value (items 7–16) and
3. Technical value (items 17–27)

Classical test theory (CTT) makes an assumed characterisation of a person through a total dichotomous (0 and 1) summed-score. Although the Rasch measurement theory (RMT) scores test-items in the same way as CTT, RMT uses the total person-score as the sufficient statistic due to the model (Andrich & Marais, 2019). There are marked differences between these two measurement techniques. CTT has no practical way to see whether test-items are working as expected. In contrast, RMT uses the probability that a *"person n with given proficiency βn responds correctly to an item i with difficulty σi "* (Andrich, 2010, p. 162).

The item characteristic curves (ICC) discussed previously, graphically display this fit concept by comparing the observed mean value of each RMT-class category

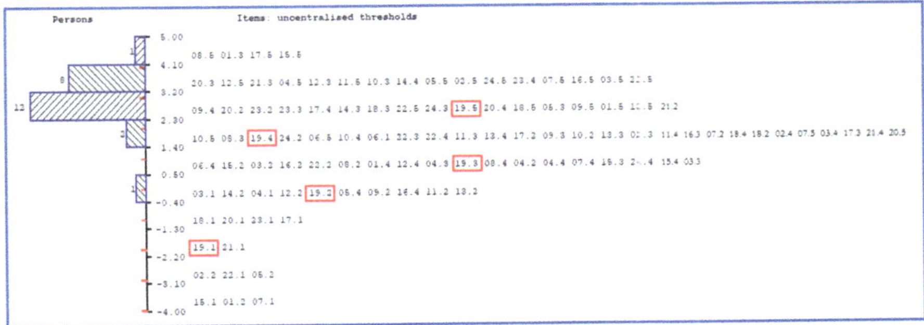

Fig. 6 Final analysis item variable map

(black dots) against the model derived expected value curve for each question. The left-hand plot in Fig. 7 illustrates that test item-22 (asking if the environment is easy to run?) has an excellent fit to the model curve. The fit residual mean is only 0.293.

5.2 *The Category Characteristic Curve (CCC)*

The category characteristic curve (CCC) illustrates the probability of a participant responding to the category answer and the likely person's logit value. And so at any logit value, the sum of probabilities for each question will add up to 100%. Using Item-22 as a typical model distribution, showing a normal progression of Likert-scale responses, the right-hand of Fig. 7, illustrates that a participant with a logit value of a '1' would have a 40% probability of answering at the level- 2, a 30% probability of answering at level-1, a 20% probability of answering at level-3 and a 10% probability of answering at Likert level-4.

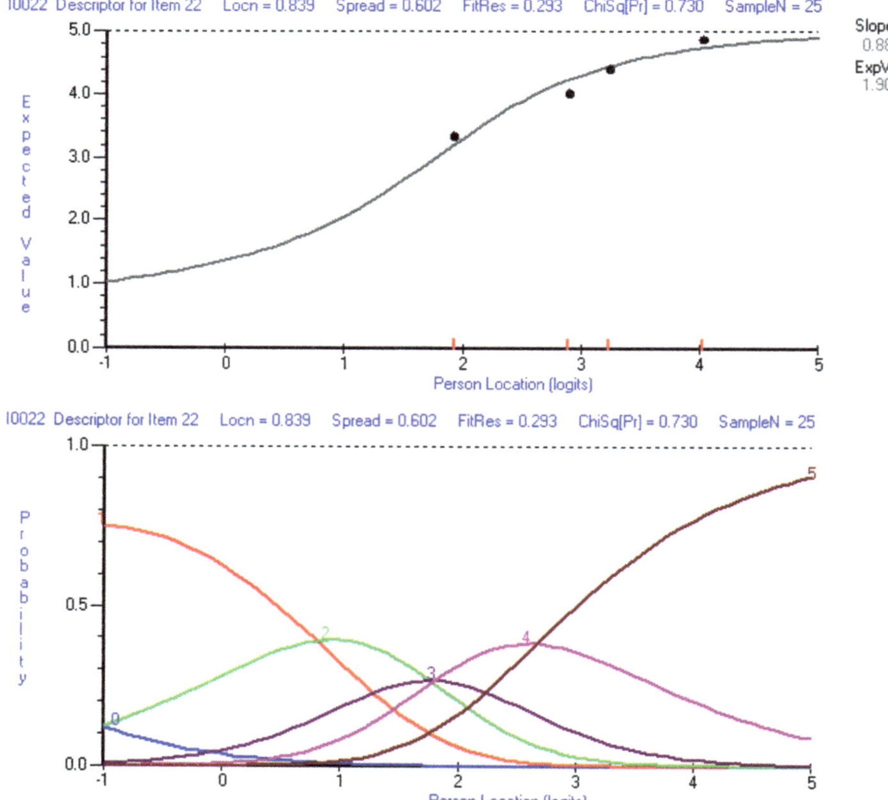

Fig. 7 Final analysis item-22 ICC and CCC probability showing a good fit

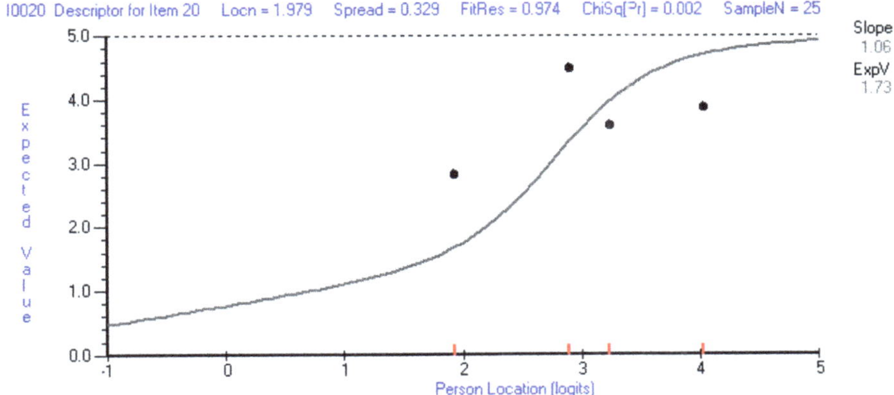

Fig. 8 Final analysis item-20 ICC showing a poor fit

Looking at the agreement-scale endpoints, a participant with a logit value of −1.0 or lower has over a 75% probability of answering question-22 at the level-1 agreement-level (negative). A person with a logit value of '5' would have a 90% probability of answering question-22 at the level-5 agreement level (positive). The brown curve indicated that a person with a logit value of '1' had no chance of answering item-22 at the level-5 and that a logit-value of almost '3' is required to have a 50% probability of answering with a '5' response.

Conversely, Fig. 8 illustrated that test item-20 (asking whether sound has technical value) had a bad fit to the expected curve, with all observed class category, means plotted away from the model expected curve. The fit residual mean has increased to 0.974. This item may need further evaluation to determine if participants understood what was asked or whether the response indicated an anomalous distribution of attitude towards sound use.

In the final analysis, the remaining items have a model fit between these two endpoints and would be suitable for future experiments.

6 Conclusions

Following a Rasch measurement approach to data analysis has profound rewards, not possible through standard statistical evaluation. The interactivity of the person/item behaviours relative to each other and measured on a unidimensional (logit) scale, provides a robust tool to illustrate this complex environment. The category characteristic curve (CCC) and the item characteristic curves (ICC) are keys to understanding this powerful measurement model.

Rash measurement CCC plots each response's probability as a function of person proficiency and item characteristic curves (Andirch & Marais, 2019, p. 242). For instance: the category probability plot for item-22, which asked for an opinion on the Priscilla environment being easy to run, provides a robust comparison of students' probability to answer this question relative to their overall test-score. A participant with a '−1' overall logit-score has a 75% probability of having a negative agreement (a '1' on the Likert-scale). Whereas a participant with a logit-score of '3' has over 50% chance of having a positive agreement (a '5').

Conversely, item characteristic curves (ICC) reveal a fine-grained analysis of expected/observed score-values. For instance: test-item-20, which related to sound, did not fit the Rasch measurement model as observed mean-scores were erratic and did not follow the anticipated performance curve. Moreover, the fit residual mean indicated to the researcher to examine separately to determine whether students understood the question, or whether something else about using sound was responsible for the responses.

This pilot study data analysis resulted in the removal of two items with extreme scoring outcomes; item-25 – relating to hardware requirements for working with the environment not being excessive, had 23 of 26 participants score at level-5 (positive agreement), while item-26 – relating to cost not being excessive/free, had 25 level-5 answers (with only participant-17, who scored most items as a '1,' scoring differently). Consequently, removing these items afforded a more accurate and practical estimate. Examining the person-item statistics identified two outlier participants, who may have carelessly answered the questionnaire. Only one participant was removed from the final analysis. Evidence for this likely haphazard approach to participant scoring outcomes is seen by examining the Final Analysis Item Variable Map (often referred to as a Wright Map (Boone et al., 2014)); where not all items followed a regular progression along the five-level agreement Likert-scale.

There can be no doubt that running a pilot study has merits for validating the measurement instrumentation's reliability and the schedule of events before running the main experiment. In this case, the observation concerning the participant criteria/information on the five-category Likert-scale suggests detail regarding each of the five-level Likert-scale is necessary to elicit reliable outcomes from all test-items. To increase discrimination between participant's agreement levels, a seven-level Likert-scale could also be considered.

The one of the main aims of the FITPED Project was reducing the number of students because of failure to learn programming in the first years' study on IT specialisation via introduction Priscilla platform and elaborating above 2000 microcources of a programming language. Computer programmers are responsible for the following tasks: Translating program designs into code; Mastering computer languages; Borrowing from code libraries; Testing and troubleshoot programs; Using integrated development environments (IDEs) (Walter, 2020). The first research results showed that the students were generally good at evaluating the Priscilla environment. Simultaneously they should be additionally improved in several other issues, like: minor technical problems; correcting bugs and adding more theories in some sections before formulating queries (note: in some microcourses); sometimes the generator compiles the same tasks/exercises for execution. The authors of the Priscilla platform and the international team of other authors offer more than

2000 microcources that continue improving the environment and didactic tools using permanent monitoring and feedback.

Acknowledgments This research was funded by European Commission under the ERASMUS+ Programme 2018, KA2, grant number: 2018-1-SK01-KA203-046382 "Work-Based Learning in Future IT Professionals Education".

Appendix

Fitped Survey Evaluating the Priscilla Environment (students – Databases – UŚ) Evaluation of the Priscilla environment according to the proposed criteria.

Please rate the Priscilla environment values on a scale from 1 to 5 according to the following criteria – where 1 means negative and 5 means positive. * Required

1. **Substantive value***
    1. Substantive correctness
    2. Formulating information contained in the environment/microcourses
    3. Instructions
    4. Adequacy of the environment/micro-courses to the age of the learners
    5. The information contained in the environment/micro-courses takes into account the current knowledge
    6. Adherence to ethical standards, tolerance and gender policy in the program
2. **Didactic value***
    7. Individualisation of teaching
    8. The approach to the presented problems
    9. Ability to work with the environment/micro-courses of more than one person
    10. Is it possible to make multiple attempts to solve the problem in the program?
    11. The interactivity of the environment/micro-courses
    12. The environment/micro-courses are adjusted to the level of development of students
    13. The environment/micro-courses leave the lecturer free in terms of methodology
    14. The use of the environment/micro-courses causes that other teaching aids are not so effective
    15. Adequacy of information describing the environment to the package contents
    16. The environment/micro-courses contain content compatible with the text-book/script/teaching materials
3. **Technical value***
    17. Is the workflow in the environment efficient and clear?
    18. Is the environment "user friendly"?

19. Graphics
20. Sound
21. Does the environment/micro-courses predict user errors or mistakes?
22. The environment is easy to run
23. It is possible to change the way information is presented
24. The environment/micro-courses make the most (properly) use of the student's time
25. The hardware requirements for working with the environment are not excessive
26. Program cost (not (excessive), free)
27. Is the workflow in the environment efficient and clear?

4. **Please send your suggestions to improve and enhance the Priscilla environment and programming language learning micro-courses**

References

Andrich, D. (2010). Rasch models. In P. Peterson, E. Baker, & B. McGaw (Eds.), *International encyclopedia of education* (3rd ed., pp. 111–122). Elsevier.

Andrich, D. (2011). Rating scales and Rasch measurement. *Expert Review Pharmacoeconomics Outcomes Research, 11*(5), 571–585.

Andrich, D., & Marais, I. (2019). *A course in Rasch measurement theory: Measuring in the educational, social and health sciences*. Springer Texts in Education.

Beaudin, J. S., Intille, S. S., Tapia, E. M., Rockinson, R., & Morris, M. E. (2007). *Context-sensitive microlearning of foreign language vocabulary on a mobile device*. Lecture Notes in Computer Science (including subseries Lecture Notes in Artificial Intelligence and Lecture Notes in Bioinformatics) Volume 4794 LNCS, Springer Verlag, 2007, Pages 55–72 European Conference on Ambient Intelligence, AmI 2007; Darmstadt; Germany; 7 November 2007 through 10 November 2007; Code 70979.

Boone, W. J., et al. (2014). *Rasch analysis in the human sciences*. Springer.

Draxler, F. (2020, October). Environment-triggered microlearning. *MobileHCI'20: 22nd international conference on human-computer interaction with mobile devices and services*. Article No.: 40, pp. 1–3 https://doi.org/10.1145/3406324.3409259.

Javorcik, T., & Polasek, R. (2019). Practical application of microlearning in education of future teachers. *Proceedings of the European conference on e-Learning*, ECELVolume 2019-November, 2019, pp. 254–259. *18th European Conference on e-Learning, ECEL 2019*; Aalborg University Copenhagen; Denmark; 7 November 2019 through 8 November 2019; Code 155850.

Frisbie, D. A. (1988). Reliability of scores from teacher-made tests. *Instructional Topics in Educational Measurement (ITEMS)*. Spring, pp. 25–35.

Gill, A. S., Irwin, D. S, Ng, R. Y.- K., Towey, D., Wang, T., & Zhang, Y. (2020, December). The future of teaching post-COVID-19: Microlearning in product design education. *Proceedings of 2020 IEEE international conference on teaching, assessment, and learning for engineering*, TALE 20208, Article number 9368322, pp. 780–785. *2020 IEEE International Conference on Teaching, Assessment, and Learning for Engineering, TALE 2020*; Virtual, Takamatsu; Japan; 8 December 2020 through 11 December 2020; Category number CFP20TAL-ART; Code 167764.

Hug, T. (2005, May 6–8). *Micro learning and narration. Exploring possibilities of utilization of narrations and storytelling for the designing of "micro units" and didactical microlearning arrangements*. Paper presented at the fourth Media in Transition conference, MIT. https://www.researchgate.net/publication/237558117_Micro_Learning_and_Narration_Exploring_possibilities_of_utilization_of_narrations_and_storytelling_for_the_designing_of_micro_units_and_didactical_micro-learning_arrangements. Accessed 10 Sep 2017.

Mikhailov, V. (2018). Microlearning – Features, advantages and disadvantages. *Education*. https://edu-russian.ru/mikroobuchenie-osobennosti-preimushchestva-i-nedostatki.html

Mulyani, H., et al. (2020). Quality analysis of teacher-made tests in financial accounting subject at vocational high schools. *Jurnal Pendidikan Vokasi, 10*(1).

RUMM-2030 (2015). *RUMM2030 getting started manual*. WA, RUMM_Laboratory_Pty_Ltd.

Skalka, J., & Drlik, M. (2020). Automated assessment and microlearning units as predictors of at-risk students and students' outcomes in the introductory programming courses. *Applied Sciences, 10*(4566), 1–24. https://doi.org/10.3390/app10134566

Skalka, J., Drlik, D., Benko, L., Kapusta, J., Rodríguez del Pino, J.C., Smyrnova-Trybulska, E., Stolinska, A., Svec, P., & Turcinek, P. (2021). Conceptual Framework for Programming Skills Development Based on Microlearning and Automated Source Code Evaluation in Virtual Learning Environment. *Sustainability, 13(6),* https://doi.org/10.3390/su13063293 https://www.mdpi.com/2071-1050/13/6/3293 ISSN:2071–1050

Walter, J. (2020). *Learning to code? Strong language skills matter more than being good at math*. https://www.discovermagazine.com/mind/learning-to-code-strong-language-skills-matter-more-than-being-good-at-math

Microlearning Formats in Crisis? Theses in the Field of Tension Between Corona-Induced Short-Term Solutions, Apodictic Rhetoric's of no Alternatives and Perspectives Open to the Future

Theo Hug

1 Introduction

The expression 'microlearning' has been used for approximately 15 years. It can be found predominantly in web discourses unrelated to educational science and in on-the-job education and training, in contrast to approaches and concepts of microteaching, which have been applied since the 1960s mainly in teacher education. Quite frequently, microlearning is used synonymously with 'on-demand learning', 'nano-learning', 'crowd-based learning', 'ubiquitous learning', 'rapid learning', 'bite-' or 'byte-sized learning' and similar metaphorically pointed descriptions of forms of learning with digital media. The formats range from programmed push-systems for behavioral modification and apps for acquiring rote knowledge, to learning with short tutorials, animations, infographics and simple diagrammatic representations, to small-sized AI-based language assistance systems for learning purposes and elements of educational robotics. The guiding principles are usually oriented more toward imaginations of automatized learning technologies than toward imaginations of open-ended personality formation (*Persönlichkeitsbildung*) or co-creative forms of dealing with microformats in the context of knowledge building.

As far as programming skills in higher education are concerned, automated assessment and efforts of optimization of learning processes, for example by means of learning analytics, are important in corresponding discourses and practices (cf. Skalka & Drlík, 2020; Skalka et al., 2020). However, bricoleur styles of working as described by Turkle and Papert (1990) are often neglected regardless of its potentials in the field of microlearning in programming languages teaching. This is not only a question of claims of disposition, surveillance and control or an issue of

T. Hug (✉)
Innsbruck University, Innsbruck, Austria
e-mail: theo.hug@uibk.ac.at

E. Smyrnova-Trybulska et al. (eds.), *Microlearning*,
https://doi.org/10.1007/978-3-031-13359-6_8

logics and prediction but also a matter of style as the authors illustrate by means of an analogy: "In cooking, this would be the style of those who do not follow recipes and instead make a series of decisions according to taste. While hierarchy and abstraction are valued by the structured programmers' planner's aesthetic, bricoleur programmers prefer negotiation and rearrangement of their materials" (Turkle & Papert, 1990, p. 136).

The individual characterizations of microlearning formats vary, with micro-dimensions in regard to time, content, process and media usually justified in an unsystematic way. The same is true for micro-dimensions of learning in the context of repetitive, instrumental, incidental, reflective, expansive, emotional, social, playful, mobile, action-oriented as well as task-, practice-, goal- or problem-oriented forms of learning and their localization in the context of learning-theoretical research. To be sure, both applied research close to the market as well as academic basic research concede that, in regard to microlearning concepts, not only individual steps of learning and single, isolated events have to be considered, but also the contexts of learning and teaching, educational contexts and diverse meso- and macro-dimensions. However, this acknowledgment is not usually taken into account in a differentiated way, whether conceptually, theoretically, performatively or practically.

As far as microlearning formats in crisis are concerned, this article is not aimed at an evaluation of microlearning offers directly related to COVID-19 – see for example https://www.ecdc.europa.eu/en/news-events/online-micro-learning-activities-on-COVID-19 or https://www.meduplus.de/microlearning/coronavirus/ (accessed: 2021-12-14) – or at questions of the practicality of such offers in corona-induced contexts of crisis in consideration of different content orientations, methodological emphases and didactic framings. Neither is it about the handling of micro-content in an "infodemic" in the context of COVID-19 (Hua & Shaw, 2020), about Corona-intensified dynamics of educational inequality (van Ackeren et al., 2020), didactic self-delusions in connection with short-term transfers of face-to-face formats to digital formats, or a typology of didactic arrangements for the reorganization of small learning steps for self-study, for distance learning and for those hybrid forms of remotely-, externally- and self-controlled formats which have recently become significant at the juncture of home learning and home schooling. However, this is not supposed to derogate the relevance of current research on these and similar topics. For example, the contributions in the *Medienimpulse* special issue, *Nähe(n) und Distanz(en) in Zeiten der COVID-19-Krise* (Barberi et al., 2020) offer numerous links for determining the relationships between micro-, meso- and macro-perspectives of learning, even if the individual contributions do not contain an explicit relationing and contextualization of microlearning formats in crisis. The case is similar for current programmatic contributions published of late due to current events in various educational contexts around the globe (see for example Brandenburg, 2020; Gallo & Trompetto, 2020; Luyben et al., 2020; Saxena, 2020).

Instead, the following deals with explorations and reflections on desiderata which tie in with the declining hype around microlearning. These will be put up for discussion in the form of seven concise theses. A German version of this paper has been be published by Kopead (cf. Hug, 2021a).

2 Theses on Microlearning in Crisis

The current corona crisis does not only exacerbate existing social, economic, educational, knowledge-, gender- and milieu-related dynamics of inequality, it also contributes to increasing calls for digitization in education. While microlearning formats are quite noticeable in continuing professional development (see for example Koch et al., 2012; Kapp & Defelice, 2019) and initial AI-capable microlearning solutions are being advertised for Industry 4.0 (see https://www.it-daily.net/shortnews/23942-erste-ai-faehige-microlearning-loesung-fuer-die-industrie-4-0 and https://www.aveva.com/ both accessed: 2021-12-14), pertinent "pedagogically sound and technically executable learning designs" (Miao et al., 2009) have so far been used in isolated instances rather than comprehensively in schools, universities and adult education. The reasons are not only to be found in unresolved technical issues, inadequate equipment, education-political conditions, lacking offers for further education and widespread doubts about the pedagogic and didactic soundness, but there are also various reasons related to learning and media culture, generational differences, milieu, ethics and anthropology.

While in some places the clearing up of myths around e-learning (see for example Kaiser-Müller, 2015) has not even arrived, the streaming of lectures is considered as a prototype of "digital university teaching" or the moocification of education offers is recklessly promoted, some educational authorities and parents as well as some researchers in the fields of education, learning and media are increasingly uneasy with strategies of digitization which focus on pre-fabricated microlearning formats in preparation for 'Work 4.0'. Occasionally this leads to assumptions that the magic word 'blended' could easily relate to 'blinded'. It is one thing what the fairly coarse blends of teaching and learning formats mix and combine, whether in a well-founded or rather casual way; it is quite another thing, however, what is concurrently highlighted or blinded out. Even without education-economic or education-political background information and without distinctive competencies in metaphor analysis it can be surmised that references to 'Learning 4.0', 'School 4.0' or 'University 4.0' are connected to macro-perspectives and structural transformation dynamics which always affect the microclimate in education and learning cultures.

As is generally known, the reference to a Fourth Industrial Revolution, which the German federal government combined with the label '4.0' in the context of the development of a high-tech strategy, is aimed at a profound change in processes of production, business and adding value and at the creation of highly complex, interconnected structures in which (partly) autonomous people and machines as well as digital technologies and cyber-physical systems (CPS) cooperate in a result-oriented and profitable way. That digitization as a technicization of processes of learning and education contributes significantly to the fulfillment of education-technological promises of quality improvement, the sustainable development of educational institutions or the increased educational equality is everything but easily justified. Questions about the reasons for competences, the weighting of experiences, the perception of benefits and damages, the information- and knowledge-ecological consequences and the distribution of gains and losses have to be asked and broadly discussed. This is supported not least by the learning- and education-technological invasions of the global education industry (Verger et al., 2016), whose relevance for national education systems as well as individual educational institutions and for the design of microlearning formats is commonly substantially underestimated.

A determination of the relationship of media- and education-technological aspects of an ecology of invasions with the biological concepts of invasions (Kowarik, 2010) and with a General Ecology (Hörl & Burton, 2017) has to be left open here. It could contribute to a better understanding of co-creative microlearning dynamics at the junctures of human and machine productivity in particular and the enabling conditions of viral microformats in general. Among the latter are, for example, jokes, GIFs and memes as well as learning-technologically prefabricated quiz formats which are distributed in large quantities. From a media-theoretical perspective and based on the considerations of Krämer (2008), these formats can be specified according to modalities of "infection by means of transcription" (ibid., p. 138–159).

Paradoxically, the corona crisis has shown that, on the one hand, very many things could be different, even in education, and that, on the other hand, the willingness to accept legally questionable infrastructures of the big internet companies is very high. The problem here is less the corona-induced shift of evaluation criteria but rather the resonating suggestion of a lack of alternatives. Development dynamics from ad-free public educational institutions to the micro-soft manipulation of pedagogic processes in school contexts to the mental image of the temporary interruption of Apple or Google promotions for the sake of pedagogic inserts may seem exaggerated and dystopian. The question remains as to why long-known organizational, media-didactic, learning-technological and media-cultural alternatives for the design of microlearning formats and educational processes are not discussed on a broad basis. The following theses offer some starting points for a differentiated discussion.

2.1 *Thesis 1: The Microlearning Discourses Are Characterized by Substantial Historical Amnesia*

The expression 'microlearning' is frequently used in learning- and education-technological contexts of application and relatively rarely in the context of basic research in education and learning sciences. On closer examination this term often refers to the application of concrete tools and specific features connected with conceptual characterizations aimed at technological promises and drawing on rhetorics of 'WebSpeak' or 'Edtech-Speak'. Especially the learning-technological discourses consider neither the history of the idea or concept of microlearning, nor phenomenal aspects of micro-dimensions of learning *avant la lettre* which can be historically reconstructed. This regards informal learning contexts and well-known microformats such as anecdotes, aphorisms, jokes, graffiti, epigrams, short stories or short films but also more recent formats such as GIFs, memes, micro-movies, microgames, podcasts, digital storytelling, flash fiction or tweets. Concepts from the history of education and examples of the relevance of 'learning in small steps' and its references to the learning of structures and complex interrelationships (see Hierdeis, 2007) are generally ignored.

2.2 *Thesis 2: The Microlearning Discourses Are Characterized by Substantial Media and Education Amnesia*

Although microlearning discourses often deal with digital or "new" media, media- and education-theoretical differentiations remain disregarded to a large extent. This concerns the reflection on medial forms in historical-medial constellations and fundamental questions of mediality with regard to educational contexts, but also conceptualizations of education which do not reduce it to measurable outputs, certifiable qualifications and tradable commodities. Stereotypical framing references to established concepts of mediatization which function as a "brand label for an approach" (Billig, 2013, p. 114) are only of limited use for the differentiated analysis and design of learning practices. The same applies to contextualizations of microprocesses of learning against the background of educational products as market-relevant goods.

On the one hand, the different forms of mediatization in the sense of an institutionalized "making mediate", the power-based assertion of "media logics" and the creation of new dependencies are frequently underestimated when it comes to their significance for formats of microlearning. On the other hand, what also falls short is the reflection on dynamics of medialization in regard to medial constellations, medial forms and enabling conditions in cultural and social systems as well as media-epistemological dimensions and the autonomy potentials of processes of learning and education.

Beyond that, the media and education amnesia also applies to the reflection on tendencies of "learnification" (Biesta, 2010) and pedagogic responsibilities (Biesta, 2011, p. 190; Friesen, 2019) as well as media-anthropological dimensions, from the "micrologization of perception" (Faßler, 2009, p. 290f) to questions of *Coevolution* (Lee, 2020) to perspectives of *Co-creation* (Cizek et al., 2019). In this respect, said media- and education amnesia can be combined into a thesis about media education amnesia.

2.3 Thesis 3: Rhetoric and Imagery of the Forms of Articulation Are Based on Education-Technological Promises

Statements like “Training ‘snippets’ can be viewed as cost-effective programs that serve as quick and meaningful training” (Khan, 2019, p. 278) stand in the tradition of e-learning myths and ICT rhetorics in the field of education (Haugsbakk & Nordkvelle, 2007; see also Haugsbakk, 2020 and the contributions in the special issue “30 years of ICT and learning in education – major changes and challenges”). Illuminating and masking dimensions of the metaphoric use of expressions like ‘snippets’, ‘nuggets’, ‘bites’, ‘facets’, ‘episodes’ or ‘fragments’ are not explicitly described in relevant discourses. Aspects of the effectiveness of learning and promises of sustainability are rarely evaluated. It remains open as to what degree and under which conditions promises like the following are fulfilled: “The outcome of well-designed meaningful, low-cost, reinforcing snippets contribute to the successful change of behavior and performance improvement for trainees” (Khan, 2019, p. 282).

This relates not only to instrumental forms of learning but also to prevalent promises of salvation in digitization which need to be reflected on (see Bauer et al., 2020). Furthermore, metaphoric ways of expression generally play a prominent role, for example in transformatory approaches. See, for example, Björk (2011) and the apps on her *Biophilia* album which highlight a reflection on the relationships between nature and technology and intuitive possibilities of creative and multimodal music production (cf. https://bjork-biophilia-ios.soft112.com/). For instance, claims of a corrective “to ocularcentric banking pedagogies where knowledge is fixed and progress is unidirectionally measured” (Abramo, 2014, p. 78) are also waiting to be redeemed and justified.

2.4 Thesis 4: The Relevance of Micro-, Meso- and Macro-Structural Interdependencies of Techno-Economic and Education-Political Dimensions as Well as the Role of the Global Education Industry Are Commonly Misjudged and Underestimated

The view to contents and didactics of microlearning can easily hide the fact that organizational designs as well as institutional, technological and political parameters play a significant role in the development and normalization of concrete formats and routines. Even more, the routines of getting used to specific formats of microlearning, the strategies of the normalization of concrete learning-technological applications and the preference for specific hardware and proprietary software for educational purposes at the same time represent essential requirements of enabling and promoting macrosocial dynamics and macroeconomic market developments in the educational sector. Especially the industrially prefabricated microlearning formats of the dominant internet corporations may be regarded as an application of those global microstructures which, as forms of coordination, "span global areas but at the same time are of a microsocial nature" (Knorr Cetina & Bruegger, 2005, p. 145).

The emergence of a *Global Education Industry* (Verger et al., 2016) has not just undermined existing prohibitions of advertising in schools and reflective equilibriums regarding the framework conditions for public and private educational institutions. The formation of this concept, like in the case of medical-industrial complex, is analogous to the expression military-industrial complex (see Picciano, 1994; Picciano & Spring, 2013). Research in this field is still in the early stage (see Parreira do Amaral et al., 2019), and desiderata include, among others, similarities and differences in the strategic communication, in the tactical overcoming of regional expectations of normality or in the rhetorics of innovation in the three societally relevant complexes.

This goes hand in hand with a basic reframing of fields of education – interdependent all along, but partly autonomous – in western-oriented societies especially in Europe and North America which make free spaces for educational processes for their own sake an anomaly and consistently organize processes of learning in the mode of commercialized forms of communication. The tendencies towards limiting the relative autonomy of micro-orders and towards the continued sellout of public education (Lohmann, 2009, p. 57) with digital means are just as hard to comprehend among the broad public as the various data-based payment modalities and "management models for 'micro contexts'" (Faßler, 2014, p. 26). The need for research, information and action in regard to data protection and the consequences of platform economy in education is diverse and far-reaching. If sustainability in education is not supposed to be an empty pedagogic formula and no synonym for antidemocratic notions of education, it takes data-economic alternatives to the prevalent web-based business models in due consideration of commons orientations and privacy protection (see Ochs et al., 2019). General licenses in the field of education for using software products by the Microsoft corporation and similar contracts with other Internet corporations run counter to this. The fact that the agreements with Microsoft have recently been renewed in Germany as well as Switzerland and Austria highlights the need to raise awareness about this topic.

2.5 *Thesis 5: Microlearning Formats Correspond with Social-Technological Forms of Microcontrolling Which Are Linked to Specific Challenges in the Face of New Versions of Well-Known Pedagogic Antinomies and Paradoxes*

Forms of microcontrolling were known in pedagogy long before the semiconductor chips used today in vast numbers in microcontroller architectures. The miniaturization of devices and many other factors such as scalability, transfer rate, production costs, mobility and interoperability have contributed in recent years to the realization of microtechnologies for monitoring and surveillance, to a degree and with scopes which make many a science fiction novel of the twentieth century look tame in comparison. This does not mean that microlearning formats *per se* have to be an integral part of surveillance-capitalist routines. Depending on the media-, information- and learning-ecological constellations, self-determined formats and expansive forms of learning may be suitable as well. This applies in particular to some offers of free education initiatives and forms of subversion (see Glauser et al., 2019) as well as cultural hacking and media-activist interventions. The latter is not meant to belie the fact that Google, for example, has since its founding reached a quasi monopoly in the search engine market and today offers numerous services, including Google Classroom, while the GWEI project (https://gwei.org/) was stopped shortly after its launch.

In effect, however, many microlearning formats are based on prefabricated learning-technological routines which allow ongoing control and monitoring of learning processes. This intensifies familiar antinomies and paradoxes in educational contexts such as freedom and coercion or external and self-determination as they have been discussed for decades (see, for example, Winkel, 1986; Helsper, 1996), as institutions of public education, private education and continuing professional development provide for the routine use of proprietary software, "involuntary mediatization" (Adolf, 2014) is not being regarded as a serious problem in large parts of educational research and policy, and "eduveillance" as an application of *Surveillance Capitalism* (Zuboff, 2019) represents an issue essentially only for a small academically interested minority. Where micro(learning) formats play a pivotal role in the context of monitoring and surveillance orientations in private or public education that are not to be questioned, the reference to informational self-determination becomes a euphemism. This is true for elements of e-portfolios in early education which are managed in companies or agencies just as for the intransparent use of user data from learning platforms and MOOCs or for tracking and face recognition in schools and universities.

Similar arguments can be made for such contradictory relationships as uniformity and polymorphism, mobilization and stabilization, adaptation and resistance, surveillance and subveillance, proximity and distance, disciplinary strategies and undisciplined risks, educational promises and open-ended processes, assumptions of certainty and experiences of uncertainty or the call for error culture and concrete criteria for assessment. These and many other paradoxical constellations represent heightened requirements for a successful dilemma management. These constellations include for example votes for free educational media and media-colonization of worlds of learning or digitization in the service of red-tape interests and the promotion of creativity and innovation. For other examples of contemporary paradoxical structures and fields of tension see Hug (2018, p. 11).

This applies particularly in the context of developing and implementing media concepts in educational institutions of all levels. If for instance "collective willingness to change [is described] as a crucial factor of success of digitization processes at universities" (Graf-Schlattmann et al., 2020), it does not just beg the question how the interplay of action variables such as coordination and integration, transparency and visibility or perceptible benefit (ibid., p. 26–33) can be accommodated in practice. Moreover, there are additional questions arising as to the starting conditions and the limitations of the horizons of change. The former relate to aspects such as degrees of openness and transparency in regard to initial expectations, goals and scopes for designing organizational, communicative, technological and evaluative dimensions. If the autonomy of the academic staff and the existing remains of democratic decision-making structures at universities are supposed to be respected, this is not compatible with corporate top-down-routines or expectations of submission to the strategies of tech-elites (Schmalz, 2020). Also, as far as the limitations of the horizons of change are concerned, there is a major difference whether we are dealing with modalities of *re-acting, re-structuring, re-designing, re-framing* or *re-generating* (see Peschl & Fundneider, 2008), especially since these open up different possibilities of dealing with paradoxical requirements.

2.6 *Thesis 6: Limitations of Datafication, AI Applications and Big Data Analyses Are Scarcely Reflected on*

The microstructures of the global education industry are oriented to the monetization of digital interfaces and not to their humanization. This should not be overlooked in the face of AI applications and Big Data finding their way also into various contexts of learning and education in the past few years. For some companies, agencies and providers of learning technologies, increasingly bigger and better-structured amounts of data are available not only for individual analysis but also in combination with other available data sets. In this context, even the analysis of microdata and their structures is raising high hopes: "Data analytics can help institutions to develop the most strategic and persuasive approach to enhance learning environments, which in turn contribute to a greater return-of investment for both individuals and institutions" (Corbeil et al., 2017, p. 8).

In the mainstream of data-positivist basis orientations, not only pedagogic legitimations and ethical justifications receive inadequate attention, but limitations do as well. The latter concern different types of data and their connections, perspectives of data criticism, epistemological and political dimensions of datafication, unintentional institutional and organizational effects and not least tendencies of data-induced discrimination which are frequently denied or trivialized in everyday media discourses. A differentiated examination of these topics is among the desiderata in microlearning discourses, although there is no lack of relevant points of contact (see, for example, Dander, 2014, 2018; Williamson, 2017, 2020; Allert & Richter, 2017; Eubanks, 2018; Noble, 2018; AlgorithmWatch, 2019; Sander, 2020; Swertz & Barberi, 2020). Such an examination requires an expansion of contextual thinking beyond lexical contexts of meaning, personal contexts and discourse contexts (van Goor et al., 2004, p. 176) towards user-generated, data-driven and computer-based contexts. Relevant indications can be found for example in the concept of "learner-generated contexts" (Seipold, 2017), in cultural-anthropological analyses of the work of algorithms (Seaver, 2018) and models of calculating causally effective factors (Pearl & Mackenzie, 2018).

2.7 *Thesis 7: The Mainstream of Microlearning Discourses Is Characterized by Tendencies Informed by Availability-Rationalism and a Belief in the Calculability of the World*

While individuals with knowledge about education theory hold rather cautious and deliberative views regarding the assumed impact of processes of learning and, the mainstream of microlearning discourses is characterized by rhetorics of the implementation and availability of processes and results. Where learners are turned into customers or "participants" who are funneled through personalized microlearning programs for the purpose of modifying their behavior (Kapp & Defelice, 2019, p. 89–108), what matters are calculable outputs and not subjectively significant learning experiences. Demands for controlling processes of teaching and learning, for the algorithm-based production of specific effects, the tech-based timing of learning steps, the predefined time management or the planning of education with a definitive, failproof outcome can be informally understood as an expression of tendencies of availability rationalism (*Verfügungsrationalismus*). In detail, these tendencies may well be based on different concepts of rationalism, for example in regard to the minimization of effort in view of concrete goals (purposive rationality) or the consistent orientation towards certain values or principles (value rationality *sensu* Max Weber). Tendencies of availability rationalism are not bound to a special rationality or version of rationalism. They refer to all forms of rationalism which are marked by an inclination to absolutize the determination of initial situations, modalities of assessment, means, intended purposes or processes and instances for the intentional production of concrete behaviors or specific circumstances (see Hug et al., 2007).

There is no doubt that, along with today's structural-mathematical developments, there have emerged potentials for the generation of realities (Löffler, 2019) which can also be applied in the designing of microformats and in the field of education in general. Nevertheless, this does not render unnecessary the question of the limits to the calculability of the world in general (Pietsch et al., 2017) and of pedagogic worlds in particular, much less that of the limits to the corporate optimization mindset.

3 Conclusion

Microformats play a tremendous role in formal and informal contexts of learning and education. This is true not only for those technological applications which have been associated with 'microlearning' for approximately 15 years, but also for numerous historical and contemporary forms of organizing content units and learning activities in a microdidactic way.

Today, datafication, AI applications and Big Data analyses offer diverse possibilities for designing innovative microlearning formats. The use of these possibilities on the basis of technological offers by the global education industry corresponds with complex medial dynamics of inclusion and exclusion and with an enormous potential for the transformation of social, cultural and societal meso- and macro-structures in the field of education. The deep structures, subtle dynamics of change and transformation modes are still largely misunderstood, particularly since micro-political and micro-social concretizations of the microlearning formats and local and regional adaptations of the global development dynamics are quite different.

The mainstream of digitization industries relies on instrumental logics of digital innovation and transformation, frequently spreading suggestions that there is no alternative to the path of innovation, something which needs to be called into question (see Mansell, 2018). This applies to learning and education as much as to other societally relevant areas. Efforts to make contingencies in the field of microlearning and microteaching visible, as well as attempts to make processes of transformation comprehensible and point out and test alternative paths of development occur in niches rather than within well-funded research programs which are inspired by education-political initiatives for sustainability.

If we agree that there are many pathways of innovation in dealing with microformats in learning and educational contexts generally and in the field of programming skills in higher education especially, questions about sound pedagogy practices remain (cf. Hug, 2021b). However, the theoretical reflections presented in this chapter do not allow for a final recipe-like message. We are always challenged to reflect the relevance of micro-, meso- and macro-structural interdependencies and the limitations of the application of instrumental logics in contexts of learning and education. There is no all-embracing pedagogy that could function as a solid and proven framework for designing microlearning objects. Moreover, complex challenges of sustainability in education, ecology and society go far beyond the challenges related the demand for improving ICT skills and algorithmic thinking. In order to be able to deal successfully with this complexity, contextual, critical and creative forms of thinking and acting are needed, too. Depending on the situation, problem and purpose, different combinations of these and other forms of thinking can open up viable solutions and a sustainable management of dilemmas and paradoxical constellations.

Microlearning formats have to be neither the scene of a *War on Learning* (Losh, 2014) nor the centerpiece of tendencies of "learnification" (Biesta, 2010). Also, there is no reason to utilize or tacitly approve the widespread everyday acceptance of algorithm-based educational, marketing and manipulation programs serving political or economic interests in public educational institutions. If microlearning formats are critically designed and employed along the lines of the outlined theses, they can be part of educational processes which focus neither on elite, highbrow traditions nor primarily on marketable qualification processes. Instead, open-ended perspectives correspond with notions of education as bricolage in which the public and the private are reflected on and respected. In this case, microlearning formats correspond with comprehensible didactic arrangements, with transparent software architectures that both teachers and learners can freely configure and not least with a healthy dose of skepticism towards education-technological promises, bearing in mind the long history of the imagination of automatized learning technologies.

References

Abramo, J. (2014). Music education that resonates: An epistemology and pedagogy of sound. *Philosophy of Music Education Review, 22*(1), 78–95.

Adolf, M. T. (2014). Involuntaristische Mediatisierung. Big Data als Herausforderung einer informationalisierten Gesellschaft. In H. Ortner, D. Pfurtscheller, M. Rizzolli, & A. Wiesinger (Eds.), *Datenflut und Informationskanäle* (pp. 19–35). Innsbruck University Press.

AlgorithmWatch. (2019). *Atlas der Automatisierung. Automatisierte Entscheidungen und Teilhabe in Deutschland.* Retrieved from https://atlas.algorithmwatch.org/wp-content/uploads/2019/04/Atlas_der_Automatisierung_von_AlgorithmWatch.pdf. Accessed 22 June 2021.

Allert, H., & Richter, C. (2017). Das Politische der Algorithmen in der Bildung. Subjektivierungsprozesse und Digitalität. In S. Eder, C. Mikat, & A. Tillmann (Eds.), *Software takes command. Herausforderungen der "Datafizierung" für die Medienpädagogik in Theorie und Praxis* (pp. 69–83). kopaed (Schriften zur Medienpädagogik).

Barberi, A., Grünberger, N., & Schmölz, A. (Eds.) (2020). Nähe(n) und Distanz(en) in Zeiten der COVID-19-Krise. *Medienimpulse-Themenheft, 58*(2). Retrieved from https://journals.univie.ac.at/index.php/mp/issue/view/291. Accessed: 22 June 2020.

Bauer, R., Hafer, J., Hofhues, S., Schiefner-Rohs, M., Thillosen, A., Volk, B., & Wannemacher, K. (Eds.). (2020). *Vom E-Learning zur Digitalisierung. Mythen, Realitäten, Perspektiven* (Medien in der Wissenschaft) (Vol. 76). Waxmann. (in print).

Biesta, G. (2010). *Good education in an age of measurement: Ethics, politics, democracy.* Routledge.

Biesta, G. (2011). Disciplines and theory in the academic study of education: A comparative analysis of the Anglo-American and continental construction of the field. *Pedagogy, Culture & Society, 19*(2), 175–192. https://doi.org/10.1080/14681366.2011.582255

Billig, M. (2013). *Learn to write badly* (How to succeed in the social sciences). Cambridge University Press.

Björk. (2011). *Biophilia.* [LP, CD, digital]. One Little Indian Records/Well Hart.

Brandenburg, U. (2020). Internationalisation in higher education for society – IHES in the times of corona. *Sociální Pedagogika / Social Education, 8*(1), 11–24.

Cizek, K., Uricchio, W., Anderson, J., Agui Carter, M., Harris, T. A., Holmes, M., & Stephenson, M. (2019). *Part 1: 'we are here': Starting points in co-creation.* Retrieved from https://wip.mitpress.mit.edu/pub/collective-wisdom-part-1. Accessed 22 June 2021.

Corbeil, M. E., Corbeil, J. R., & Khan, B. H. (2017). A framework for identifying and analyzing major issues in implementing big data and data analytics in e-learning: Introduction to special issue on big data and data analytics. *Educational Technology, 57*(1), 3–9. Retrieved from https://www.jstor.com/stable/44430534. Accessed 2022-08-15.

Dander, V. (2014). Von der 'Macht der Daten' zur 'Gemachtheit von Daten'. Praktische Datenkritik als Gegenstand der Medienpädagogik. *Mediale Kontrolle unter Beobachtung*. (3.1). Retrieved from https://d-nb.info/1058904396/34. Accessed 14 December 2021.

Dander, V. (2018). Zurück in die Zukunft der Medienpädagogik. «Subjekt», «Bildung» und «Medien*Kritik» im Lichte | im Schatten digitaler Daten. *MedienPädagogik: Zeitschrift für Theorie und Praxis der Medienbildung, 23*, 1–134. https://doi.org/10.21240/mpaed/diss.vd.X

Eubanks, V. (2018). *Automating inequality. How high-tech tools profile, police, and punish the poor*. St. Martin's Press.

Faßler, M. (2009). Vom Sichtbaren des Denkens. In U. Ratsch, I.-O. Stamatescu, & P. Stoellger (Eds.), *Kompetenzen der Bilder* (Funktionen und Grenzen des Bildes in den Wissenschaften) (pp. 289–314). Mohr Siebeck.

Faßler, M. (2014). Das Soziale. In *Entstehung und Zukunft menschlicher Selbstorganisation*. Fink.

Friesen, N. (2019). Educational research in America today: Relentless instrumentalism and scholarly backlash. *Erziehungswissenschaft, 59*(30), 77–83. https://doi.org/10.3224/ezw.v30i2.09

Gallo, G., & Trompetto, M. (2020). The effects of COVID-19 on academic activities and surgical education in Italy. *Journal of Investigative Surgery*, 1–2. https://doi.org/10.1080/08941939.2020.1748147

Glauser, C., Harder, S., Gruber, A., Schürch, A., Willenbacher, S., Moersch, C., & Sack, M. (2019). *Kalkül und Kontingenz: Kunstbasierte Untersuchungen im Kunst- und Theaterunterricht: Chewing Reality*. Kopaed.

Graf-Schlattmann, M., Meister, D. M., Oevel, G., & Wilde, M. (2020). Kollektive Veränderungsbereitschaft als zentraler Erfolgsfaktor von Digitalisierungsprozessen an Hochschulen. *Zeitschrift für Hochschulentwicklung, 15*(1), 19–39. https://doi.org/10.3217/zfhe-15-01/02

Haugsbakk, G. (2020). Special issue: 30 years of ICT and learning in education – major changes and challenges. *Seminar.Net, 16*(2). https://doi.org/10.7577/seminar.4043

Haugsbakk, G., & Nordkvelle, Y. (2007). The rhetoric of ICT and the new language of learning: A critical analysis of the use of ICT in the curricular field. *European Educational Research Journal, 6*(1). https://doi.org/10.2304/eerj.2007.6.1.1

Helsper, W. (1996). Antinomien des Lehrerhandelns in modernisierten pädagogischen Kulturen: Paradoxe Verwendungsweisen von Autonomie und Selbstverantwortlichkeit. In A. Combe & W. Helsper (Eds.), *Pädagogische Professionalität. Untersuchungen zum Typus pädagogischen Handelns* (pp. 521–569). Suhrkamp.

Hierdeis, H. (2007). From meno to microlearning: A historical survey. In T. Hug (Ed.), *Didactics of microlearning: Concepts, discourses and examples* (pp. 35–52). Waxmann.

Hörl, E., & Burton, J. (Eds.). (2017). *General ecology: The new ecological paradigm* (Theory). Bloomsbury Academic, an imprint of Bloomsbury Publishing Plc.

Hua, J., & Shaw, R. (2020). Corona virus (COVID-19) "Infodemic" and emerging issues through a data lens: The case of China. *International Journal of Environmental Research and Public Health, 17*(7), 2309.

Hug, T. (2018). Herausforderungen für Lernen und Bildung im Medienzeitalter – Zur Einführung. In T. Hug (Ed.), *Medienpädagogik – Herausforderungen für Lernen und Bildung im Medienzeitalter* (pp. 7–17). Innsbruck University Press.

Hug, T. (2021a). Mikrolernformate in der Krise? Thesen im Spannungsfeld coronainduzierter Kurzzeitlösungen, apodiktischer Alternativlosigkeit und zukunftsoffenen Perspektiven. In: Moormann, P., Zahn, M., Bettinger, P., Hofhues, S., Keden, H. J., & Kaspar, K. (Hrsg.), Mikroformate. Interdisziplinäre Perspektiven auf aktuelle Phänomene in digitalen Medienkulturen (pp. 83–98). Kopead.

Hug, T. (2021b). Sound pedagogy practices for designing and implementing microlearning objects. In J. R. Corbeil, B. H. Khan, & M. E. Corbeil (Eds.), *Microlearning in the digital age. The design and delivery of learning in snippets* (pp. 35–57). Routledge Taylor & Francis Group.

Hug, T., Friesen, N., & Rourke, L. (2007). Nutzenerwartungen und Wissenswandel – kritische Betrachtungen im Spannungsfeld von nutzloser Nützlichkeit und nützlicher Nutzlosigkeit am Beispiel der Learning Sciences. In G. Reinmann & J. Kahlert (Eds.), *Der Nutzen wird vertagt … Bildungswissenschaften im Spannungsfeld zwischen wissenschaftlicher Profilbildung und praktischem Mehrwert* (pp. 173–197). Pabst-Verlag.

Kaiser-Müller, K. (2015). Ideologiekritik des E-Learnings. *Medienimpulse, 53*(1) Retrieved from https://journals.univie.ac.at/index.php/mp/article/view/mi773. Accessed 22 June 2021.

Kapp, K. M., & Defelice, R. A. (2019). *Microlearning: Short and sweet*. ATD Press.

Khan, B. H. (2019). Microlearning: Quick and meaningful snippets for training solutions. *International Journal of Research in Educational Sciences (IJRES), 2*(2), 275–284. Retrieved from http://iafh.net/index.php/IJRES/article/view/107. Accessed 22 June 2021.

Knorr Cetina, K., & Bruegger, U. (2005). Globale Mikrostrukturen der Weltgesellschaft. Die virtuellen Gesellschaften von Finanzmärkten. In P. Windolf (Ed.), *Finanzmarkt-Kapitalismus. Analysen zum Wandel von Produktionsregimen. Sonderheft 45/2005 der Kölner Zeitschrift für Soziologie und Sozialpsychologie* (pp. 145–171). VS Verlag.

Koch, J., Heidemann, W., & Zumbeck, C. (2012). *Weiterbildung im Betrieb mit E-Learning, Web 2.0, Mikrolernen und Wissensmanagement*. Hans-Böckler-Stiftung.

Kowarik, I. (2010). *Biologische Invasionen. Neophyten und Neozoen in Mitteleuropa* (2nd ed., with contributions by Wolfgang Rabitsch). Eugen Ulmer Verlag.

Krämer, S. (2008). Medium, Bote, Übertragung. In *Kleine Metaphysik der Medialität*. Suhrkamp.

Lee, E. A. (2020). The coevolution. In *The entwined futures of humans and machines*. MIT Press.

Löffler, D. (2019). *Generative Realitäten I. Die Technologische Zivilisation als neue Achsenzeit und Zivilisationsstufe. Eine Anthropologie des 21. Jahrhunderts*. Velbrück.

Lohmann, I. (2009). Momentaufnahme der gegenwärtigen Regierungsweise des Bildungssystems. In I. Sylvester, I. Sieh, M. Menz, H.-W. Fuchs, & J. Behrendt (Eds.), *Bildung – Recht – Chancen. Rahmenbedingungen, empirische Analysen und internationale Perspektiven zum Recht auf chancengleiche Bildung* (pp. 47–60). Waxmann.

Losh, E. (2014). The war on learning. In *Gaining ground in the digital university*. MIT Press.

Luyben, A., Fleming, V., & Vermeulen, J. (2020). Midwifery education in COVID-19-time: Challenges and opportunities. *Midwifery, 89*, 102776. Retrieved from https://www.ncbi.nlm.nih.gov/pmc/articles/PMC7263260/. Accessed 22 June 2021.

Mansell, R. (2018). Transformative communication technologies: The accountability challenge. 36th Boehm-Bawerk Lecture – Inauguration of the Department of Media, Society and Communication. *Kleine Medienreihe* (Vol. 2). IUP.

Miao, Y., van der Klink, M., Boon, J., Sloep, P., & Koper, R. (2009). Enabling teachers to develop pedagogically sound and technically executable learning designs. *Distance Education, 30*(2), 259–276. https://doi.org/10.1080/01587910903023223

Noble, S. U. (2018). *Algorithms of oppression: How search engines reinforce racism*. Combined Academic Publ. New York University Press.

Ochs, C., Friedewald, M., Hess, T., & Lamla, J. (Eds.). (2019). *Die Zukunft der Datenökonomie: Zwischen Geschäftsmodell, Kollektivgut und Verbraucherschutz*. Springer VS.

Parreira do Amaral, M., Steiner-Khamsi, G., & Thompson, C. (Eds.). (2019). *Researching the global education industry*. Palgrave Macmillan.

Pearl, J., & Mackenzie, D. (2018). *The book of why: The new science of cause and effect*. Basic Books.

Peschl, M. F., & Fundneider, T. (2008). Emergent innovation and sustainable knowledge co-creation. A socio-epistemological approach to "innovation from within". In M. D. Lytras et al. (Eds.), *The open knowledge society: A computer science and information systems manifesto* (pp. 101–108). Springer.

Picciano, A. G. (1994). Technology and the evolving educational-industrial complex. *Computers in the Schools., 11*(2), 85–101.

Picciano, A. G., & Spring, J. H. (2013). *The great American education-industrial complex: Ideology, technology, and profit*. Routledge.

Pietsch, W., Wernecke, J., & Ott, M. (Eds.). (2017). *Berechenbarkeit der Welt? Philosophie und Wissenschaft im Zeitalter von Big Data*. Springer VS.

Sander, I. (2020). Critical big data literacy tools—Engaging citizens and promoting empowered internet usage. *Data & Policy*. Cambridge University Press, 2, https://doi.org/10.1017/dap.2020.5

Saxena, R. (2020). Corona crisis: Implications for higher education in India. *Business World*, 2020-05-07. Retrieved from http://bweducation.businessworld.in/article/Corona-Crisis-Implications-For-Higher-Education-In-India/07-05-2020-191442/. Accessed 22 June 2021.

Schmalz, G. (2020). Mein fremder Wille. In *Wie wir uns freiwillig unterwerfen und die Tech-Elite kassiert*. Campus.

Seaver, N. (2018). What should an anthropology of algorithms do? *Cultural Anthropology, 33*(3), 375–385. Retrieved from von https://journal.culanth.org/index.php/ca/article/view/ca33.3.04/90. Accessed 10 June 2021.

Seipold, J. (2017). Lernergenerierte Contexte. Raum für personalisiertes und selbstgesteuertes Lernen und Ideengeber für ein "Ökologiemodell von Aneignung". In K. Mayrberger, J. Fromme, P. Grell, & T. Hug (Eds.), *Jahrbuch Medienpädagogik 13. Vernetzt und entgrenzt – Gestaltung von Lernumgebungen mit digitalen Medien* (pp. 29–43). Springer VS.

Skalka, J., & Drlík, M. (2020). Automated assessment and microlearning units as predictors of at-risk students and students' outcomes in the introductory programming courses. *Applied Sciences, 10*, 4566. https://doi.org/10.3390/app10134566

Skalka, J., Drlík, M., Obonya, J., & Cápay, M. (2020). Architecture proposal for micro-learning application for learning and teaching programming courses. *IEEE Global Engineering Education Conference (EDUCON), Porto, Portugal* (pp. 980–987). https://doi.org/10.1109/EDUCON45650.2020.9125407.

Swertz, C., & Barberi, A. (2020). Personal Data für Entscheidungsimpulse setzende Akteurinnen und Akteure. *Zeitschrift MedienPädagogik (Jahrbuch Medienpädagogik 15)*, 15–34. https://doi.org/10.21240/mpaed/jb15/2020.03.02.X

Turkle, S., & Papert, S. (1990). Epistemological pluralism: Styles and voices within the computer culture. *Journal of Women in Culture and Society, 16*(1), 128–157.

van Ackeren, I., Endberg, M., & Locker-Grütjen, O. (2020). Chancenausgleich in der Corona-Krise. Die soziale Bildungsschere wieder schließen. *Die Deutsche Schule, 112*(2), 245–248.

van Goor, R., Heyting, F. G., & Vreeke, G.-J. (2004). Beyond foundations: Signs of a new normativity in philosophy of education. *Educational Theory, 54*(2), 173–192. https://doi.org/10.1111/j.1741-5446.2004.00013.x

Verger, A., Lubienski, C., & Steiner-Khamsi, G. (2016). *World yearbook of education 2016: The global education industry*. Routledge.

Williamson, B. (2017). *Datafication of education. The digital future of learning, policy and practice*. Sage.

Williamson, B. (2020). Datafication of education. A critical approach to emerging analytics technologies and practices. In H. Beetham & R. Sharpe (Eds.), *Rethinking pedagogy for a digital age* (3rd ed., pp. 212–226). Routledge. https://doi.org/10.4324/9781351252805

Winkel, R. (1986). Antinomische Pädagogik und Kommunikative Didaktik. In *Studien zu den Widersprüchen und Spannungen in Erziehung und Schule*. Schwann.

Zuboff, S. (2019). *The age of surveillance capitalism: The fight for a human future at the new frontier of power*. Public Affairs.

Theo Hug is Professor in Educational Sciences at the Department of Media, Society and Communication at the University of Innsbruck, Austria, and coordinator of the Innsbruck Media Studies research group. His areas of interest include media education and media literacy, mobile learning and microlearning, theory of knowledge, methodology and philosophy of science.

A Comprehensive Discussion of Emerging Automatic Programming Assessment in Learning Management Systems: The VPL Example

Juan Carlos Rodríguez-del-Pino, Zenón J. Hernández-Figueroa, María Dolores Afonso-Suárez, and José Daniel González-Domínguez

1 Introduction

Computer programming is a subject present in a wide variety of curricula, not only in higher education, but at all educational levels. Programming assessment is an especially costly task since different correct solutions may vary substantially from each other in terms of the involved logic constructions. Manual evaluation of these solutions could be a long and tedious process, especially if the number of students and the code is large. Large-size classes usually require the intervention of several evaluators, which could produce inconsistency and heterogeneity in mark grades, especially when assessment criteria and rubrics are not strictly stablished. As Tharmaseelan (Tharmaseelan et al., 2021) says, the automation of evaluation has the intrinsic value of "provide consistency and standardization across the mark distribution especially in large classes where multiple human-markers are involved". Thus, from the perspective of the programming teacher, the main motivation for using automatic assessment tools is to perform the assessment with less effort and greater accuracy.

From the students' point of view, the main benefit of automatic evaluation is that feedback from their results is faster than when the evaluation is manual and is usually accompanied by the possibility of reworking successive submissions to improve those results. In this sense, there are studies (Chen et al., 2020) that suggest the

J. C. Rodríguez-del-Pino (✉) · Z. J. Hernández-Figueroa · M. D. Afonso-Suárez
J. D. González-Domínguez
Department of Informatics and Systems, University of Las Palmas de Gran Canaria, Las Palmas, Spain
e-mail: jc.rodriguezdelpino@ulpgc.es; zenon.hernandez@ulpgc.es; marilola.afonso@ulpgc.es; josedaniel.gonzalez@ulpgc.es

E. Smyrnova-Trybulska et al. (eds.), *Microlearning*,
https://doi.org/10.1007/978-3-031-13359-6_9

convenience of limiting the number of allowed resubmissions, to avoid students ending up solving their problems by a trial-and-error approach supported by automatic evaluation, instead of implementing the tests to make sure the code they have written works correctly.

2 Automated Programming Assessment Systems

An Automated Programming Assessment System (APAS) involves, at least, three legitim actors (Teacher/Evaluator, Student/Learner, and APAS Developer), plus a non-legitim one (Student/Cheater), as Fig. 1 shows. Each actor has different needs and interests. Furthermore, actually, each actor can be considered a set of diverse persons with the same role but not the same interests-skills. There are also entities, and relationships to consider. The entities are tasks description, tests, submissions/drafts, feedback, marks, and the APAS that includes test frameworks. Relationships are between actors an entities: teachers/evaluators write tasks descriptions and develop tests for a specific test framework or APAS. Students read the task description and submit a proposal of solution that the APAS assess using the tests. The APAS generate a report that may content feedback and marks. The cheating student tries to get an unfair mark or other benefits by sending manipulated submissions to the APAS. The APAS developer tries to get the best system for teachers, allowing the best assessment and feedback to students, and avoiding unfair use by cheaters.

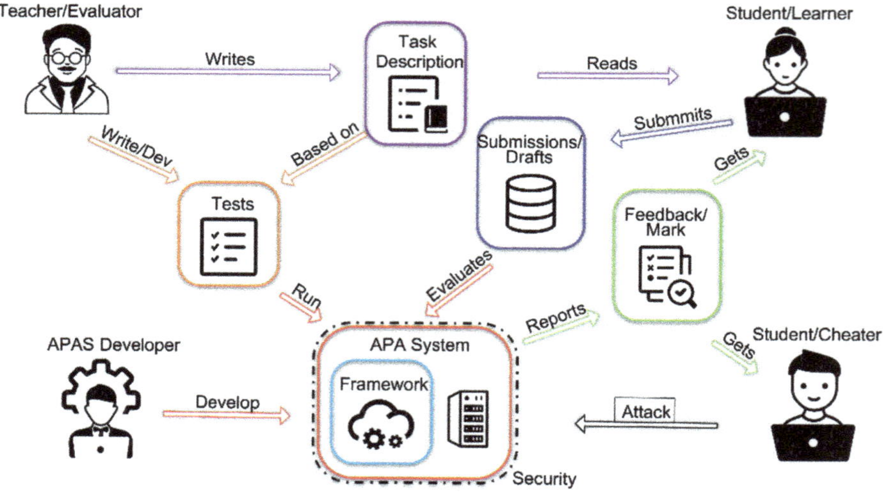

Fig. 1 Actors, entities and relationships on an automated programming assessment system

2.1 Teachers/Evaluators

Teachers use APAS to improve the student's learning process and reduce the evaluation time and effort. In this context, they develop programming activities to support different teaching approaches. Teachers may range from a basic school instructor to a university professor, all of them with different skills to develop automated assessment activities. Not all types of APA Systems are suitable for the skills of all teachers. For example, not all teachers of the basic school can write tests using a xUnit framework. The teacher may or not be an evaluator, but if the teacher and the evaluator are different persons, they must work in close coordination, that is why we have identified them as the single actor Teacher/Evaluator.

The roles of the Teacher/Evaluator are to design the automatic assessment and to check its proposed results. The teacher/evaluator must write a full description of the task to be solved and build the proper tests to assess it. Based on our experience of more than 20 years developing an APAS and using it as evaluators, we think that the best way to design the evaluation is by applying what we call "Test-Driven Assessment", due to its similarity to the well-known "Test-Driven Development" used in software engineering. First, the Teacher/Evaluator must know what kind of automatic assessment the APAS allows. Techniques for program assessment are usually divided into two types: static and dynamic (Ala-Mutka, 2005). Static assessment is carried out by analysing the software code without running it. It could be useful for syntax error discovery, style analysis, software metrics evaluation, plagiarism detection, and more (Rahman & Nordin, 2007). Dynamic assessment, on the other hand, implies the execution of the code using a set of test cases to detect malfunctioning and possibly also determine its efficiency. Some systems allow combining both types of assessment.

The Teacher/Evaluator must know the APAS' limitations. Notice that not all types of APAS can test all types of programing tasks. For example, a teacher can write a task description asking the student to build a recursive solution for a problem, but not all APA Systems or test frameworks can check if the code uses recursion.

The Teacher/Evaluator must build assessment tests accordingly to the features and limitatios of the available APAS, must formulate the task requirements accordingly to the tests, and must write the task description to make those requirements clear for the proper functioning of the assessment.

2.2 Students

The students form a heterogeneous group that face each programming task differently due to the different abilities required to resolve it. Some students can resolve correctly the task with no help, and others may be facing an unsolvable problem according to their current programming skills. With the correct task description and proper feedback during the development, many of the students may improve their programming skills and successfully pass the task. The target of many of the students is to learn and improve their skills, but others may have as a primary target to pass the task. Anyway, almost all of them want to pass the task with minimal effort.

The Student/Learner needs formative feedback to improve his learning and the Teacher/Evaluator must include such feedback in a suitable way to the student. The feedback provided should consider the student profile. The first-course student does not require the same type of feedback that a student following an advancing programming course. The type and complexity of the task to solve is another factor to consider, and, overall, the Teacher/Evaluator must know the different types of feedback that he must provide. For example, Keuning (Keuning et al., 2018) lists five types of elaborate feedback components: Knowledge about task constrains, Knowledge about concepts, Knowledge about mistakes, Knowledge about how to proceed, and Knowledge about meta-cognition.

Some students sometimes turn into cheaters. The Student/Cheater is a type of learner that, for different reasons as lack of skills, short time to solve tasks, social or economic environment pressures, or enjoy cheating among others tries to pass the task without resolving the problem. The other actors that participate in the learning process must be aware of this type of student; not only for trying to get an unfair grade but also for the effect that this can have on the rest of the students.

2.3 APAS Developer

The APA developer must be in coordination with developers of other related system features that can include the management of task description, tests definitions, submissions, reports, integration with LMS, etc. However, the main coordination is with the teachers/evaluator because the main feature of APAS is to run the tests developed by evaluators for a specific submission.

2.3.1 Controlling the Use of Resources

A common feature of all APAS is to control de resources used by the tests process. The types of resources to control may be CPU time, memory used, the number of processes, the disk used, the network bandwidth used, etc. If the APAS has no limit of resources for running tests, the type of test may be limited to static ones that do not run student code. Running student's code without resource limits may lead to exhaust some of the resources and the affected machine become unusable due to being unavailable or having low throughput. The developer must offer the evaluator a way to set the limit of resources that needs each test, especially if the test runs the student's code. It may be appropriate to have a default value for not established limits by evaluators.

2.3.2 Defining Tests and Feedback

The APAS must provide a way to define the tests for the student's code. The test types can range from a specific test framework, which commonly is or mimics a general-purpose test framework, e.g. JUnit, to a specific language for describing tests. The election of this feature must be coordinated with evaluators.

Commonly a test represents a set of tests cases. Each test case tries to check if the student program passes a specification of the problem or of the code. To generate a proper report for students, when the tests case fails the system adds default information to the feedback; also, the test case definition may contain text that the system adds to the feedback. This text may show the data of the test case, hints to pass the test, where the student can get information to resolve the problem found, etc.

2.3.3 Security

The APAS as all types of software must consider security as a high priority requisite. Notice that cheaters may have a strong motivation to get an unfair benefice and that cheaters are learning aspects of computer science that can give knowledge of how to attack a system, also the cheater can know peers that can help to prepare an attack. The systems hosting APAS are often connected to a network, giving the attacker two attack vectors and two targets. The vectors of attack are the network and the student's code. The targets may be the host system and the APA system itself. Possible path of attack can see in Fig. 2.

The system administrators can palliate attacks against the host system using the network with common measures used on other systems connected to networks. The APAS developers can palliate attacks using the network with a proper authentication system from the evaluation requester to the APAS. The APAS developers can reduce attacks to the host system using an isolation approach of the tests executions. The APAS developers and evaluators can mitigate attacks on APAs using student's code with the correct APA design and the proper use of the test definition by the evaluator. For example, in the latter case, an evaluator can write test cases that

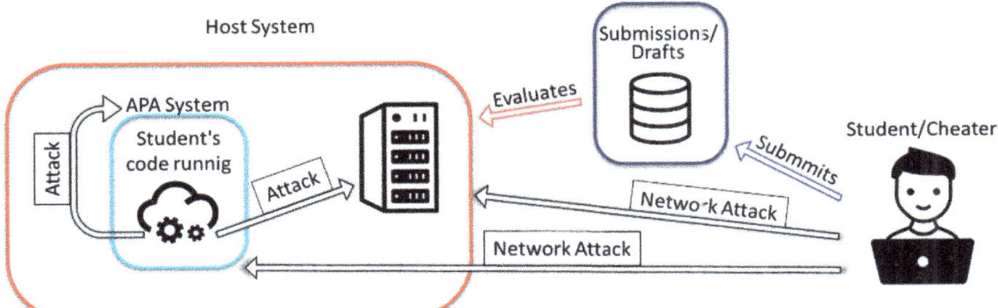

Fig. 2 Cheater attacks

inform the student of the details of the test case failure, including the data values used and the expected outcome. This is common practice because if not the student can be frustrated with unknown fails. If the system allows repeated submissions, a cheater con passes the tests cases with a simple program with a sequence of "if known value return expected result" obtained from the failed cases. To resolve this attack the evaluator must write test cases of the same "class of equivalence" that does not give the values used and expected, and only inform of the type of failed case. The use of a submission versioning system and a proper log of all run tests can help to found attacks using student's code.

3 Existing Solutions for Automatic Assessment in LMS

Several Automated Programming Assessment Systems (APAS) exist (Christian & Bhushan, 2016) (Keuning et al., 2018), but many of them have been developed and used in a research context, are not publicly available, or have been abandoned once the research comes to an end. Among them, and from our own perspective and experience, the most valuables are those which are integrated into a Learning management System (LMS). A LMS usually provides a full ecosystem of modules for teaching and learning activities as well as a grading system capable of combining marks from many of those activities. An automated programming assessment tool could be integrated into an LMS as an activity module and could beneficiate from the interaction with the background provided by such a system, simultaneously contributing to the overall learning design.

Currently, there are a variety of available LMS, some of them proprietaries as Blackboard and Brightspace D2L, and others open source as Moodle, Canvas, and Sakay.

As can be seen from Fig. 3 (Hill, 2017), in 2017 Moodle was the dominant LMS at degree-granting institutions in Europe, Latin America, and Oceania, and the second one in North America.

To the best of our knowledge and among the first 30 items (sorted by relevance) returned by a search[1] in the Moodle Plugin Directory using the terms "computer programming learning automated assessment" (without quotation marks) we found that three of them were really related to the automated assessment of programming code. The first one was "Virtual Programming Lab" (VPL),[2] described as "an activity module to manage programming assignments". At the time of the search, it was being used in, at least 1725 sites, and had 5000 downloads in the last previous 90 days as Fig. 4 shows.

[1] Realized 07/28/2021.

[2] https://moodle.org/plugins/mod_vpl

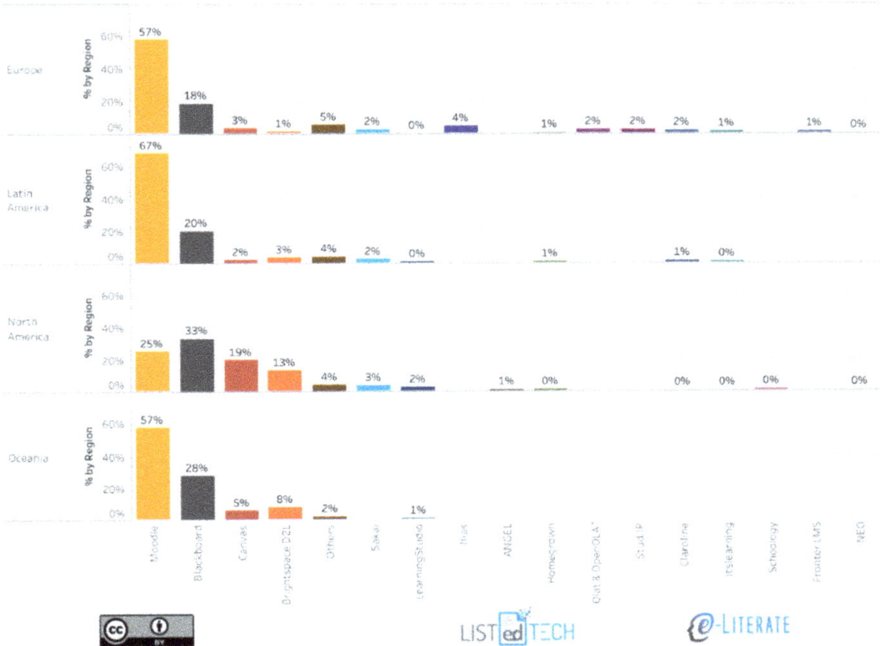

Fig. 3 Spring 2017 market share: higher Ed LMS in 4 global regions

The second one was "ProFormA Programming Task",[3] described as "Quiz question type for automatically graded programming questions". At the time of the search, it was being used in, at least 50 sites, and had 81 downloads in the last previous 90 days.

The third one was "Source-code Plagiarism Plugin",[4] described as "A plugin integrating 2 source code detection engines MOSS and JPlag into Moodle for programming assignments", but, although plagiarism is a topic related to assessment, obviously this is not a plugin for full-automated assessment. At the time of the search, it was being used in, at least 8 sites, and had 19 downloads in the last previous 90 days.

Within the first 60 items we find two more. The fourth one was CodeRunner, described as "A question type that allows question authors to set programming questions in which the student answer is code in some programming language". This plugin has around 1430 downloads in last 90 days and is installed in 2002 sites around the world (Table 1).

The last related plugin was VPL Question described as "VPL Questions are questions that can fit within a Moodle quiz. They are intended to create small to

[3] https://moodle.org/plugins/qtype_proforma

[4] https://moodle.org/plugins/plagiarism_programming

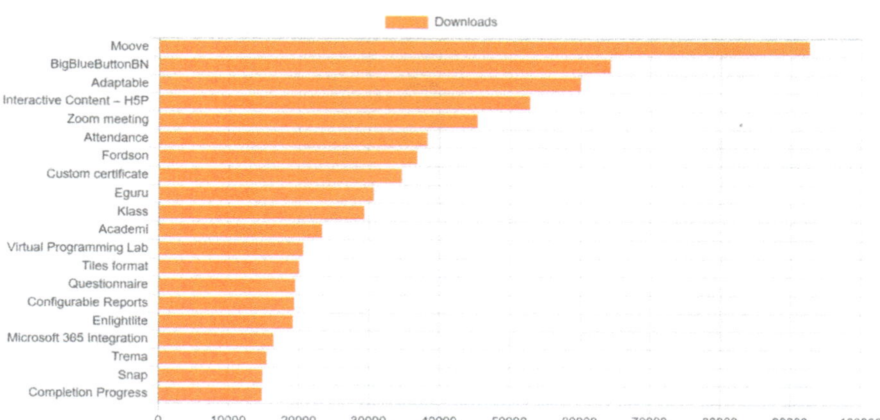

Fig. 4 Top plugin downloads in Moodle in the last 12 months (07/26/2021)

Table 1 Detail of programming related Moodle plugins

Plugin	Type	Downloads	Sites	Likes
VPL	Activity	>5000	1725	102
ProFormA	Question	76	50	8
CodeRunner	Question	>1000	2002	89
VPL question	Question	140	210	19

medium coding exercises, based on the Virtual Programming Lab plugin". This new Quiz plugin developed at the university of Grenoble has 139 downloads in the last 3 months and is installed in 210 Moodle sites (Table 1).

VPL seems to be the dominant activity plugin in Moodle for managing programming assignments, including assessment, although its short description on the plugin homepage is a bit scant about it. As of the date of the search, it was ranked 12th in the top 20 global Moodle plugin downloads (Fig. 4). VPL supports software development, from edition to running, debugging, and assessing, in several languages. Currently, it is distributed with support for Ada, C, C++, C#, D, Erlang, FORTRAN, Go, Groovy, Haskell, Java, JavaScript, Kotlin, MIPS, Lua, Octave, Pascal, Perl, PHP, Prolog, Python, R, Ruby, Scala, Scheme, SQL, and VHDL, but it is designed to be language-independent, and any user could install support for other languages (Rodríguez-del-Pino et al., 2012). It also provides a feature to search for similarities in students' code in the same or another course, so supporting counter-plagiarism actions.

4 Adapting Unit Testing Frameworks for APAS and LMS

Dynamic techniques for program assessment have a lot of similarities with unit testing techniques. Both take a piece of software, run it against a set of test cases, and produce a report from such execution. The main difference is both the software to be tested and the report that is generated. Unit test frameworks are designed to test "real" software and inform developers about detected errors, according to the applied test cases. Programming assessment tools take apprentice software, prone to have errors which are unlikely for a professional, like infinite loops, unexpected exceptions, security shortcomings and more. A programming assessment tool takes such sort of code and not only have to report error occurrences, but also produce useful feedback for the students, inform the instructors about the student skills, and, usually, propose a mark.

A well-known family of unit testing frameworks is xUnit. The xUnit family of unit testing frameworks has ground in most of the current main programming languages with great popularity. The architecture of xUnit frameworks is composed of a set of basic elements:

- Tests cases, which define the test data as pairs of input data and expected results.
- Tests fixtures, which define the context for the tests.
- Tests suites, which are a set of text sharing the same fixture.
- Test runners, which execute the tests and report the results.

Given the popularity of the xUnit Family, it seems to be a good idea to use them as models or tools for automated programming assessment systems. The ProFormA plugin homepage explicitly says that "Java questions using JUnit can be created directly in Moodle", so adhering to this criterion by using JUnit. VPL provides two ways to automate the assessment of programming activities:

1. The simplest way is using the basic input/output test evaluation system (BIOTES) provided by VPL out of the box. This system uses the input/output of the student's program to test it. We have to fill the file vpl_evaluate.cases (see Fig. 5) to define the test cases using a simple test case description language. This language allows defining, for each case, the input we want to provide to the student's program and the output we expect. We can also configure other stuff, as the penalization for failed tests (see the "VPL Test Case Description Language"[5]). The advantage of this approach is having an APAS independent of the programming language, easy to use, an allows write the tests without programming. The drawback is that its basic aim is to test programs by input/output.
2. VPL allows evaluators to take full control of the evaluation process with the only requirement that the output report must have a proper format (See the "Filtering and Formatting of VPL Evaluation Output"[6] document for more details). This

[5] https://vpl.dis.ulpgc.es/images/FITPED/VPL_Test_Case_Description_Language.pdf

[6] https://vpl.dis.ulpgc.es/images/FITPED/Filtering_and_Formating_VPL_output.pdf

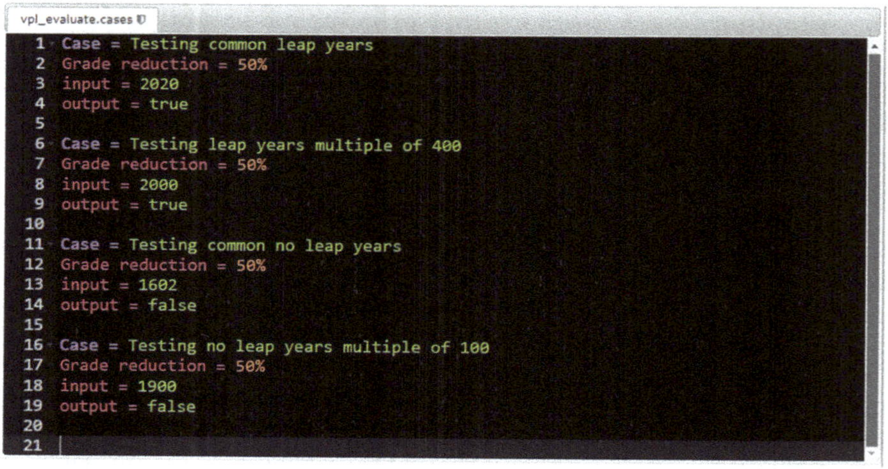

vpl_evaluate.cases

```
Case = Testing common leap years
Grade reduction = 50%
input = 2020
output = true

Case = Testing leap years multiple of 400
Grade reduction = 50%
input = 2000
output = true

Case = Testing common no leap years
Grade reduction = 50%
input = 1602
output = false

Case = Testing no leap years multiple of 100
Grade reduction = 50%
input = 1900
output = false
```

Fig. 5 Example of test cases definition for check leap years in the evaluation system (BIOTES) provided by VPL

advanced evaluation requires the evaluator developing a program to test the code submitted by the student, usually using the same programming language. This program could be written from scratch for each activity or be based on a customizable testing framework. Notice that VPL, in this approach, acts as a meta-APAS by supporting many other APA systems by writing the proper code.

Desirable features for a framework suitable to serves as a base for advanced evaluation using VPL may be:

- Must be integrable within VPL.
- Must allow giving clear and meaningful feedback to the students.
- Its learning curve for evaluators must be as low as possible.
- Evaluation should not require any interaction with the input/output of the student program (although such interaction must be possible).
- When possible, should be able to evaluate partial programs.
- The development effort needed to evaluate the students' code must be as simple as possible.
- The grading system provided by the framework must be suitable for a wide range of grading approach.
- Must be robust to the fatal fails of the students' code and report them.
- Must provide a tool for the internationalization of the reports.
- Must consider cheating risks.

Evaluate.java

```
import org.junit.*;
import static org.junit.Assert.*;
public class Evaluate {
    @Test
    public void isLeapYear() {
        assertTrue(StudentCode.isLeapYear(2000));
    }
    @Test
    public void isNotLeapYear() {
        assertFalse(StudentCode.isLeapYear(2001));
    }
}
```

Fig. 6 Example of simple JUnit test

5 Integrating xUnit in Assessment Systems

In this section, we discuss the drawbacks of xUnit frameworks to serve as assessment tools "as they are", and present proposals to shortcut such drawbacks. We focused on JUnit as a representative example of the xUnit family.

Junit is a framework for writing tests for Java. It is one of the first frameworks of this type to gain high popularity and based on the community dzone.com is still (2020) one of the best Java testing frameworks.

Writing tests for Java using Junit require writing classes with test methods that check the program behavior by testing asserts. The parametrization of the tests and the indication of what methods contain asserts or need to be run after or before each test is done using the Java annotation feature (format @annotation(param1, param2, ...). Java annotations allow tagging classes, methods, etc. Junit consults this information using the java reflection feature to orchestrate the tests, as the developer requires. Annotations must be set just before the element to tag. An example of JUnit annotations is @Test that tag a method to be run in test and containing asserts to check (see Fig. 6).

Some of the following frameworks use annotations to control the APAS tests. Some of these annotations are compatibles with JUnit doing the use of these test frameworks easier for evaluators with JUnit knowledge.

5.1 ProFormA

ProFormA allows to provide JUnit tests suites as external files and offers a setup option to specify the grading weight of such tests (see Fig. 7).

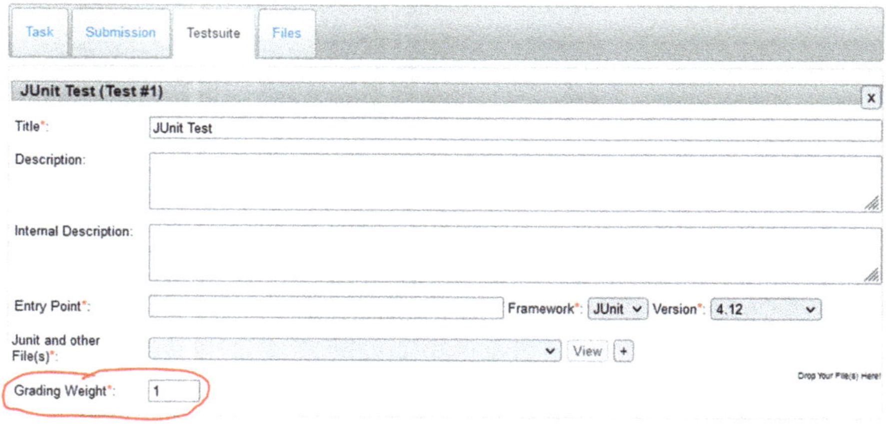

Task | Submission | Testsuite | Files

JUnit Test (Test #1)

Title*: JUnit Test

Description:

Internal Description:

Entry Point*: Framework*: JUnit Version*: 4.12

Junit and other File(s)*: View +

Grading Weight*: 1

Drop Your File(s) Here!

Fig. 7 Setup window of ProFomA

```
import caseine.format.javajunit.Grade;

import org.junit.Test;

import static org.junit.Assert.*;

public class Vpl_tests {
    @Test
    @Grade(33)
    public void testCompil() {
        Point p1 = new Point(0.0, 0.0);
        Point p2 = new Point(1.0, 1.0);
        Point p3 = new Point(2.0, 2.0);
        PointTriplet triplet = new PointTriplet(p1, p2, p3);
        assertEquals("P1 ", p1, triplet.getP1());
        assertEquals("P2 ", p2, triplet.getP2());
        assertEquals("P3 ", p3, triplet.getP3());
    }

```

Fig. 8 Grade annotation from Caseine Project

5.2 *The Grenoble University Approach*

The project Caseine (https://moodle.caseine.org), led by Grenoble University, modifies the basic input/output test evaluation system of VPL to merge different types of evaluation, including those based on JUnit tests suites. In addition, it creates a new Java annotation to establish the grade for each test, as Fig. 8 shows.

5.3 The University of Las Palmas de Gran Canaria Approach

At the University of Las Palmas de Gran Canaria we have developed a package, called JUnit4VPL, suitable to use the JUnit system without having to do any change to VPL. This framework was developed in the context of the project FITPED (Work-Based Learning in Future IT Professionals Education). JUnit4VPL modifies the Test annotation available in JUnit adding the attributes "description" and "penalty" while accepting the "expected" and "timeout" attributes available in the original JUnit Test annotation; Although the timeout behaviour is slightly different because in JUnit4VPL a timeout always exist: if the "timeout" attribute of Test is not set, the defaultTestTimeout of TestClass is used. The timeout may need be adjusted to do not surpass the global timeout. JUnit4VPL also adds new annotations.

5.3.1 The TestClass Annotation

TestClass is an annotation for classes which is not present in Junit (Fig. 9). TestClass sets global parameters to be applied to the test:

- defaultTestTimeout. Sets the default timeout in milliseconds for each test method. The default value is 2000 and can be overridden for a method by defining the timeout attribute of Test.
- globalTimeout. Sets the global timeout in milliseconds for the whole test suite. The default value is 30,000, but the global timeout used is the minimum of globalTimeOut and the value set at the VPL activity options settings form. When a overall timeout is reached, all pending tests are stopped, the evaluation is terminated and a 100% penalty is applied.
- timeoutPenalty. Sets the penalty to apply when a test method reaches its timeout. By default, the same penalization as for assertion fails is applied.
- exceptionPenalty. Sets the penalization to apply when an unexpected exception is raised. By default, the same penalization as for assertion fails is applied.
- expectedPenalty. Sets the penalization to apply when an expected exception is not raised. By default, the same penalization as for assertion fails is applied.

```
@TestClass (
    defaultTestTimeout = 1000,
    globalTimeout = 10000,
    exceptionPenalty = "30%"
)
public class TestFraction {
```

Fig. 9 TestClass annotation example

5.3.2 The ConsoleCapture Class

This class allows creating objects that can capture the standard output of the application. Capturing the output of the application has two goals: be able to check the output of the student's code and avoid that the student's code interferes with the test report sent to VPL. ConsoleCapture has the following methods:

- startCapture(). This procedure saves and reassigns the out and err streams to new on-memory streams.
- stopCapture(). This procedure restores the saved out and err streams.
- getCapturedOut(). Returns the text sent to the out stream from the last captureStart()
- getCapturedErr(). Returns the text sent to the err stream from the last captureStart()
- print(String text). Sends the text to the saved out stream (out of the capturing).

The best practice is to capture the streams as soon as possible and before starting the test. After ending the test, do not stop the capture: send the test report to VPL using the ConsoleCapture print method.

5.3.3 JUnit4VPL Internationalization

JUnit4VPL use internationalized text by taken the text to show from an object of JUnitI18n or a derived class. The default language is English, but other languages are available, as Spanish. To select an available language you must call the static function JUnitI18n.setLang() with new language object as parameter. The call to setLang() must be done before calling to JUnitCore.runClasess() or JUnitCore.main() methods to take effect.

To add a new language to JUnit4VPL it is necessary to extend the JUnitI18n class and override the methods that define the text to output. Some of the text strings are parametrized with one or two parameters that must be in the string. The current values replace the parameters when the text is used.

For example, the method expectedButWas() returns a string with two parameters <expected> and <was> (Fig. 10).

The translated text for the Spanish language must contain also the two parameters (Fig. 11). If assertEquals("", 2, 3) fails, the output text for English is "Expected 2, but was 3" and for Spanish is "Se esperaba 2, pero fue 3".

The name of the new class must be JUnIt18nLC where, LC is the language code capitalized, and must belong to the "es.ulpgc.junit4vpl.i18n" package.

```
public class JUnitI18nEN extends JUnitI18n {
    String expectedButWas() {
        return "Expected <expected>, but was <was>";
    }
```

Fig. 10 Junit4VPL internationalization example (1)

```java
public class JUnitI18nES extends JUnitI18n {
    @Override
    String expectedButWas() {
        return "Se esperaba <expected>, pero fue <was>";
    }
```

Fig. 11 Junit4VPL internationalization example (2)

6 Conclusions

This chapter provides insight into the more used existing solutions to the Automatic Programming Assessment applied to the assessment in computer programming subjects. Specifically, those that can be used from a Learning Management System, contributing to extend different approaches to teachers, developers and also students.

The teachers as users or future users and the researchers could also use the features and findings presented to enhance their experience in the assessment of programming subjects from different points of view: they want to know about new APAS tools or start using them or just study these frameworks from a scientific point of view.

The examples exposed offer a much better understanding of the scenarios that the roles defined in an Automated Programming Assessment System may find, facilitating a perspective from which to understand how to make better use of these tools.

Moreover, the use and studies of these systems as well as the contributions made by an international community of teachers and students in their different roles will surely lead to the improvement of these systems.

Acknowledgements This research was funded by European Commission under the ERASMUS+ Programme 2018, KA2, grant number: 2018-1-SK01-KA203-046382 "Work-Based Learning in Future IT Professionals Education".

References

Ala-Mutka, K. M. (2005). A survey of automated assessment approaches for programming assignments. *Computer Science Education, 15*(2), 83–102.

Chen, H. M., Nguyen, B. A., Yan, Y. X., & Dow, C. (2020). Analysis of learning behavior in an automated programming assessment environment: A code quality perspective. *IEEE Access*, 167341–167354.

Christian, M., & Bhushan, T. (2016). A comparison of existing tools for evaluation of programming exercises. In *Proceedings of the second international conference on information and communication Technology for Competitive Strategies* (pp. 1–6).

Hill, P. (2017). *Academic LMS market share: A view across four global regions*. Obtenido de. https://eliterate.us/academic-lms-market-share-view-across-four-global-regions/

Keuning, H., Jeuring, J., & Heeren, B. (2018). A systematic literature review of automated feedback generation for programming exercises. *ACM Transactions on Computing Education (TOCE), 19*(1).

Rahman, K. A., & Nordin, M. J. (2007). A review on the static analysis approach in the automated programming assessment systems. *National Conference on Programming 07*

Rodríguez-del-Pino, J. C., Rubio-Royo, E., & Hernández-Figueroa, Z. (2012). A virtual programming lab for Moodle with automatic assessment and anti-plagiarism features. *WorldComp12.* Las Vegas, USA.

Tharmaseelan, J., Manathunga, K., Reyal, S., Kasthurirathna, D., & Thurairasa, T. (2021). Revisit of automated marking techniques for programming assignments. *IEEE global engineering education conference (EDUCON)* (pp. 650–657).

Database and SQL Microlearning Course

Pavel Turčínek and Radim Farana

1 Introduction

The range and complexity of competencies required for teaching in the twenty-first century are constantly evolving (Nikou, 2019). Requirements for all educators to meet technology standard is visibly increasing (Reinhardt & Elwood, 2019) as well. The digital technology development allowed for the expansion of the possibilities of e-learning. As Javorcik and Polasek (2019) found out: "The current trends and society's demands have changed the form of e-learning." One of the trends is microlearning.

This paper presents the results of the international project Work-based Learning in Future IT Professionals (Grant No. 2018-1-SK01-KA203-046382) aimed at creating comprehensive study support in the field of information systems using microlearning technology, see (web project https://fitped.eu, 2021). The following text focuses on the description of one of the created courses, namely the Database and SQL course. Three universities participated in its creation: Constantine the Philosopher University in Nitra, Slovakia, Mendel University in Brno, Czech Republic, Pedagogical University of Silesia in Katowice, Poland. The course was created in English and subsequently translated into Czech, Polish, Slovak and Spanish.

P. Turčínek (✉) · R. Farana
Mendel University in Brno, Faculty of Business and Economics, Department of Informatics, Brno, Czech Republic
e-mail: pavel.turcinek@pef.mendelu.cz; radim.farana@mendelu.cz

E. Smyrnova-Trybulska et al. (eds.), *Microlearning*,
https://doi.org/10.1007/978-3-031-13359-6_10

2 Methods

Microlearning technology was used to create the course. According to Giurgiu (2017) studies indicated that a short content may increase information retention by 20%. As Gabrielli et al. (2006) state: "Microlearning activities, by definition, rely on access to learning resources which may happen at the time of breaks or gaps in learners daily work/life activities." Shatte and Teague (2020) found out in their scoping review that: "Overall, the application of microlearning to higher education has demonstrated a range of benefits for both objective and subjective student outcomes." Leong et al. (2021) concluded: "microlearning enables work-based learners to gain new knowledge or skills just in time to meet their immediate needs in this fast-changing world; in addition, microlearning can also help work-based learners to achieve a specific, actionable task." Buchem and Hamelmann (2010) state that "microlearning combines different approaches to learning. Microlearning facilitates self-directed lifelong learning, as short activities can be easily integrated into everyday activities. Small learning steps with small chunks of information can be used for learning in-between and on-demand. In this way microlearning enables individuals to stay up-to-date in today's knowledge society and offers a viable supplement to more time-consuming and formalized modes of learning, such as classroom courses or web-based trainings."

The basic principle is to use the possibilities of current personal devices, especially mobile phones or tablets for the presentation of individual parts of the curriculum. The whole teaching text corresponding to the scope of one semester of teaching is thus divided into hundreds of short parts containing both an explanation of the subject, preferably in the scope of one screen, and a verification task to verify its correct understanding. The processing time for one part should not exceed 5 minutes. The student thus has the opportunity to make optimal use of his time to study, especially if his time pool is very limited. This course was developed using the framework PRISCILLA described by Skalka and Drlík (2018) and Skalka et al. (2021).

3 Course Content

The structure of the created microlearning course corresponds to the requirements of microlearning technology and at the same time also to the requirements of subjects dealing with the field of database systems. The micro-tasks used in the course can be divided into three types:

- Contents (explanation)
- Question
  - Short answer
  - One correct

  - More correct
  - Drag&drop
  - Linear reorder

- Program (code in the given language)

The teaching of database systems and SQL is different from the teaching of procedural programming languages. The first task is to understand how the data to be worked on is related. But even earlier, it's important to understand what data is. Before the course gets to the SQL language itself, it is necessary to clarify the basic terminology and explain the principles of how to store data correctly. The first and second chapters are used for this. The whole structure of the course, as seen by the students, is shown in Fig. 1. The overview also shows the progress of the student.

The first chapter introduces the student to basic concepts such as data, attribute, domain, etc. Experiencing these concepts is important for a good understanding of the following parts of the course. Texts that explain the issue predominate here. There are 11 of them in this chapter. Whether the student has understood the content can be verified with six questions. An example of one of the questions is in the following Fig. 2.

The student has the task to assign the correct terms to the individual definitions.

The second chapter deals with data modeling. It is divided into four sections, in which the student has to understand how the data are related and ideally acquire the skill to design a data model appropriately. The issue of data modeling is very complex. There may be more suitable solutions. The course, therefore, focuses mainly on the explanation of the basic elements of data modeling such as entities, the

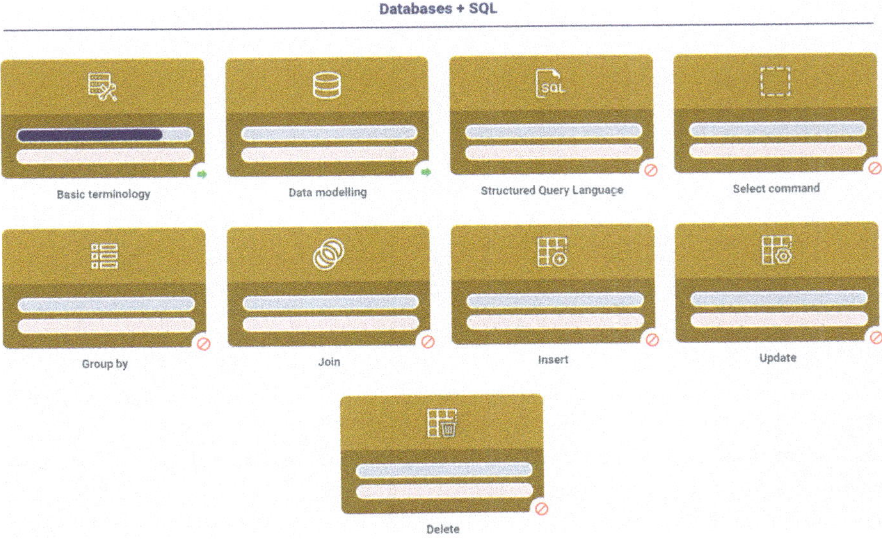

Fig. 1 Structure of the course

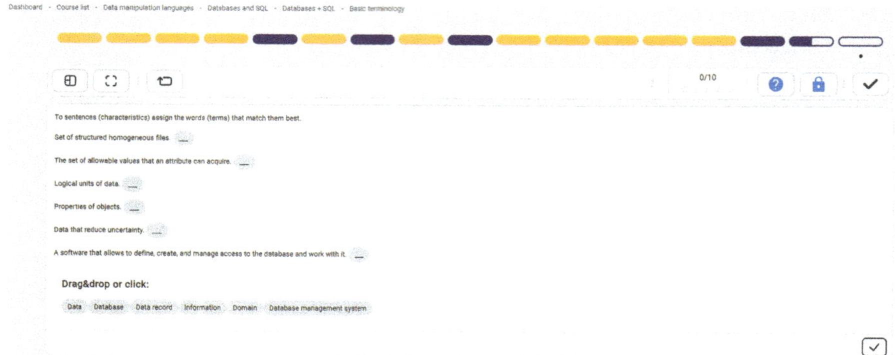

Fig. 2 Example of drag&drop question

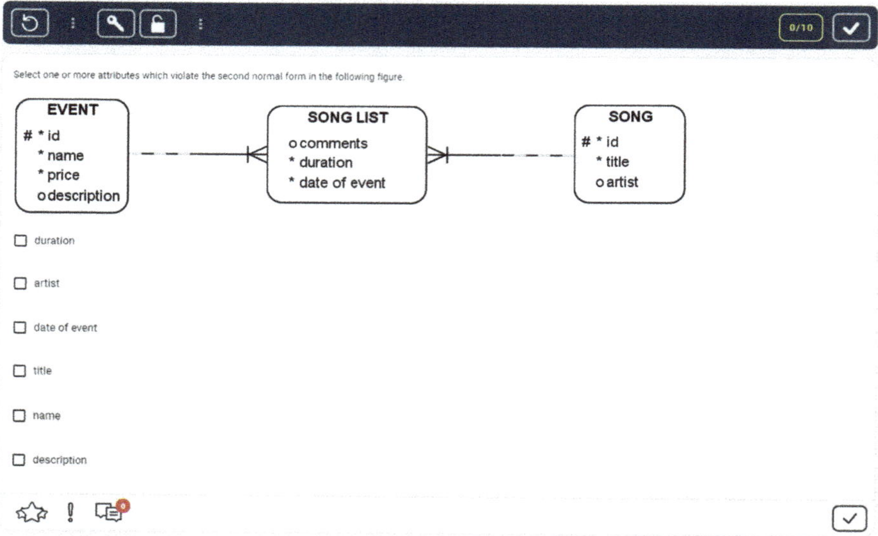

Fig. 3 Example of multiple-choice question

relationships between them, the principle of normalization, and the conversion to a physical model. From 35 short texts, the student can learn what to look out for. The texts are supplemented by 35 questions, which often point out the traditional errors that can occur during the design (example in Fig. 3).

Baker's notation was chosen to display the model. Unfortunately, it is not possible to verify more complex tasks, where the student would create something himself/herself, using microlearning. Such examples are also important for the student's explanation of what he meant and the subsequent feedback from the teacher, who can explain what is right, what is not right, or show alternatives and, above all, explain why this is the case.

In the next chapter of the course, students will be introduced to the SQL language. The first part explains the difference compared to procedural languages and also presents the division into subsections of the language (DDL, DML, DQL, DCL). The second part of the chapter deals with the DDL language, which builds on the previous chapter of the course devoted to the design of a data model. This chapter contains a total of 19 teaching texts and 13 verification questions. You can see one of them in the following Fig. 4. The following chapters deal with DML and DQL separately.

In chapter "Learning by Designing, Imagination and Programming", students will learn how to query the relational database. It gradually reveals the secrets of the SELECT statement. Only the basics are described here, which are followed by other chapters. The fourth chapter is divided into six parts, four of which have a similar character as in the previous chapters (changing of explanations and questions), and two are set aside for writing SQL queries. Here, in contrast to the design of the data model, the correctness of the answer can be verified. As you can see in Fig. 5, it is possible to verify students' knowledge in various forms. Here, their task is to properly sort the order of the individual parts of the SELECT statement.

Figure 5 also shows the evaluation when the student correctly aligned the parts of the SELECT statement and received the full number of points for it. The following Fig. 6 shows how students will be shown a task to practice a SELECT statement.

The entire fourth chapter contains 21 explanatory texts, 14 questions, and 22 tasks for practicing the SELECT statement. The student will get acquainted with the projection, selection, sorting, and use of single-line functions.

The fourth chapter is followed by the fifth chapter. It deals with grouping in four parts. The nine texts explain the basics of grouping principles, aggregation functions, and the use of the HAVING clause. The acquired knowledge can be verified on nine questions. The last part is devoted to SELECT statements to verify skills. There are also 9. You can see an example and evaluation in Fig. 7.

The last chapter on the SELECT statement deals with joining tables. Everything important is explained in 11 texts supplemented by 8 questions and 9 examples for practice. The chapter describes the principle of an inner and outer join. It shows how to join using both the JOIN clause and the constraints in the WHERE section. Figure 8 then demonstrates one of the questions where the student's task is to correctly arrange the individual lines to achieve the desired result.

The remaining three chapters are devoted to the field of DML. Each of them deals with one of the INSERT, UPDATE, and DELETE statements. This issue is explained in 9 texts and verified on 11 questions and 50 examples. You can see one of the questions in Fig. 9.

The following Table 1 demonstrates the structure of individual chapters and the numbers of individual microtasks.

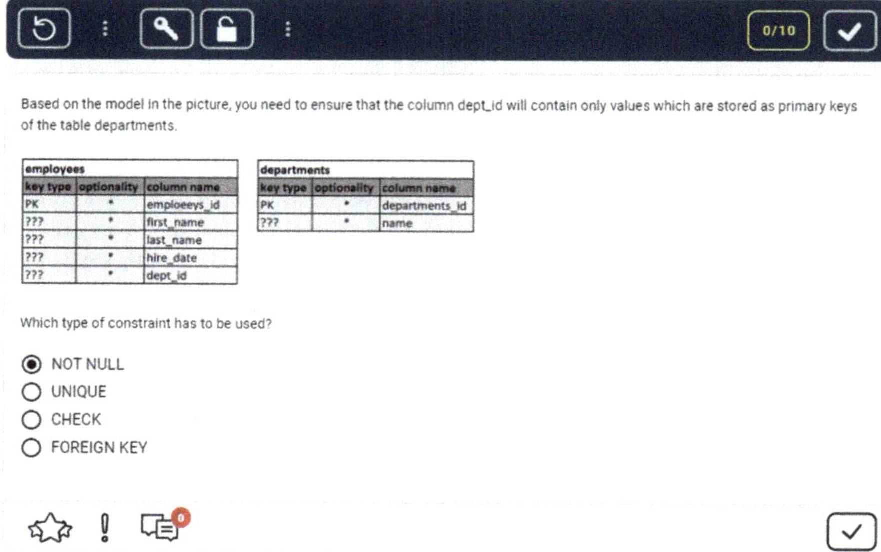

Fig. 4 Example of one-choice question

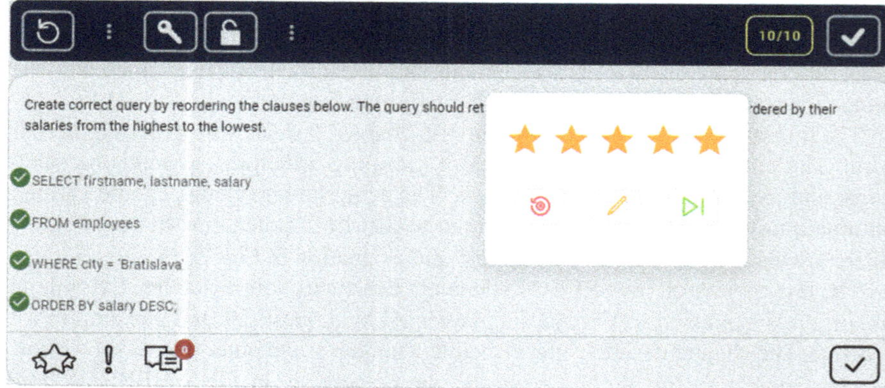

Fig. 5 Example of evaluated linear reorder question

4 Results

The created microlearning course was made available to students of Mendel University in Brno in the summer semester of the academic year 2020/2021 as one of the study materials for the study of Database Systems and Database Design. At the same time, students had at their disposal a previously created teaching text in the

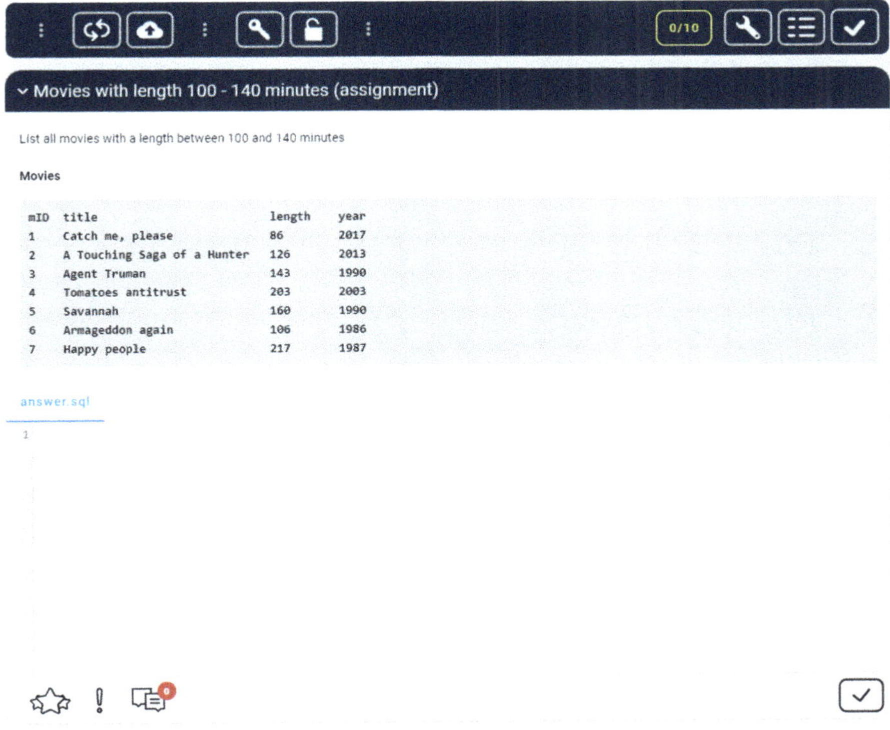

Fig. 6 Example of SQL query task

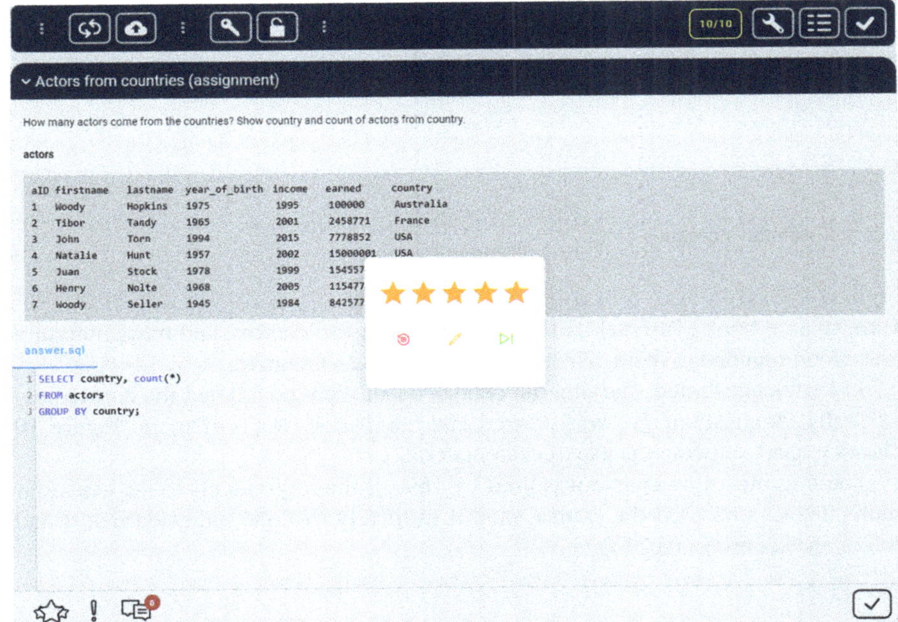

Fig. 7 Example of evaluated SQL query task

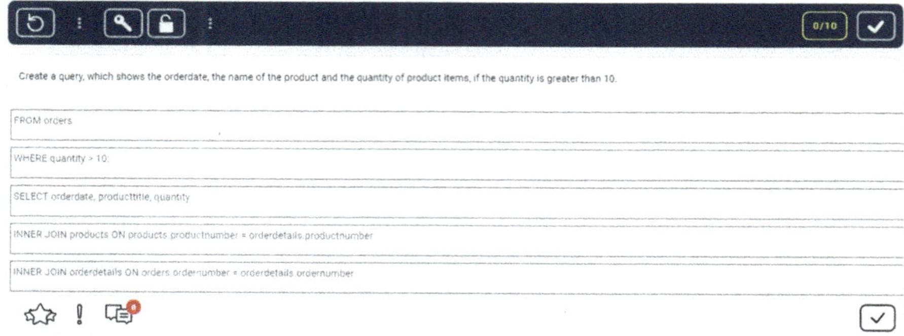

Fig. 8 Example of linear reorder question

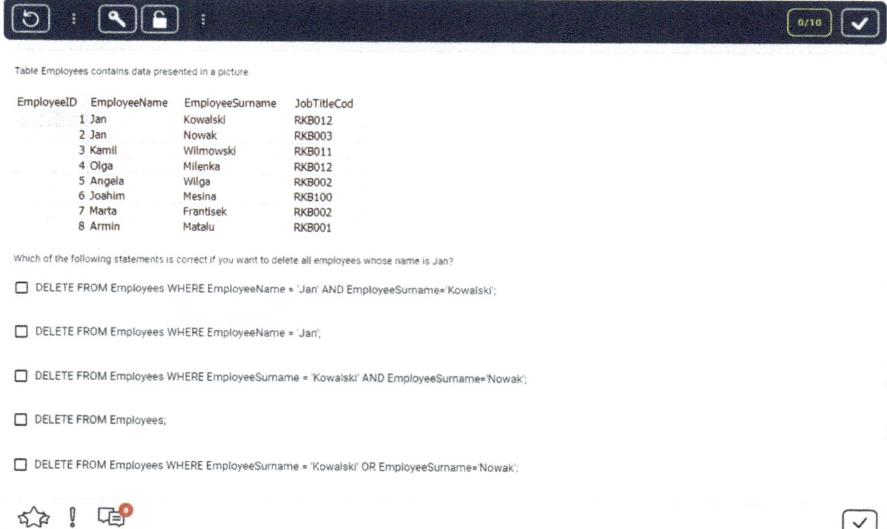

Fig. 9 Example of question

form of an e-book (Turčínek, 2018), presentations for lectures, and other literature was recommended to them. The use of materials was voluntary.

114 students started studying the course. 71 of them completed the course successfully. A questionnaire was created and completed by 50 of them. Figure 10 shows a chart showing the use of each material.

The microlearning course was used by 16% of the respondents to the questionnaire. Those who used the course rated it positively. No one indicated that it had major shortcomings (see Fig. 11).

Table 1 Structure of individual chapters

	Contents	Questions					Program	Total
		Short answer	One correct	More correct	Drag & drop	Linear reorder		
Basic terminology	**11**	**0**	**1**	**3**	**2**	**0**	**0**	**17**
Data modelling	**35**	**3**	**20**	**9**	**3**	**0**	**0**	**70**
Entities	11	0	2	4	2	0	0	19
Relationships	11	0	11	0	0	0	0	22
Normal forms	9	0	3	5	0	0	0	17
Physical model	4	3	4	0	1	0	0	12
Structured Query Language	**19**	**0**	**11**	**1**	**1**	**0**	**0**	**32**
SQL	6	0	3	1	1	0	0	11
DDL	13	0	8	0	0	0	0	21
SELECT command	**21**	**0**	**9**	**3**	**1**	**1**	**22**	**57**
Basics	4	0	2	1	0	0	0	7
ORDER BY Clause	3	0	1	0	0	1	0	5
Basics (exercises)	0	0	0	0	0	0	12	12
Functions	8	0	3	1	1	0	0	13
WHERE Clause	6	0	3	1	0	0	0	10
WHERE clause (exercises)	0	0	0	0	0	0	10	10
GROUP BY	**9**	**1**	**4**	**3**	**1**	**0**	**9**	**27**
Aggregation functions	6	0	2	3	0	0	0	11
Grouping	2	0	1	0	1	0	0	4
HAVING Clause	1	1	1	0	0	0	0	3
Procvičování	0	0	0	0	0	0	9	9
JOIN	**11**	**0**	**3**	**1**	**2**	**2**	**9**	**28**
Multi-table Queries	4	0	2	1	0	0	0	7
Simple Join Using WHERE Clause	2	0	1	0	0	1	0	4
Preferred Approaches to Join Tables based on JOIN Clause	5	0	0	0	2	1	0	8
JOIN (exercises)	0	0	0	0	0	0	9	9
INSERT	**5**	**0**	**1**	**1**	**1**	**0**	**20**	**28**
INSERT INTO statement	5	0	1	1	1	0	0	8
INSERT exercise I.	0	0	0	0	0	0	10	10
INSERT exercise II.	0	0	0	0	0	0	10	10
UPDATE	**2**	**0**	**2**	**1**	**2**	**0**	**20**	**27**
UPDATE statement	2	0	2	1	2	0	0	7
UPDATE exercise I.	0	0	0	0	0	0	10	10
UPDATE exercise II.	0	0	0	0	0	0	10	10

(continued)

Table 1 (continued)

	Contents	Questions					Program	Total
		Short answer	One correct	More correct	Drag & drop	Linear reorder		
DELETE	**2**	**0**	**1**	**2**	**0**	**0**	**10**	**15**
DELETE statement	2	0	1	2	0	0	0	5
DELETE exercises	0	0	0	0	0	0	10	10
TOTAL	**115**	**4**	**52**	**24**	**13**	**3**	**90**	**301**
		96						

When we compare the achieved results of those who used the microlearning course with those who did not use it, it turns out slightly better, as the following Table 2 demonstrates.

However, the number of students is still too small to generalize the results achieved. In order to obtain feedback from students, both a quantitative survey in the form of a questionnaire and qualitative research in the form of a guided interview were carried out. Students who used the textbook especially appreciated its concept, which they used for the appropriate timing of their preparation. One of the students, for example, stated in an interview, quoting: "I appreciated the opportunity to study individual parts of the text while traveling by bus from school to home."

5 Discussion and Conclusions

We are not aware of any other micro-learning course dealing with the area of database systems. There are some short video tutorials that can be meant as microlearning content dealing with SQL such as videos at teradata.com[1] and others. However, we didn't find any micro-learning course about database systems like ours which would have also a possibility to verify the acquired knowledge.

The fact that such courses are a novelty at Mendel University in Brno could also play a role in the small interest of students in using the microlearning course, similarly to the whole in the Czech Republic. Students are not used to them and prefer more traditional materials. It is very likely that with the occurrence of more courses, the experience with them will increase and thus their more frequent use. Those who used the course evaluated it positively.

It is not yet possible to draw conclusions regarding the acquired knowledge and skills, resp. their improvement. From the first phase of verification, we can only state that the students who chose this textbook achieved similar results as users of

[1] https://www.teradata.com/Resources?assetTypeFilter=video

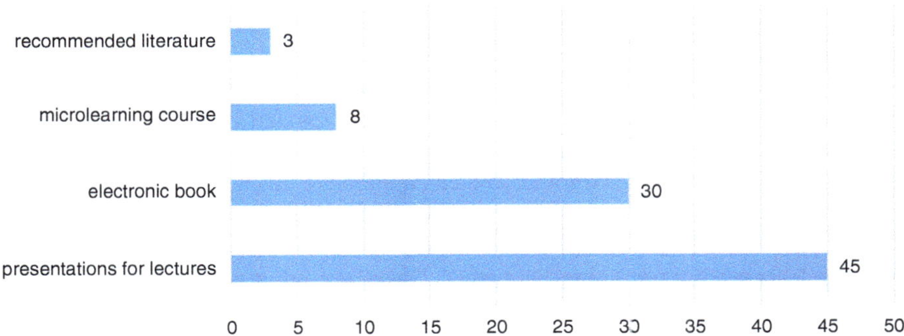

Fig. 10 Use of given materials

How do you evaluate the microlearning course?

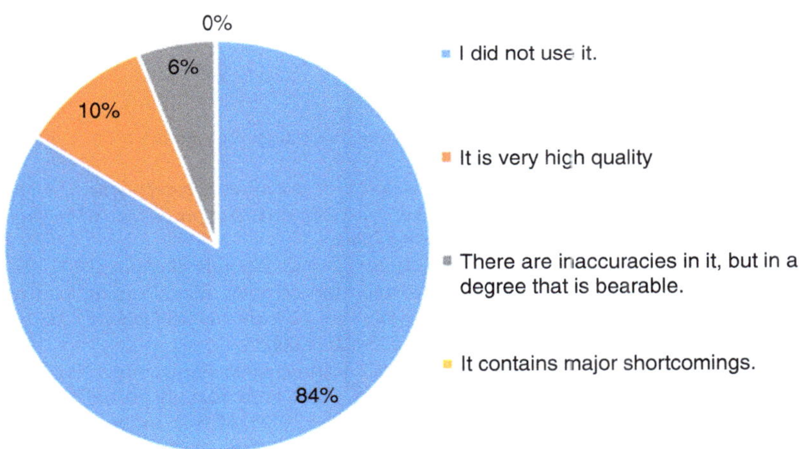

Fig. 11 Evaluation of microlearning course

Table 2 Structure of individual chapters

	A	B	C	D	E	F	Not specified	Total	Grade average
Did not use	7	4	9	13	7	2	0	42	2,2
Used	2	1	1	1	2	0	1	8	2

classical textbooks. From the teachers' point of view, we agree with Jomah et al. (2017) that micro-learning should not be used as the only tool where students need to acquire complex skills. We think that micro-learning is a suitable complement to other study materials, seminars, and lectures.

Due to the focus of the course on the basics of creating database information systems, it proves to be an interesting possibility to expand its usability for vocational education at secondary schools. Current high school students are very adept at using mobile devices in particular and can appreciate this approach.

As authors of microlearning courses in the system PRISCILLA we can state, that this system is easy to use and it is very helpful with creating microlearning courses even for learning programming languages. There are other tools such as Content Management System for Creating Microlearning Courses described by Javorcik (2021). However, we do not have any experience with other systems.

Acknowledgements This research was funded by European Commission under the ERASMUS+ Programme 2018, KA2, grant number: 2018-1-SK01-KA203-046382 "Work-Based Learning in Future IT Professionals Education".

References

Buchem, I., & Hamelmann, H. (2010). Microlearning: A strategy for ongoing professional development. *eLearning Papers, 21*(7), 1–15.

Gabrielli S., Kimani S., & Catarci T. (2006). The design of microlearning experiences: A research agenda (on microlearning). In: *Microlearning: Emerging concepts, practices and technologies after e-learning, Proceedings of microlearning 2006.*

Giurgiu, L. (2017). Microlearning an evolving elearning trend. *Scientific Bulletin, 22*(1), 18–23.

Javorcik, T. (2021). Content management system for creating microlearning courses. In *Proceedings – 2021 international symposium on educational technology, ISET 2021* (pp. 223–227). https://doi.org/10.1109/ISET52350.2021.00053.

Javorcik, T., & Polasek, R. (2019). Transformation of e-learning into microlearning: New approach to course design. *AIP conference proceedings 2116*, 2019. https://doi.org/10.1063/1.5114051.

Jomah, O., Masoud, A. K., Kishore, X. P., & Aurelia, S. (2017). Microlearning: A modernized education system. *BRAIN. Broad Research in Artificial Intelligence and Neuroscience, 7*(1), 103–110.

Leong, K., Sung, A., Au, D., & Blanchard, C. (2021). A review of the trend of microlearning. *Journal of Work-Applied Management, 13*(1), 88–102. https://doi.org/10.1108/JWAM-10-2020-0044

Nikou, S. (2019). A micro-learning based model to enhance student teachers' motivation and engagement in blended learning. In K. Graziano (Ed.), *Proceedings of Society for Information Technology & Teacher Education International Conference* (pp. 509–514). Association for the Advancement of computing in education (AACE). Retrieved January 4, 2022 from https://www.learntechlib.org/primary/p/207690/

Reinhardt, K. S., & Elwood, S. (2019). *Promising practices in online training and support: Microlearning and personal learning environments to promote a growth mindset in learners* (Handbook of Research on Virtual Training and Mentoring of Online Instructors) (pp. 298–310). IGI Global.

Shatte, A. B. R., & Teague, S. J. (2020). *Microlearning for improved student outcomes in higher education: A scoping review*. OSF Preprints. https://doi.org/10.31219/osf.io/fhu8n

Skalka, J., & Drlík, M. (2018). Conceptual framework of microlearning-based training mobile application for improving programming skills. *Adv. Intell. Syst. Comput., 725*, 213–224. https://doi.org/10.1007/978-3-319-75175-7_22

Skalka, J., et al. (2021). Conceptual framework for programming skills development based on microlearning and automated source code evaluation in virtual learning environment. *Sustainability, 13*(3), 3293. https://doi.org/10.3390/su13063293

Turčínek, P. (2018). *Databázové systémy a návrh databází*. Mendelova Univerzita v Brně. ISBN 978-80-7509-576-3, online: https://emendelu.publi.cz/book/526-databazove-systemy-a-navrh-databazi

The Architecture of Visual Design in Modern Web Applications

David Sabol and Ján Skalka

1 Introduction

Agile methodologies are currently one of the most common approaches in software development. According to Maleki and Ramsin (2018), agile methodologies are suitable candidates for developing web systems but choosing the right one can be a severe challenge for web development teams. An essential requirement for developing a system that is expected to be constantly and long-term evolved is the ability to implement changes quickly and, in visual design, support rapid updates based on styles, inheritance, and interconnectedness.

Currently, many methodologies and frameworks describe the steps of software development. Still, they are often oriented to the system as a whole and design, as the entire presentation of the elements of the system, is not described separately (Torrecilla-Salinas et al., 2015; Al-Zewairi et al., 2017). In commercial applications, the visual elements and the positive user experience are critical elements in attracting and retaining users (Wang & Emurian, 2005; Yazid & Jantan, 2017). Designing an architecture that can cover features for quickly switching users' looks while implementing developer requirements with minimal code changes is a challenging task (Taivalsaari et al., 2017).

The paper focuses on the description of advanced approaches in designing web applications, their strengths and weaknesses and their implementation in the web application *Priscilla* (Skalka & Drlík, 2018) based on a conceptual framework (Skalka et al., 2021) covering educational activities in the teaching of programming languages. From the front-end point of view, the web application *Priscilla* is developed using *Vue.js*, a technology that defined the selection of used tools and techniques and design definition options. Although the application also includes

D. Sabol · J. Skalka (✉)
Constantine the Philosopher University in Nitra, Nitra, Slovakia
e-mail: david.sabol@student.ukf.sk; jskalka@ukf.sk

E. Smyrnova-Trybulska et al. (eds.), *Microlearning*,
https://doi.org/10.1007/978-3-031-13359-6_11

gamification elements, the primary emphasis is on the simplicity of the user interface and the ability to switch the visual appearance quickly.

The article consists of three chapters. The first chapter describes essential skinning technologies used in web application design development. They use *CSS* (Cascading Style Sheets) as the basic styling element, preprocessors, and custom properties to generate the final code. The second chapter focuses on different methodologies of the *CSS* content generation and the division of the generation process into layers to provide the most efficient method for constantly updating the design of the web application. The last chapter presents the application of the selected methodology to define the visual design of the web portal *Priscilla*. This section describes the procedures and best practices for skinning web applications and the approach used to describe and set up the day, night, and colour-blind appearance.

2 Basic Design Definition Techniques

Skinning provides the ability to control and change the look of application parts by selecting pre-created designs or skins (Eastabrook, 2020). In this context, the skin or theme is understood as the visual side of the elements organized into the user interface (UI) (Dowden & Dowden, 2020). The settings are usually contained in a file or files from which the design module loads them. The combination of files describes the visual properties of individual elements, such as colour, border, font, shadows, and the like. These features can be reused in different contexts and for different elements of a web application. By using skins, it is possible to influence the appearance and, to a large extent, also the usability of the application. Still, it is not possible to affect the functionality itself by the application of skins.

The goal of skinning code creation is primarily to separate the graphical user interface (*GUI*) and the functionality and business logic of the application. This approach allows the definition of the *GUI* using external files that can be linked to the application code later. The collaboration and mutual understanding between the business logic and the application skin must be implemented to ensure the link between user and application (Fomitchev et al., 2007).

Many techniques and options currently allow defining, changing, applying, and saving a change of visual themes, respectively, skins within a web application. Despite the number of approaches, however, it is possible to observe that quite often, these are only modified versions of the solutions presented in the following subchapters.

2.1 *CSS Custom Properties Approach*

CSS custom properties are native variables in *CSS*. They are often mentioned as one of the most common current approaches to implement changeable visual UI themes in the web application skinning process (Tzucker, 2019). They are usually defined as a key: value pair, where the key must be prefixed with two hyphens (--). These native *CSS* variables must be defined within a declaration block, which can be any selector. If it needs to declare globally available properties, it is necessary to use the pseudo-selector: root. Defined values can be accessed and applied by calling the native *CSS* function var() (Kudrna, 2019).

CSS variables thus allow defining a variable that can be referenced from multiple places throughout *CSS*. This feature is crucial for skinning because it is possible to share a property between thousands of elements. Change request processing thus only means a change of one value of the variable. It is not necessary to update the *CSS* of each element individually (Tzucker, 2019). The dynamic nature of *CSS* variables offers flexibility for all forms of theming and skinning – for pre-prepared and user-customized themes (Williams, 2017).

The theme of the graphical appearance can be generally defined in the form of a set of native *CSS* variables using this technique. These are unified within a specific declaration block of *CSS* rules with a selector specifying a specific skin. Other UI themes can be created similarly by redefinition or rewriting of values of existing *CSS* variables through a new *CSS* rule (Fig. 1) (Tzucker, 2019). Skins defined by the default theme in this way can be overridden after the user-initiated change. Rewriting functionality is provided by adding specificity in a class or attribute to the top-level element of an *HTML* document, such as an <body> element. Switching classes or values of element attributes can be done using *JavaScript*.

CSS custom properties can be accessed directly and manipulated in a browser using *JavaScript*. This approach makes it possible to specify new values for custom properties on a web page or application. Using this technique, *JavaScript* allows changing the appearance of the current theme dynamically in the browser. In this way, it is possible to modify selected parts of the design immediately, even when the web application is running. Using a few lines of *JavaScript*, it is possible to apply changes that, due to the inheritance of *CSS* styles, affect many elements of the web application (Grant, 2018).

Harrell (2017) introduces the advantages of this technique thanks to *CSS* custom properties, individual variables, and properties in the browser. These properties can

Fig. 1 Example of *CSS* custom properties using specificity and inheritance (Tzucker, 2019)

```
body, body[data-theme="light"] {
    --primaryColor: white;
    --secondaryColor: black;
}
body[data-theme="dark"] {
    --primaryColor: black;
    --secondaryColor: white;
}
body, button {
    background-color: var(--primaryColor);
}
p, button {
    color: var(--secondaryColor);
}
```

be easily redefined in media queries or *JavaScript*. The significant advantage of *CSS* custom properties is the nativity, which allows using custom properties without the need for a *CSS* preprocessor.

The disadvantage of the technique is its excessive detail, as it requires the element to be styled with an excessive number of properties. If individual elements contain not only style definitions but also many rows with variables, this approach often doubles the size of the element declaration block. Rewriting the properties, taking into account the appearance of several themes or skins of the web application, is again too detailed and enlarges *CSS* files.

2.2 CSS Preprocessor Approach

CSS preprocessors such as *SASS* (Syntactically Awesome Style Sheets), LESS (Leaner Style Sheets) and Stylus are tools that provide *CSS* with added capabilities and functionality that are not available in native *CSS* (Attardi, 2020). The use of preprocessors changes the way of code writing. The content is organized in a specific way and designed differs from the native *CSS* code. They offer the possibility of calculating values, but these values are not available outside of preprocessors. On the one hand, it is possible to use *DRY* (Don't repeat yourself) semantic code, but on the other hand, it is necessary to add another step in which the code must be compiled into native *CSS* (Dowden & Dowden, 2020).

Figure 2, based on Watson-Nolan (2019), shows a survey of developers who use *CSS* preprocessors. At first glance, dominance is evident of the *SASS* preprocessor. It can be proof that that choosing this preprocessor is a good choice when preparing web application themes.

Mixins are a language concept that allows a programmer to inject some code into a class. Mixins let developers create properties and values that can be easily reused across the entire application. Using the *@include* directive, assigning a previously defined mixin to a new context includes it in the class definition (Dowden & Dowden, 2020). It is also possible to define mixins that accept parameters similar to conventional programming functions (Grant, 2018).

Visual themes support the *SASS* map declaration, which can stylize *CSS* properties with their values for a specific theme. It is usually a separate file in a project imported into files with real element styles (Borody, 2017).

Borody (2017) mentioned that the main idea of the illustrative approach presented in Fig. 3 is to wrap the properties of the themes in a *themify* mix. It accesses these properties (which are defined in themes) by calling the *themed()* function with the name of the desired property. Any call to the *themed()* function outside the @ *themify* block will not work.

Figure 4 concisely illustrates the use of *@mixin*, *@function*, *@include*, and other valuable options that the *SASS* preprocessor offers for web applications skinning.

With the capabilities of preprocessors, it is also possible to improve the technique using *CSS* custom properties. Feigenbaum (2020) states that fallback values

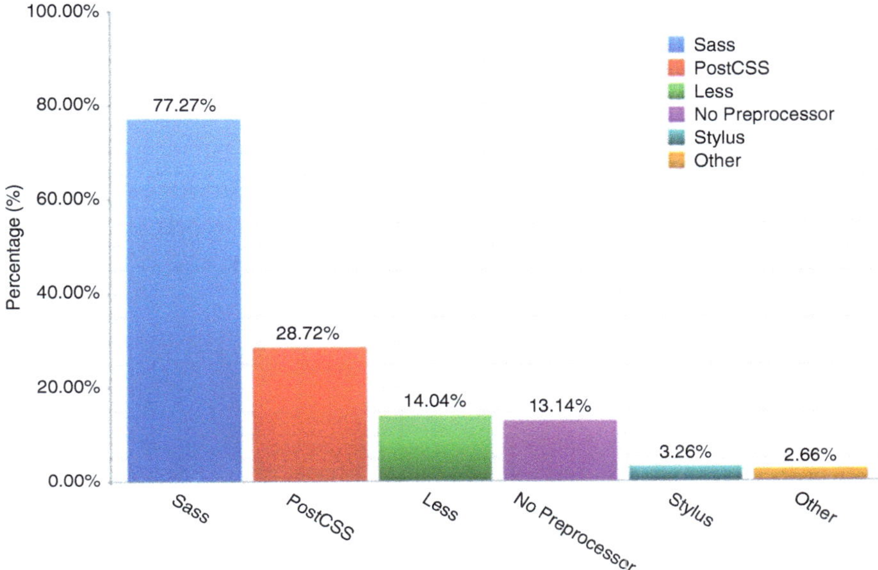

Fig. 2 The popularity of *CSS* Preprocessors – Front-End Tooling Survey 2019 (Watson-Nolan, 2019)

Fig. 3 Example of defining themes using the *SASS* map (Borody, 2017)

```
$themes: (
  light: (
    backgroundColor: #fff,
    textColor: #408bbd,
    buttonTextColor: #408bbd,
    buttonTextTransform: none,
    buttonTextHoverColor: #61b0e7,
    buttonColor: #fff,
    buttonBorder: 2px solid #fff,
  ),
  dark: (
    backgroundColor: #222,
    textColor: #ddd,
    buttonTextColor: #aaa,
    buttonTextTransform: uppercase,
    buttonTextHoverColor: #ddd,
    buttonColor: #333,
    buttonBorder: 1px solid #aaa,
  ),
);
```

or properties can partially solve the lack of support for Internet Explorer and older browsers. Users of these unsupported or outdated versions of browsers will not change colour modes, but they will see the default theme. Writing these backup

```
// Implementation of themes

@mixin themify($themes) {
  @each $theme, $map in $themes {
    .theme-#{$theme} & {
      $theme-map: () !global;
      @each $key, $submap in $map {
        $value: map-get(map-get($themes, $theme), '#{$key}');
        $theme-map: map-merge($theme-map, ($key: $value)) !global;
      }
      @content;
      $theme-map: null !global;
    }
  }
}

@function themed($key) {
  @return map-get($theme-map, $key);
}

// Actual styles for the app

.app-container {
  display: flex;
  flex-direction: column;
  flex: 1;
  align-items: center;
  justify-content: center;

  @include themify($themes) {
    color: themed('textColor');
    background-color: themed('backgroundColor');
  }
}
```

Fig. 4 Example of *SASS* mixin implementation and function (Borody, 2017)

solutions is often time-consuming, so this process can be automated using the *SASS* preprocessor mixin. Böck (2020) argues that combining static variables of *CSS* preprocessors with *CSS* custom properties is the correct approach because they both do different things.

2.3 Independent Templates and Themes of CSS

Independent templates and themes can be defined in external *CSS* files. Each of these files usually contains specific styles for a certain theme (Morgan, 2021).

Themes can be applied to web applications in several ways. A common approach to applying a theme is to change the href attribute of the *HTML* link element, which is used to import external *CSS* styles of the application skin or the mentioned themes or templates. This change can be achieved using *JavaScript* or a server-side programming language such as PHP, Java, or others.

Pickering (2019) mentions a performance issue using this approach that can occur in some cases. The rewriting theme requires a large amount of additional *CSS* code to load when changing. In most cases, this approach also causes a problem with code maintenance, as it is necessary to maintain several distinct styles of individual user interface themes during further development.

2.4 Alternative Skinning Approaches

Analyzing approaches to processing the request for skinning a web application can be distinguished individual techniques according to where the logic of skinning or theming occurs, either on the server-side or the client-side.

2.4.1 Server-side Skinning

Assuming the use of a server-side language such as PHP, it is possible to modify and apply the UI theme in a way that does not require *JavaScript*. Users send GET or POST requests with an URL address with the parameter of the required theme. The server responds with pre-prepared PHP code. It can assign a corresponding *CSS* class to the element body according to the user's preference after reloading the page (Adhuham, 2020).

The essential disadvantage is the need to refresh the page or application to apply changes. Despite this disadvantage, this approach is still considered helpful in preserving the user's theme selection even after reloading the page or web application.

2.4.2 Client-side Skinning

Creating modular styles of multi-developer web applications requires adhering to agreed conventions and avoiding conflicting object names. Some communities of web developers began experimenting with alternative approaches and turned to *JavaScript*. The proposed technique uses inline styles in a form known as *CSS* in *JavaScript*. This approach requires *JavaScript* to create class names guaranteed to be unique or that individual *CSS* styles can be applied to a page using the *HTML* attribute style.

Grant recommends keeping in mind this principle even though it is still experimental (Grant, 2018). It should be noted that this principle only works for applications that are fully rendered using a library or *JavaScript* framework, such as *Vue.js*, *React*, *Angular*, or others.

3 *CSS* Code Design and Maintenance Methodologies

CSS is considered a simple and easy-to-learn language for web application development. However, if we focus on the language features, it doesn't seem easy to write *CSS* code in a sustainable and scalable form intended for manual maintenance by developers. With an inappropriate approach to defining the structure of *CSS* code, its management can be difficult or impossible as web projects grow. The main consequences are then redundancy or poor performance.

Web application skinning is a typical example of the need to have *CSS* code unambiguously structured and adequately targeted individual web application elements through proven naming conventions. In this context, Dowden & Dowden mentioned that experts often prefer a combination of several proven maintenance methodologies and *CSS* code writing (Dowden & Dowden, 2020).

3.1 Object-Oriented CSS

Object-Oriented *CSS* (*OOCSS*) was initially presented by Nicole Sullivan at the Web Directions North conference (Dowden & Dowden, 2020). This methodology borrows concepts from object-oriented design to provide a *CSS* structure and defines an object as a repetitive visual pattern that can then be generalized to independent snippets of *HTML*, *CSS*, and possibly *JavaScript*. This object can be once created and many times reused on the entire web page or in the application.

OOCSS is based on two principles:

- separation of the structure layout and the visual skin, or the theme,
- separation of the container and the content.

The first rule demands the separation of the structure and the application skin. The structure layout refers to features that are not directly visible to the user. In principle, these are instructions that affect the size or location of the elements. These *CSS* properties include, for example, width, height, margin, padding, overflow, etc. Through the web application skin, it refers to the visual properties of elements, which are, for example, colour, font-family, box-shadow, etc.

With *OOCSS*, these properties are defined separately. Subsequently, visual patterns common to several elements are identified and used as parents to inherit individual characteristics (Arsenault, 2019).

The second principle separates the container and the content and helps to create a more consistent and predictable user environment. In this case, the content covers elements such as images, paragraphs, and div elements embedded into other elements used as containers. As a general rule, *CSS* styles should never be targeted to specific containers for possible reuse of styles without the need for subsequent rewriting. To avoid child selectors is a suitable strategy to maintain the separation of the contents and the container components.

3.2 Block Element Modifier

Block Element Modifier (*BEM*) is the name for the *CSS* methodology and naming convention created by the Yandex team. Michálek considers the most significant benefit of *BEM* to be the naming convention, which represents only a specific part of the original *CSS* methodology (Michálek, 2017).

Within the naming convention, the naming of individual classes is directed by the following pattern:

- **Block** – a separate element (.block) that is reusable,
- **Element** – an element within a block (.block__element); it cannot be used alone and is linked to the block in which it is contained,
- **Modifier** – designation of blocks (.block – modifier) or elements (.block__element – modifier), the use of which will achieve a change in appearance, behaviour, or state.

Dowden & Dowden (2020) introduced that the use of modifiers in *BEM* contradicts the recommendations of the *OOCSS* methodology, which aims to create versatile and reusable styles that represent skin or theme.

Michálek (2017) stated that when using the *Bootstrap* template (or other similar libraries) to supplement the primary *CSS* code, it is advisable to consider the prefix of selections of these libraries or the primary code.

3.3 Scalable and Modular Architecture for CSS

Scalable and Modular Architecture for *CSS* (*SMACSS*) is a *CSS* methodology described by Snook (2012) as follows: "The core of *SMACSS* is categorization. By categorizing *CSS* rules, we begin to see patterns, and we can define better practices for each of these patterns.". Snook divides cascading styles into five types of categories:

- **Base** – basic *CSS* rules that define the default values of *HTML* elements in agreement with Dowden & Dowden (2020). In this category, it is also possible to define default styles of attribute selectors, pseudo-classes, etc. However, it is essential to note that nesting elements should be avoided in this category of rules.
- **Layout** – rules for the layout of the elements divide a page into sections. These elements include e.g. header, sidebar, article, and footer.
- **Module** – the category covers the reusable modular parts of the design are defined. It can include various sidebar sections, navigation bar, etc. – various elements with repeated use in the application.
- **State** – rules that describe the appearance of individual modules or layouts when they are in the appropriate state. Such states include, e.g. hover, focus, visible/ hidden, active/inactive, etc.
- **Theme** – declarations that affect appearance but do not affect layout and functionality. These declarations are similar to the *OOCSS* skin concept of Dowden & Dowden (2020).

3.4 Inverted Triangle CSS

Inverted Triangle *CSS* (*ITCSS*) is a methodology focused on a sustainable way of organizing scalable *CSS*. The motivation for creating the methodology was to find an effective way to manage and develop large-scale web projects (Roberts, 2014). However, the solution is not a library but a definition of the way of thinking. The main principle of *ITCSS* is to divide the *CSS* code into layers arranged according to how the *CSS* works. The essence of the methodology lies in the exact ordering of styles according to specificity. The specificity means how the web browsers decide to apply the most relevant values of defined *CSS* properties to individual elements of a website or application.

The organization of specificity is defined in *ITCSS* by a series of seven layers (Roberts, 2014):

- **Settings** – the layer that contains variable definitions and various settings and is intended for *CSS* preprocessors.
- **Tools** – layer reserved for mixins and functions, similar to the previous layer. This one belongs to the preprocessor, and in general, the first two layers should not contain the classic *CSS* output or code.
- **Generic** – generic, normalization (normalize.*CSS*) or reset (reset.*CSS*) style files.
- **Elements** – the layer of basic styles of standard *HTML* elements, element selectors.
- **Objects** are the class selector layer that defines reusable non-decorative styles or patterns such as objects (described above in the subchapter *OOCSS*).
- **Components** – the layer of specific user interface components.
- **Trumps/Utilities** – helper classes that override previous *CSS* rules. Within these rules, it is possible to use the importance of rules in the form !important (Table 1).

Table 1 Example of the division of objects into layers (Kudrna, 2019)

Category	Layer	Example
Preprocesor	Settings	$primary-color, $border-width
	Tools	@mixin breakpoint-up()
HTML	Generic	h1, h2, h3, p
	Elements	h1, h2, h3, p
CSS classes	Objects	.container, .media
	Components	.button, .card, .alert
	Utilities	.mb-3, .p-4, .text-center

3.5 *Settings Change Processing*

The changes of themes based on the web application skinning process should be saved as user preferences. Adhuham mentions this fact in (Adhuham, 2020) as an essential user element enabling the change and preservation of the appearance even the next time when he enters the application. The user's choice can be saved into a *localStorage* of the browser, or as a limited alternative, to the *cookies* storage.

For web applications with an authentification, the preferences should be saved in the relational or *NoSQL* databases, in which this information can be linked to a specific user account.

Due to the current ability to set light or dark mode directly in operating systems, *media features* known as *prefers-color-scheme* have been added to *media queries*. When skinning web applications, they detect whether the user prefers a light or dark colour theme at the operating system level.

Kalifa (2020) states that respecting the operating system's preferences in the web application is a good first step to customization user preferences. But an even better approach is to give the user more control over changing the theme. Blažek (2019) considers accepting a theme from the operating system beneficial but warns that the user may require a different (light) theme in the operating system and a different (dark) in the application.

4 *ITCSS* Methodology Application

The presented approach of skinning and theming was applied to the educational system *Priscilla* (Skalka & Drlik, 2018, 2020) with a focus on achieving a better user experience and educational effect. The web version of the application is a typical e-learning system focused on programming.

Within this web application, the requirement for the design and implementation of philosophy with practical skin output for daily, nightly, and colour-blind mode were defined as the primary task. The front-end part of the application is developed by the *JavaScript* framework *Vue.js* using UI components library *Vuetify*. This library is based on the recommendations of the *Material Design* design language.

4.1 Skinning Technique Selection

The current scope of the application and its active development excluded approaches to define themes as separate templates. This approach would not solve the efficient organization of *CSS* styles and, in addition, would result in the need for manual management of each of the template files of the required skins when changing the design of the application.

The *Vuetify UI library* used by the application offers the possibility to define the properties of several themes. This technique applies an approach known as *CSS* in JS, which lies in the inefficient sustainability of *CSS* styles (usually determined at the component level). This approach limits the use of defined properties only within the specified library components and does not support universal use for all *HTML* elements. With the subsequent changes in the user interface design, it would be necessary to trace the styles in the components and edit them manually at various points in the application.

According to the *ITCSS* description, the first prerequisite for modern styling is defining logical division and arrangement of individual styles. This step contributes to the effective sustainability of *CSS* design code and skins, preventing style redundancy and, last but not least, improving the performance of the application itself. *ITCSS* was chosen as the optimal methodology, which divides the *CSS* code into seven layers, the so-called inverted triangle (Fig. 5).

In the final form of *CSS*, the individual styles that the selectors represent are arranged simultaneously according to three aspects, which indicates the shape of an inverted triangle representing this methodology:

- from far-reaching styles (with great reach) to local styles,

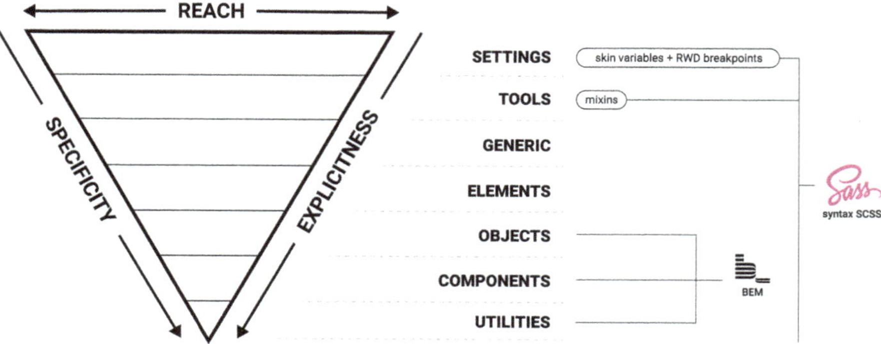

Fig. 5 Visualization of the proposed implementation of *ITCSS* in web application skinning

- from general styles to explicit styles,
- from selectors with low specificity to highly specific selectors.

This division and organization of *CSS* can maintain extensive *CSS* styles of the skinned application and more quickly respond to the growing new requirements of the system in terms of user interface design. A non-conceptual organization could cause an uncontrollable state of *CSS* style definition, increased redundancy, and problems with the specificity of *CSS* selectors. While designing and implementing the solution, it is necessary to keep in mind that ID selectors are not allowed in this methodology. Therefore the design does not contain them.

4.1.1 Settings Layer

The *CSS* preprocessor was chosen as a tool that made it possible to automate designing, defining, and applying several web application themes. For better standards compliance, the *SASS* preprocessor with S*CSS* syntax was preferred to the original *SASS* syntax. It is true that any valid *CSS* code is also a valid S*CSS*, but not the other way around. S*CSS* syntax application made it possible to apply the styles defined before the design transformation without modifications that would require new syntax.

The first layer of the *ITCSS* methodology is *Settings*. Variables with *CSS* property values for individual skins of the web application were primarily declared in this layer. Two options have been obtained for defining skin properties variables using the SASS preprocessor: native *CSS* variables and preprocessor variables. While native CSS variables dominated in the definition of specific properties for individual themes, preprocessor variables were often applied in the so-called fallback values of the application appearance.

Using only native CSS variables could result in a problem in older versions of browsers. For preprocessor variables, the size of the resulting CSS file would multiply after compilation (depending on the number of visual UI themes).

Native *CSS* variables were chosen because they are declarative, which means that changing the value of a variable will affect previous occurrences of usage and those that follow the change. Due to the lack of support for native variables in some browsers, a solution was applied in so-called fallback *CSS* values. Variables refer to the visual properties of the default theme, i.e. the daily mode styles of the application.

The *SASS* map was used to group the fallback *SASS* variables, an associative field associating the required variables and providing the certainty of displaying the application in the default mode, which would not be possible if only native *CSS* variables were used. Part of the definition is presented in Fig. 6.

The *Settings* layer was secondarily used to declare breakpoints for responsive application design. The definition of breakpoints was often preceded by an analysis of existing layout grid solutions, which describes, e.g. *Material Design* documentation (Google, 2021), *Bootstrap* (Team, 2021), *Tailwind CSS* (Tailwild Labs, 2021), and others. Due to the connection with the *Vuetify* library, four standard breakpoints

```
$fallback: (
  // ...
  readingTaskColor: #f7be16,
  questionTaskColor: #1b1464,
  programTaskColor: #e67676,
  // ...
);
```

```
body[data-theme="dark"] {
  // ...
  --readingTaskColor: hsl(36deg 100% 65%);
  --questionTaskColor: hsl(230deg 44% 64%);
  --programTaskColor: hsl(0deg 69% 67%);
  // ...
}
```

```
body[data-theme="light"] {
  // ...
  --readingTaskColor: #f7be16;
  --questionTaskColor: #1b1464;
  --programTaskColor: #e67676;
  // ...
}
```

```
body[data-theme="colorblind"] {
  // ...
  --readingTaskColor: hsl(326deg 66% 69%);
  --questionTaskColor: hsl(245deg 32% 18%);
  --programTaskColor: hsl(201deg 100% 36%);
  // ...
}
```

Fig. 6 Example of definition of variables with the properties of individual skins

for later use in the design of *SASS* mixins aimed at solving the responsiveness of a web application were defined.

4.1.2 Tools Layer

In this layer, it was necessary to define the method of assigning properties to individual elements of the web application within the declaration blocks of *CSS* rules. The first option is to skip this step by calling a directly defined native *CSS* variable from the first layer using a native function *var()*. This approach would not solve the significant problem mentioned by the lack of support in some browser versions. It would also be necessary to deal with obtaining fallback SASS map values manually.

The solution to these problems is the creation and subsequent use of mixin. Mixin in the *SASS* preprocessor provides the ability to create reusable blocks of *CSS* code. This approach can significantly automate assigning skin values to individual *CSS* properties and minimize human factors errors. It is crucial to keep in mind that none of the preprocessor layers should contain any real *CSS* output. For this purpose, a *themeStyle* mixin was created in the tools layer (Fig. 7).

Mixin *themeStyle* accepts the following three parameters:

- a standard *CSS* property that is assigned the value of a skin variable,
- the name of the variable whose value is intended to be used,
- a boolean value of true/false indicates a request to use the *!important* keyword after the CSS property value.

The last argument of the mentioned mixin can be observed as an optional parameter with a default value of *false*. This last parameter was defined to a mixin enhancement following the recommendations of the ITCSS methodology, which allows the use of the importance of the rule in the form of *!important* for rewriting previous styles only in the last layer. This structure can avoid unreasonable repetition of

```
@mixin themeStyle($property, $varName, $importance: false) {
    @if $importance == false {
        #{$property}: map-get($fallback, $varName);
        #{$property}: var(--#{$varName}, map-get($fallback, $varName));
    } @else {
        #{$property}: map-get($fallback, $varName) !important;
        #{$property}: var(--#{$varName}, map-get($fallback, $varName)) !important;
    }
}
```

Fig. 7 Mixin *themeStyle*

method calling with a *false* value due to the assumption of predominant *themeStyle* mixin calls without the need to use *!important*.

A common approach to responsive design is to unify multiple customized *CSS* styles based on a common media query condition. Although this method is a proven choice for smaller projects, other approaches have had to be considered for more complex web applications such as *Priscilla*. The solution is the use of mixins in a parameterless form. When designing these mixins with media queries, the mixins needed to be unambiguous and easy to use within any *CSS* application declaration block. The definition of the names should be based on the convention of marking the dimensions of devices with a possible prefixing of the minimum or maximum resolution according to the needs of the application.

4.2 Skin Design Procedure

The prerequisites for this phase are the definitions of parameters and variables listed in the previous steps. In this step, their application will be linked to the preparation of a specific appearance. Each of the skins listed below brought its specifics to the design, which required the gradual addition of variables with visual property values to the pre-prepared settings layer.

4.2.1 Day Skin Definition

The design of the daily mode is crucial for almost everyone skinned application. Daily mode is the default view of the *Priscilla* web application too. At the same time, some parts of the UI design of this skin were the basis for other skins. Therefore, it was necessary to pay due attention to the skin and create *CSS* styles that covered the visual needs of the entire web application.

Before skins development, the application was based primarily on components and *CSS* styles of the *Vuetify UI* library. Although they met the requirements of *Material Design*, they had to be visually unified with the newly prepared UI design and the application's components.

The reach, explicitness, and specificity of *CSS* styles were guided in the skinning process by combining the *BEM* naming convention and the ability to nest selectors using the *SASS* preprocessor. Potential class name conflicts (since *Vuetify* also uses *BEM*) have been eliminated because *Vuetify* prefixes the classes of its components with the letter *(v-)*. Simultaneously with the addition of skin variables, their application was also implemented within the declaration blocks of *CSS* code.

During the skin development, specific *CSS* styles of the application were continuously classified based on the *ITCSS* methodology into layers of components and utilities, which contain the core of the appearance of the designed skins and web application.

Rewriting of *CSS* styles originating from the *Vuetify UI* must be done in such a way as to avoid too high a specificity of selectors. The definition was based on *W3C* recommendations (Etemad & Atkins, 2018). Due to the absence of ID selectors representing the first numeric value of *a*, it was necessary to realize the sum of the number of class selectors, attributes and pseudo-classes within the value *b*. The third numerical value of the specificity *c* results from the sum of element type selectors and pseudo-elements. The *a-b-c* values thus obtained had to be subsequently concatenated to obtain the final specificity number of the selector combination without the need for unjustified use of *!important*. An example of calculating the specificity of selectors is shown in Fig. 8.

4.2.2 Night Skin Definition

At the beginning of the design of the night mode of the application, the existing dark mode solutions and benefits of their use in various web applications were analyzed (Riegler & Riener, 2019), (Pedersen et al., 2020). The critical point of the dark-mode proposal was to identify how applications approach the colour of individual elements in this mode. In addition to this information, the *Material Design* language recommendations were also valuable in designing the dark-mode.

The most fundamental recommendations are focused on the colour elevation, the colour of individual elements, and the typography of the web application. The emphasis is also placed on a sufficient contrast between the background colour and the colour of particular application elements to comply with the principles of web accessibility.

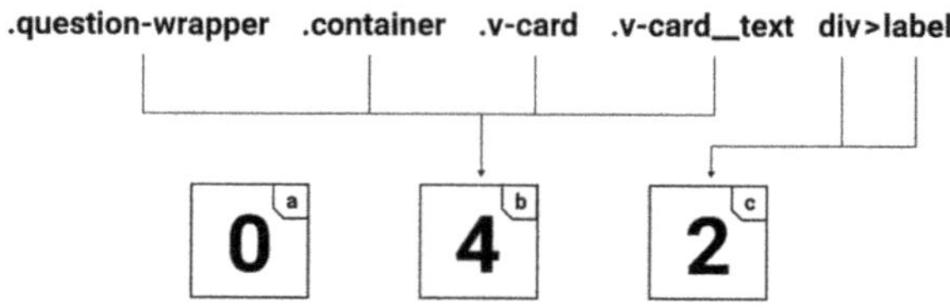

Fig. 8 Example of calculating the specificity of selectors

The colour saturation of the individual elements is reduced to achieve better visibility and less eye strain in the dark mode. The colours of the components have to be desaturated in comparison to the day/light mode. While the day mode used mainly hexadecimal colour expression from the UI design, choosing a more sophisticated colour representation in this mode was necessary. Therefore, the *HSL* colour model (hue, saturation, luminance) was used, which, in addition to the colour tone or hue, allows adjustment of the saturation and luminance of the selected colour (Fig. 9).

Another point of the design of this skin was the adaptation of the icons to dark backgrounds. For single-colour icons, the *CSS* property *filter* and its *invert* function were used. Multicoloured graphic elements, such as the logo or some control icons, are needed to create a customized version for dark mode.

4.2.3 Colour-blind Skin Definition

The third form of proposed skins was a mode for users suffering from Daltonism (colour-blind). Okabe and Ito (2002) points out that Daltonism is not a complete loss of colour vision. Colour-blind people can recognize a wide range of colours, while some specific colour ranges are difficult to distinguish. The starting points for the definition of the colour scheme were the rules of the *WCAG* (Web Content Accessibility Guidelines) accessibility methodology defined in WCAG (2012) and principles 3 (+1) Color Universal Design (Kojima et al., 2012).

Achieving acceptable colour elements of the application in the colour-blind skin is not a trivial matter. At first, it is necessary to identify proper colour combinations and exclude those that did not achieve the desired properties (e.g. contrast between

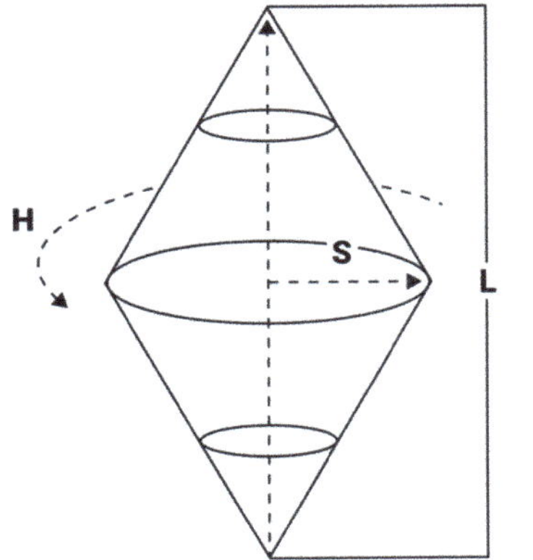

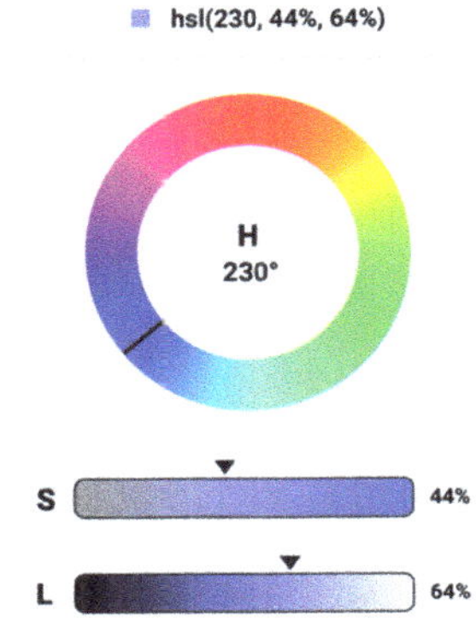

Fig. 9 Simplified *HSL* colour model (left) and interpretation of the selected colour in the night skin (right)

the background colour and text colour). A necessary validation element visualizing the appearance of the skinned application from the view of individual types of colour vision deficiencies were software tools. They visualized the appearance of the application in real-time, e.g. *Color Oracle* (Jenny, 2020), *Visolve* (Ryobi Systems Co., 2020), *WCAG color contrast checker* (Acart Communications, 2017), *WhoCanUse* (Ginnivan, 2020), *Adobe Color* (Adobe, 2021).

A first proposed solution that dynamically recalculates the colour would increase the range of the application code and solve the problem only partially. In addition, its use would disrupt the separation of code definition for design and code for application functionality.

Graphic patterns in the context of colour blindness are generally considered a valuable visual aid to distinguish similarly or even the same colours (Molina-López & Medina-Medina, 2019; Chua et al., 2015). Various SVG patterns with adapted transparency have proven to be an effective alternative to colour recalculating – the background colour with the pattern is covered with a layer of black with reduced transparency. The created colour overlay layer in the form of the *CSS* pseudo-element (*::before*) ensures a regardless of any background colour, the necessary contrast between the background colour and the font colour.

Figure 10 shows a misinterpretation of the *WCAG* for the resulting header colour values for some test results. This misinterpretation was caused because the tool could not automatically check for advanced elements with a transparent black colour at the testing time.

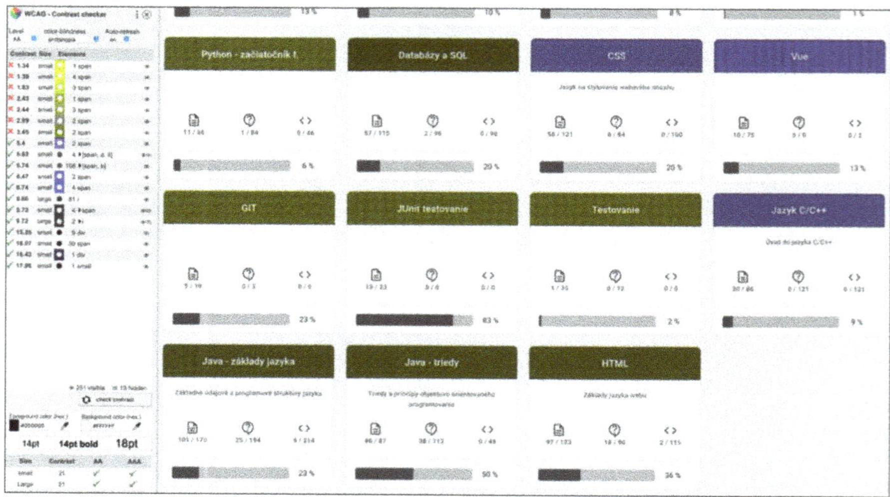

Fig. 10 Testing and simulation of colour vision deficiency – protanopia

4.3 *Skin Implementation in the Vue.js Environment*

The file structure of an application is usually determined by the development environment or framework dedicated for the application development. In the *Priscilla* web application developed in the *Vue.js* environment, one of the places that allow the implementation of created skins is the integration file *App.vue*, which is the root file of the main components of *Vue*.

The method dedicated to skin selection works with a textual value defining the application design (*theme_preference*). Based on a series of conditional statements, it evaluates the user's data-theme value and applies the appearance of the desired skin.

In assigning the skin, the lifecycle hooks of Vue components were used to access the reactive data of the application and to events at the component level to react to them by applying the correct skin. The scheme of operation in the structure of the application is presented in Fig. 11.

As part of the functionality of the skinning module, the system also included the possibility of automatically assigning a light or dark appearance based on the currently selected colour theme of the operating system (*os-preference*). This information can be accessed over a media query with a *prefers-color-scheme*. The application uses a separate setting for this way of identifying the appearance. If this information is available from the operating system, it will be used; otherwise (default link, incompatibility), the default skin of the web application is applied.

The functionality of the solution has been successfully tested in current versions of various operating systems, such as *Microsoft Windows*, *macOS*, *Android*, and *iOS*. An example of the appearance of the modes is available in Fig. 12.

The colour-blind mode of the application brings, in part, a distinctive visual design that can improve the quality of education within the system for users with colour vision deficiency. In this skin, possible colour pitfalls and visual ambiguities of the system were minimized. This approach increases the comfort and efficiency

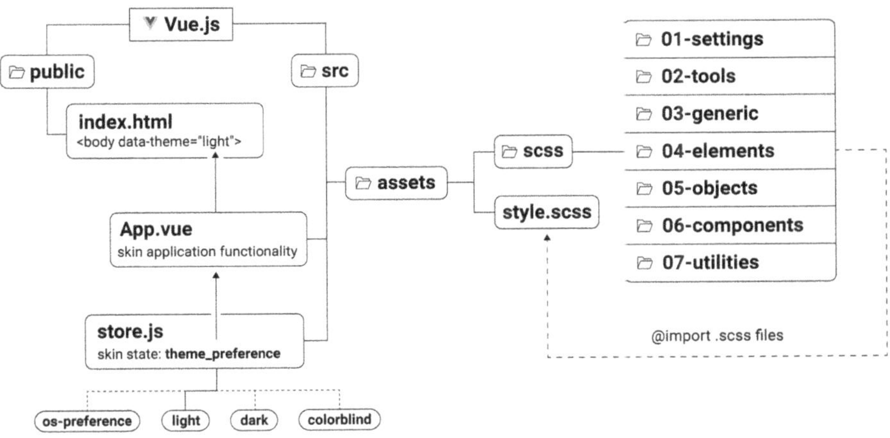

Fig. 11 The description of the skinning philosophy in *Vue.js*

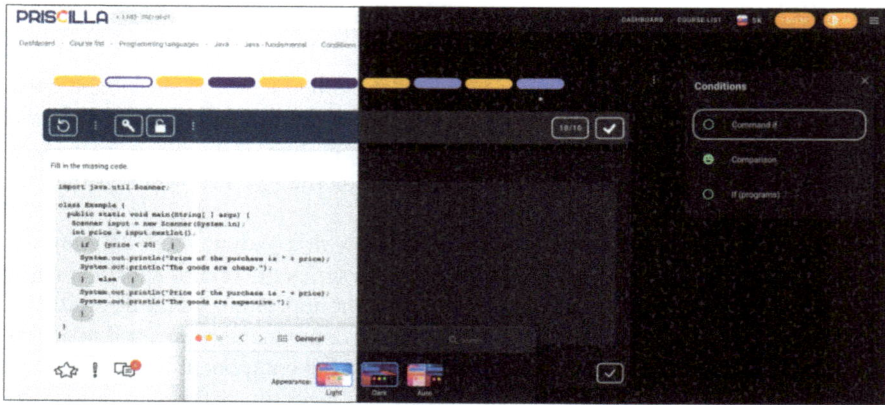

Fig. 12 Demonstration of automatic skin assignment when changing OS appearance preferences

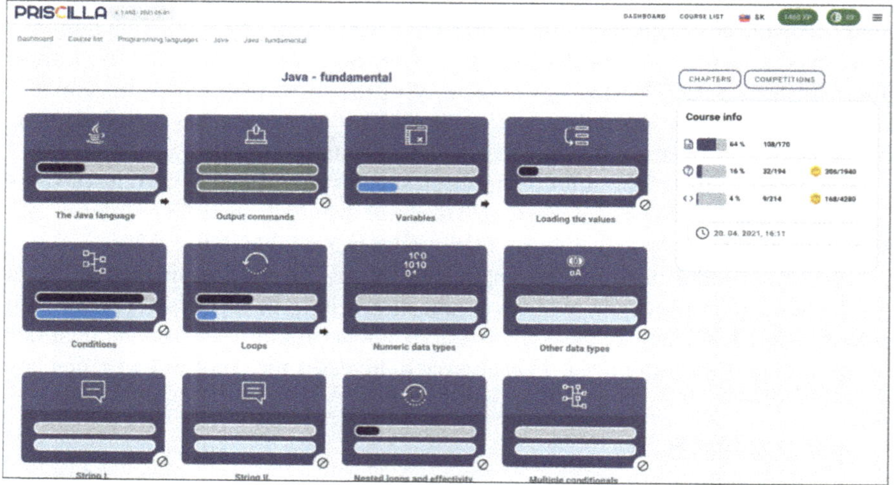

Fig. 13 Minimization of colour traps and the skin colour palette itself for colour-blind people

of colour-blind users working with the system. This skin also solves the relatively common problem of applications with the recognition of colour controls, which can be easily overlooked using the application by colour-blind users (Fig. 13).

The presented approach and created skin can be considered sufficiently adapted to individual types of colour blindness based on results from testing and simulation tools. The views of the content by users of different kinds of disabilities are presented in Fig. 14.

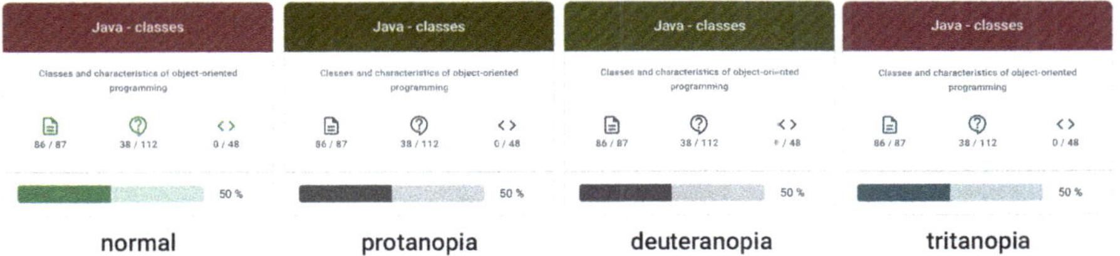

Fig. 14 Demonstration of different types of colour perception based on colour blindness diseases

5 Conclusion

The presented approach is complex and focused on large and constantly developing web applications. Although there are several applicable procedures, most of them will eventually encounter limitations or development slowdown due to code redundancy for design definition, *CSS* level issues, or non-functional inheritance between style levels.

Applying the *ITCSS* structure, methodological layers, and appropriate settings, it was possible to propose and apply a suitable responsive design that meets the defined application requirements. Using the proposed mixins with media queries and other capabilities of the *SASS* preprocessor, it was possible to target the needs of the application directly in *CSS* declaration blocks. This procedure made the *CSS* code with a responsive design more readable and unambiguous. The suitable combination of *CSS* settings allows, in addition to providing content in primary form, adaptation to mobile devices. It provides access to the educational content of the *Priscilla* system anytime and anywhere.

It should be noted that the transformation of the existing methodology for the application of styles to the levels defined by *ITCSS* is a time-consuming task. Based on the transformation made in the case study, it can be argued that the skinning process itself may get into a situation that does not allow it to be completed before the finishing development of the entire application. Therefore, it is impossible to separate the design definition and the application development process and remain only using already defined styles. The reason is, except for the new features of the application, the use of skins for users affected by Daltonism. These skins often require a specific approach that cannot be generalized or detailed in advance.

During the development of the platform and its design, several rounds of communication with users and their evaluation of the current design and content of the system took place. Although the ongoing evaluation was positive in all aspects, the authors identified several groups of improvements, which they subsequently implemented into the system.

In the final form, 77 respondents using the system for at least 2 months, commented on the design and the overall impression of the system. The results are as follows:

- the user-friendliness of the system is perceived positively by 88% of students, neutral by 7% of students;
- comprehensibility of functions in the system is at a high level according to 79% of users, 11% of users have a neutral attitude to it;
- ease of use due to the implemented functionalities is reported by 79% of users, 14% of users have a neutral attitude towards them.

In the final, 80% of users perceived graphic design positively and 10% perceived it as neutral. This assessment of the system is a confirmation of the correct direction of development and, of course, the potential for further improvement of the appearance and ease of use of the system's functions.

A potential research possibility for the future is also more detailed design research for colour-blind users. The typical problem, not only in the Priscilla system, is the representation of the flags of states in setting the language of the system, which, with their fixed and conventional colours, represent a globally unresolved and open problem for colour-blind people. In the application, this problem was solved relatively simply – by adding an international abbreviation of the language next to the flag of the state.

The application of the methodology and the rationale for its choice can help developers and designers of complex web applications select a suitable procedure for separating several levels of design and the functionality of the system.

Acknowledgements This research was funded by European Commission under the ERASMUS+ Programme 2018, KA2, grant number: 2018-1-SK01-KA203-046382 "Work-Based Learning in Future IT Professionals Education", Ministry of Education of Slovakia, grant number 004UKF-2-1/2021 "Preparation and development of teaching courses in English with a focus on artificial intelligence in the form of blended-learning", and Ministry of Education of Slovakia, grant number: 2020/8148:34-A1101 "Support for the development of practical skills of UKF students in Nitra".

References

Acart Communications. (2017). *Contrast checker*. Retrieved from https://contrastchecker.com/

Adhuham, M. (2020). *A complete guide to dark mode on the web*. Retrieved from https://css-tricks.com/a-complete-guide-to-dark-mode-on-the-web/

Adobe. (2021). *Adobe Color*. Retrieved from https://color.adobe.com/create/color-accessibility

Al-Zewairi, M., Biltawi, M., Etaiwi, W., & Shaout, A. (2017). Agile software development methodologies: Survey of surveys. *Journal of Computer and Communications, 5*(5). https://doi.org/10.4236/jcc.2017.55007

Arsenault, C. (2019). *OOCSS – The future of writing CSS*. Retrieved from https://www.keycdn.com/blog/oocss

Attardi, J. (2020). *Modern CSS: Master the key concepts of CSS for modern web development*. Apress.

Blažek, L. (2019). *Dark Mode teď prostě frčí*. Retrieved from https://blog.newlogic.cz/development/html/dark-mode-ted-proste-frci/

Böck, M. (2020). *Color theme switcher*. Retrieved from https://mxb.dev/blog/color-theme-switcher/

Borody, D. (2017). *Theming web apps with SASS*. Retrieved from https://medium.com/@dmitriy.borodiy/easy-color-theming-with-scss-bc38fd5734d1

Chua, S. H., Zhang, H., Hammad, M., Zhao, S., Goyal, S., & Singh, K. (2015). ColorBless: Augmenting visual information for colorblind people with binocular luster effect. *ACM Transactions on Computer-Human Interaction, 21*(6). https://doi.org/10.1145/2687923

Dowden, M., & Dowden, M. (2020). *Architecting CSS: The programmer's guide to effective style sheets*. Apress.

Eastabrook, J. (2020). *CSS skinning: Let your visitors choose the style*.

Etemad E. J., & Atkins, T. (2018). *Selectors level 4*. Retrieved from https://www.w3.org/TR/selectors-4

Feigenbaum, R. (2020). *The complete guide to the dark mode toggle*. Retrieved from https://ryanfeigenbaum.com/dark-mode/

Fomitchev, M., Garrood, S., Lacey, J.-D. K., & Rojas, J. J. (2007). *System and method of skinning themes*. Canada.

Ginnivan, C. (2020). *Who can use this color combination?* Retrieved from https://whocanuse.com

Google. (2021). *Responsive layout grid*. Retrieved from https://material.io/design/layout/responsive-layout-grid.html

Grant, K. J. (2018). *CSS in depth*. Manning Publications.

Harrell, J. (2017). *Unlocking the benefits of CSS variables*. Retrieved from https://www.jonathan-harrell.com/blog/unlocking-the-benefits-of-css-custom-properties

Jenny, B. (2020). *Color Oracle*. Retrieved from https://colororacle.org

Kalifa, F. (2020). *Dark mode on the web: UX, DX and technical exploration for inclusive dark mode*. Retrieved from https://fatihkalifa.com/dark-mode-web

Kojima, N., Ichihara, Y. G., Ikeda, T., Kamachi, M. G., & Ito, K. (2012). Color universal design: Analysis of color category dependency on color vision type (3). In *Color Imaging XVII: Displaying, Processing, Hardcopy, and Applications* (Vol. 8292). Retrieved from https://doi.org/10.1117/12.907669

Kudrna, A. (2019). *Dark mode s CSS custom properties: přístupnost v atraktivní podobě*. Retrieved from https://frontend.garden/dark-mode-s-css-custom-properties/

Maleki, N. G., & Ramsin, R. (2018). Agile web development methodologies: A survey and evaluation. *Studies in Computational Intelligence, 722*. https://doi.org/10.1007/978-3-319-61388-8_1

Michálek, M. (2017). *BEM: Pojmenovávací konvence pro třídy v CSS*. Retrieved from https://www.vzhurudolu.cz/prirucka/bem

Molina-López, J., & Medina-Medina, N. (2019). Design proto-patterns to improve the interaction in video games of people with color blindness. In *ACM International Conference Proceeding Series*. Retrieved from https://doi.org/10.1145/3335595.3335612

Morgan, C. (2021). *My dark theme implementation*. Retrieved from https://chrismorgan.info/blog/dark-theme-implementation/

Okabe, M., & Ito, K. (2002). *How to make figures and presentations that are friendly to color blind people.pdf*. http://Jfly.Iam.U-Tokyo.Ac.Jp/Color/Index.Html

Pedersen, L. A., Einarsson, S. S., Rikheim, F. A., & Sandnes, F. E. (2020). User interfaces in dark mode during daytime – Improved productivity or just cool-looking? In *Lecture Notes in Computer Science (including subseries Lecture Notes in Artificial Intelligence and Lecture Notes in Bioinformatics)* (Vol. 12188 LNCS). Retrieved from https://doi.org/10.1007/978-3-030-49282-3_13

Pickering, H. (2019). Inclusive components. *Smashing Magazine*.

Riegler, A., & Riener, A. (2019). Adaptive dark mode: Investigating text and transparency of windshield display content for automated driving. *Mensch Und Computer 2019 Workshop on Automotive HMIs*.

Roberts, H. (2014). Managing CSS Projects with ITCSS. Retrieved from https://csswizardry.net/talks/2014/11/itcss-dafed.pdf

Ryobi Systems Co. (2020). Visolve – the assistive software for people with color blindness. Retrieved from https://www.ryobi.co.jp/products/visolve/en

Skalka, J., & Drlik, M. (2018). Priscilla – Proposal of system architecture for programming learning and teaching environment. In *IEEE international conference on application of information and communication technologies*. Retrieved from https://publons.com/publon/27387754/

Skalka, J., & Drlík, M. (2018). Conceptual framework of microlearning-based training mobile application for improving programming skills. *Advances in Intelligent Systems and Computing, 725*. https://doi.org/10.1007/978-3-319-75175-7_22

Skalka, J., & Drlík, M. (2020). Educational model for improving programming skills based on conceptual microlearning framework BT. In M. E. Auer & T. Tsiatsos (Eds.), *The challenges of the digital transformation in education* (pp. 923–934). Springer International Publishing. https://link.springer.com/chapter/10.1007/978-3-030-11932-4_85

Skalka, J., Drlik, M., Benko, L., Kapusta, J., Del Pino, J. C. R., Smyrnova-Trybulska, E., et al. (2021). Conceptual framework for programming skills development based on microlearning and automated source code evaluation in virtual learning environment. *Sustainability (Switzerland), 13*(6). https://doi.org/10.3390/su13063293

Snook, J. (2012). *Scalable and modular architecture for CSS (second)*. Snook.ca Web Development, Inc. Retrieved from http://smacss.com/

Tailwild Labs. (2021). *Responsive design*. Retrieved from https://tailwindcss.com/docs/responsive-design

Taivalsaari, A., Mikkonen, T., Pautasso, C., & Systä, K. (2017). Comparing the Built-In Application Architecture Models in the Web Browser. In *Proceedings – 2017 IEEE international conference on software architecture, ICSA 2017*. Retrieved from https://doi.org/10.1109/ICSA.2017.23

Team, B. (2021). *Grid system*. Retrieved from https://getbootstrap.com/docs/4.0/layout/grid

Torrecilla-Salinas, C. J., Sedeño, J., Escalona, M. J., & Mejías, M. (2015). Estimating, planning and managing agile web development projects under a value-based perspective. *Information and Software Technology, 61*. https://doi.org/10.1016/j.infsof.2015.01.006

Tzucker, J. (2019). *Coding a CSS theme switcher – A multitude of web dev options*. Retrieved from https://joshuatz.com/posts/2019/coding-a-css-theme-switcher-a-multitude-of-web-dev-options/

Wang, Y. D., & Emurian, H. H. (2005). Trust in E-commerce: Consideration of interface design factors. *Journal of Electronic Commerce in Organizations*. https://doi.org/10.4018/jeco.2005100103

Watson-Nolan, A. (2019). *The front-end tooling survey 2019 – Results*. Retrieved from https://ashleynolan.co.uk/blog/frontend-tooling-survey-2019-results#css-processors

WCAG. (2012). Web content accessibility guidelines (WCAG) overview. *Web Accessibility Initiative* (December 2008).

Williams, S. (2017). *Theming with CSS custom properties*. Retrieved from https://ramenhog.com/blog/2017/06/07/theming-with-css-custom-properties

Yazid, M. A., & Jantan, A. H. (2017). User experience design (UXD) of mobile application: An implementation of a case study. *Journal of Telecommunication, Electronic and Computer Engineering, 9*, 197–200.

Virtual Programming Lab for Moodle: Automatic Program Assessment in a First-year University Course

Juan Carlos Rodríguez-del-Pino, Zenón J. Hernández-Figueroa, José Daniel González Domínguez, and Ján Skalka

1 Introduction

The ability to prepare algorithms for solving problems and rewrite them into program code is one of the necessary skills in finding work not only in the IT sector. Although pupils have been developing algorithmic skills since the first years of primary school, many fail to establish it to write programs.

In the past, difficulties were often sought in connection with mathematical thinking and skills. Gomes et al. (2006) realised a comparative study between the students' results in the programming and mathematical tests in the first year after starting university. The results pointed out that students do not have enough basic mathematical concepts concerning the number theory. They have difficulties understanding the problem description, weak abstraction levels, and a lack of logical reasoning.

Chao (2016) tried to solve these shortcomings by applying a problem-oriented approach using a visual environment. Students solve a serie of problems while observing how novice programmers use a visual programming environment to solve a computational problem. This study shows that visual problem solving is an effective approach that helps novice programmers create computational design strategies.

Bosse and Gerosa (2017) identified some typical problems of novice programmers, which can be divided into several groups. The primary cause of failure is usually a weak understanding of the basic programming principles (variables,

J. C. Rodríguez-del-Pino · Z. J. Hernández-Figueroa · J. D. G. Domínguez
Department of Informatics and Systems, University of Las Palmas de Gran Canaria, Las Palmas, Spain
e-mail: jc.rodriguezdelpino@ulpgc.es; zenon.hernandez@ulpgc.es; josedaniel.gonzalez@ulpgc.es

J. Skalka (✉)
Constantine the Philosopher University in Nitra, Nitra, Slovakia
e-mail: jskalka@ukf.sk

E. Smyrnova-Trybulska et al. (eds.), *Microlearning*,
https://doi.org/10.1007/978-3-031-13359-6_12

expressions, commands) and, subsequently, a weak ability to analyse feedback in the development environment (compiler messages, identifying the causes of run-time errors, etc.).

According to Skalka and Drlik (2020), Skalka et al. (2019) programming language courses are still the most challenging courses that students fail. The current approach to solving this problem is based on adapting the educational methodology to the habits of current students. The approach used to obtain information for young Generation Z programmers is based primarily on the use of smartphones, the limited amount of information displayed (Hug, 2005), and the provision of immediate feedback (Keuning et al., 2018; Le, 2016).

The authors (Syahanim et al., 2018) present the idea of scaffolding as a technique of teaching programming by examples with detailed instructions, which encourage students to solve problems of various kinds by allowing them to avoid frustration due to syntactic and unintentional errors. This technique is often linked to the collaborative approach of placing more advanced students in the role of teachers supporting knowledge building in novices.

Although several applications and frameworks support the use of smartphones in teaching programming, writing more complex programs in this environment is inefficient (Skalka & Drlík, 2018). An ideal tool for teaching programming at universities, which can eliminate some beginner's difficulties when set up correctly, is automated assessment (Staubitz et al., 2016; Galan et al., 2019).

Automated assessment (AA) represents a tool that automatically checks source code and provides feedback at a level defined by the instructor or module providing the AA operation. According to (Skalka et al., 2019), AA is beneficial for the following areas:

- the student gains immediate feedback whether the program is correct;
- students can use at their own pace while the teacher assists in explaining the task or getting stuck during the solution;
- the teacher gains extra time, instead of time wasted by checking the assignment and identifying and re-explaining repeated errors in past;
- it is possible to teach large groups of students without increasing the demands on teachers, which apply mainly in the case of MOOC courses;
- the learning process is more efficient and, due to the errors tracking, speed and quality of the solutions, the individual parts of the process can be fragmented, quantified and described.

The article aims to use the AA tool in the university environment and evaluate its contribution by students. The research used the Virtual Programming Lab module for LMS Moodle (VPL) (Rodríguez-del-Pino et al., 2012). VPL was integrated into the university e-learning environment. Its use with other educational materials (lectures, tests, video lessons, etc.) was used to support blended learning in the first year of bachelor's study applied informatics.

The research questions are defined as follow:

- RQ1: *How do students perceive the method of automated assessment, and how it contributes to improving their programming skills.*

- RQ2: *How do students perceive the environment of the VPL module.*

The article has the following structure. The second part describes the Virtual Programming Lab as a technological solution with its components and integration into LMS Moodle. It also describes services for running and evaluating student source code. The third part presents the structure and results of a questionnaire implemented within a group of first-year university students who used VPL as the primary tool for writing introductory programs in Java. Finally, the article concludes with a discussion and conclusion.

2 Virtual Programming Lab

Virtual Programming Lab for Moodle (VPL) is a tool aimed to manage student assignments in computer programming courses (Rodríguez-del-Pino et al., 2012). VPL is an open-source tool that supports the execution and assessment of the program code submitted by the students.

VPL is available from the official Moodle site and is developed by teachers at the University of Las Palmas de Gran Canaria (ULPGC), Spain. The following subchapters describe the structure of VPL.

2.1 Logical Structure Overview

VPL is composed of three pieces: an execution service, a Moodle plugin, and an IDE client. The execution service attends to the requests from the Moodle plugin to execute and monitor tasks while interacting with the IDE client through text or graphic terminals (Fig. 1).

The Moodle plugin manages and saves the configuration data for each assignment and the student submissions with their assessment and grading reports. It also coordinates the requests for running, debugging, or assessing student code. The user makes requests through the IDE client, and the Moodle plugin transfers them to an execution server selected to carry on such tasks. The IDE client running in a browser interacts with the users, starts requests to the Moodle plugin, retrieves and displays the responses, and establishes direct connections with the execution server.

2.2 The VPL Moodle Plugin

The VPL Moodle plugin is the piece that integrates VPL into the Moodle online learning system. It allows using VPL as an integral part of Moodle by supporting backups, restores, logs, reports, roles, groups, calendars, grade book, GDP, etc.

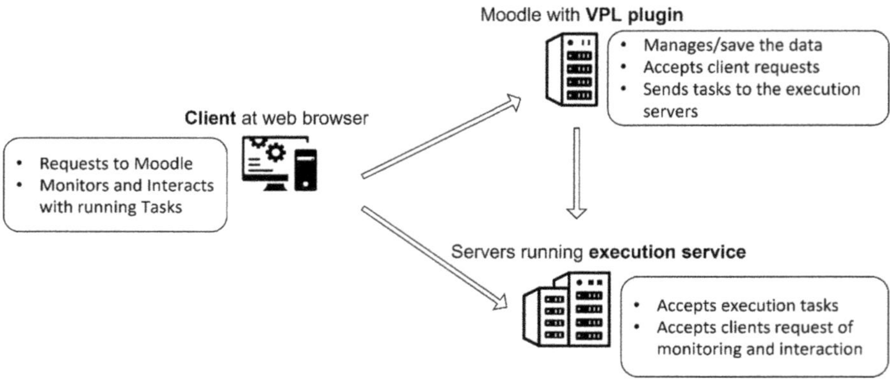

Fig. 1 Components of Virtual Programming Lab

Teachers interact with the VPL Moodle plugin to manage the VPL activities. The teachers can define all the aspects of the assignment and get live reports of each assignment status, including students' submissions and time spent in the activity. The configuration of an assignment may include an easy-to-write definition of input/output test cases, allowing automatic assessment.

The data managed by the plugin for each assignment include:

- description,
- submission limits (number of files, file size, etc.),
- execution limits (time, memory, etc.),
- initial files for the student,
- files to support running students' code,
- the submissions of each student,
- test cases definition,
- automatic and manual grading reports (Fig. 2).

From the teachers' point of view, the VPL plugin is the dashboard of the programming assignments where they can get help to manage and grade this type of activity without needing to download or run code outside this tool.

The tool out of the box supports more than 20 programming languages. This support includes the needed scripts to compile or interpret the code written in each language. It is also highly customisable, allowing teachers to add support for new programming languages or even change the behaviour for initially supported ones.

The plugin gives an always ready-to-use environment to save, develop, and test programming assignments receiving automatic feedback and the final mark from the student's point of view. All this without the need for installations or configurations in a machine. As a drawback, although the system reports the compilation and execution bugs, its auto-completion hints are not syntax-aware.

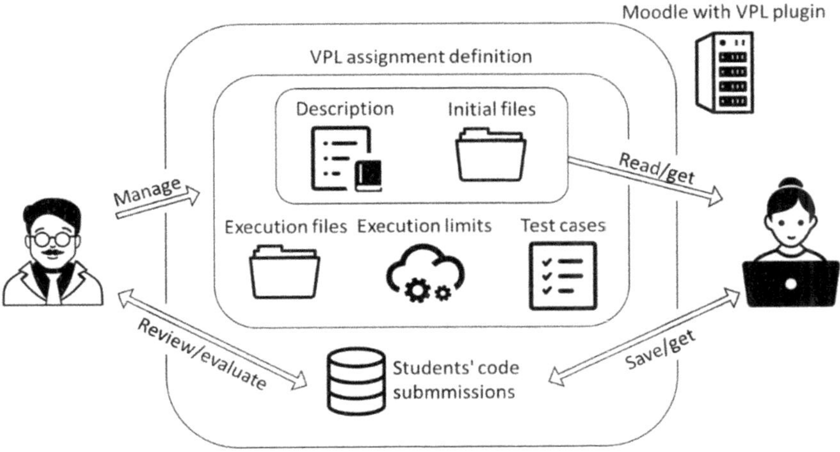

Fig. 2 Virtual Programming Lab communication in the LMS Moodle environment

2.3 The IDE Client

The IDE client is really part of the Moodle plugin, but it runs in a web browser instead of running in the Moodle server. The IDE client is a multi-file code-editing environment with syntactic highlighting for many programming languages.

It supports standard file operations like, among others, exporting files as a ZIP file, drag-and-drop, and importing files from the local machine. The import and drag-and-drop include the unpacking of ZIP files. The IDE client also consists of an interactive text terminal and a graphical environment. The client allows running many programs from classic I/O text programs, GUI programs to web applications.

The user using the IDE client triggers the execution of the code, so getting an instant compilation report and, if compilation succeeds, an interactive terminal (text or GUI) connected to the running program. The compilation report allows the student to fix the problems found.

If the assignment configuration allows it, students could also request from the IDE client the assessment of their submissions, obtaining immediate feedback on their results that they could use to rework their tasks.

2.4 The Execution Service

Running and assessing code written by students is one of the main functionalities of VPL. The execution service is the module in charge of such a task. The VPL Moodle plugin can interact with several execution services.

The execution services accept requests to run, debug, or assess students' code. The service also accepts commands to stop, get status, retrieve assessment, etc., for each task. It also allows Websocket connections to interact with running tasks and monitor them.

Security has been one of the main criteria driving the development of VPL. As internal security measures, the execution services run tasks in a controlled environment, limiting the effect of the task in the execution server. No external code runs outside the execution service. The authors recommend the service be installed on a dedicated Linux server. The service uses local installed compilers and interpreters to run code written in the different programming languages.

As perimeter security measures, VPL uses HTTPS secure connections, keys to accept tasks, transient tokens to control, monitor, and interact with tasks, and can limit the serves available to request tasks. It can also use anti-DoS algorithms (Fig. 3).

For each execution, the execution service creates a temporal user and home directory to save the data and run the code of the task. Each task runs with the limits of memory, time, processes, etc., demanded in the task request. After the job ends, the service removes the temporal user and directory assigned. The service is stateless in the sense that each execution always starts from scratch.

3 Research Methodology and Design

The preparation of the questionnaire was aimed at identifying strengths and weaknesses in the use of AA. AA was a compulsory part of completing the introductory programming course, but they were only a part of the study obligations. Students can use presentations from lectures, video recordings of lectures, video recordings of the solution of selected tasks and weekly summary tests. Education was realised in a combined form, and the teacher solved selected assignments with students. Some of the tasks were solved within the home preparation.

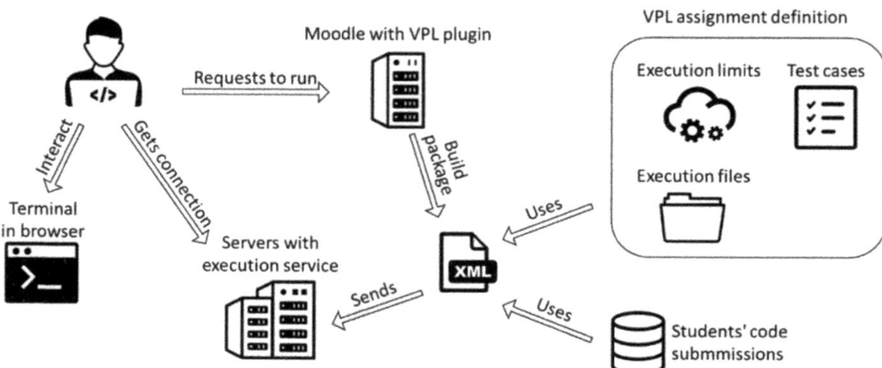

Fig. 3 Execution server with connexions from Moodle and Browser

The first part of the questionnaire examines the acceptance of principles and the use of new technology by students, and the second part is focused on the user experience of students with VPL within the introductory semester period at the university. These students were not yet in contact with the VPL or AA environment, so their perception of both elements is not affected by previous experience.

The survey population consists of 52 students aged 19–22 years of the first year of the study in the winter semester of 2019/2020 at Constantine the Philosopher University in Nitra (Slovakia). Data collection was not anonymous, but student participation was optional and voluntary in the survey.

The questions were asked in the form of a 7-level Likert scale.

3.1 Students' Attitude to the Use of AA

The first group of questions was focused on the perceptions of AA by students.

The essential characteristics of educational content are students understanding and the teacher's (or course creator's) ability to assign a task clearly and accurately. The first question (*The VPL's assignments were clear and understandable.*) focuses on identifying the unambiguity and comprehensibility of the assignment.

The second question (*The assignments of the VPL were in accordance with the content of the lectures.*) was focused on identifying whether students correctly perceive the content of lectures and can connect it with the tasks they solve through AA.

The third and fourth questions focus on identifying the role of AA in a cognitive process. The third question (*The VPL assignments helped me understand the content of programming.*) identified the importance of AA in understanding the content itself and building basic knowledge.

The fourth question (*The VPL assignments helped me practice the understood content.*) identified the importance of AA in understanding the content itself and building basic knowledge.

The summarisation of answers is presented in Table 1.

The results show that respondents perceive the most important questions significantly positively (*The VPL assignments helped me understand the content of programming. – 5.34*; *The VPL assignments helped me practice the understood content. – 5.67*), and the supplementary questions also provide information that students understand the connection between the course content and AA: *The VPL's assignments were clear and understandable. (5.19)* and *The assignments of the VPL were in accordance with the content of the lectures. (5.76)*.

The students' view of AA is illustrated by free answers, of which the most interesting observations include:

- I know the result of the task immediately; I don't have to wait for the teacher to fix it and deal with solving the problem again.
- Possibility to learn or repeat the curriculum only on the Internet. There is no need to install the program itself on my computer.

Table 1 Perceptions of AA by students in the winter semester of 2019/2020

Question	Mean	7 Strongly agree (% / N)	6 Agree (% / N)	5 Somewhat agree (% / N)	4 Neutral (% / N)	3 Somewhat disagree (% / N)	2 Disagree (% / N)	1 Strongly disagree (% / N)
The VPL's assignments were clear and understandable.	5.19	13.5% (7)	32.7% (17)	30.8% (16)	11.5% (6)	7.7% (4)	1.9% (1)	1.9% (1)
The assignments of the VPL were in accordance with the content of the lectures.	5.76	50% (26)	19.2% (10)	11.5% (6)	7.7% (4)	3.8% (2)	3.8% (2)	3.8% (2)
The VPL assignments helped me understand the content of programming.	5.34	42.3% (22)	11.5% (6)	15.4% (8)	17.3% (9)	1.9% (1)	5.8% (3)	5.8% (3)
The VPL assignments helped me practice the understood content.	5.67	51.9% (27)	11.5% (6)	13.5% (7)	13.5% (7)	1.9% (1)	0% (0)	7.7% (4)

- Thanks to the display of inputs and outputs, I can see for what inputs my program does not work.
- AA quickly detected errors in the code and saved me time searching on the Internet or in the materials from lectures in LMS Moodle.
- Possibility to practice tasks at home independently and need the opportunity to connect with a team of classmates with whom we help each other.

3.2 *Students' Attitude to the Use of VPL Environment*

The second part of the questionnaire was focused on the web IDE environment with VPL functionality to find out how students react to the web IDE environment and the behaviour of the evaluation module.

The questions were aimed to identify potential issues and their impact on student skills-building and perception of the AA environment.

The second purpose of the questions was to provide VPL module developers feedback from a group of university users.

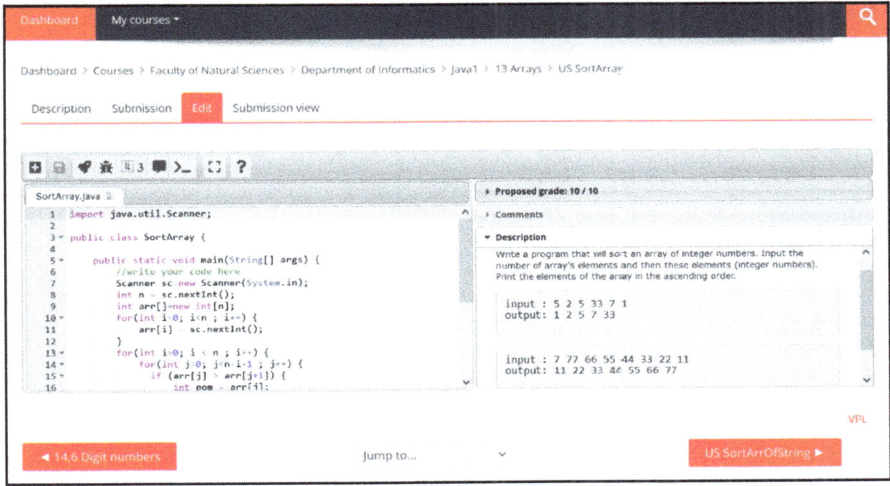

Fig. 4 User view in VPL environment

The example of an assignment evaluated in the VPL environment is presented in Fig. 4.

Questions and answers scores are shown in Table 2.

The results show that respondents are satisfied with all the functionalities of the environment to very satisfied.

Free answers bring ideas for improving the functionality of the editor and insights from practical use:

- The editor does not support the autocomplete utility and neither continuous error evaluation as the development environment.
- Sometimes there were problems with the evaluation; for example, VPL did not want to recognise the specified output, which was visually identical to the expected output - in such cases, it may be helpful to display ASCII character codes.
- The system does not prevent the student from cheating.
- The same code in NetBeans and VPL returns different results - real numbers were sometimes taken with different accuracy.

However, these observations are usually not a technological matter of the VPL environment as such. They are used to indicate that students have not identified any serious deficiencies in the VPL module within 3 months of using the system.

4 Discussion and Conclusion

The answers to the research questions can be summarised as follows.

Table 2 Perceptions of VPL environment by students in the winter semester of 2019/2020

		7	6	5	4	3	2	1
		Strongly agree	Agree	Somewhat agree	Neutral	Somewhat disagree	Disagree	Strongly disagree
Question	Mean	(% / N)	(% / N)	(% / N)	(% / N)	(% / N)	(% / N)	(% / N)
The environment was easy to use.	5.77	44.2% (23)	19.2% (10)	25% (13)	3.8% (2)	0% (0)	3.8% (2)	3.8% (2)
The functionality of the editor was sufficient.	5.15	25% (13)	25% (13)	19.2% (10)	15.4% (8)	7.7% (4)	1.9% (1)	5.8% (3)
The evaluation speed was sufficient.	5.98	51.9% (27)	21.2% (11)	17.3% (9)	3.8% (2)	0% (0)	0% (0)	5.8% (3)
Feedback on detecting syntax errors was sufficient (compiler reports).	5.53	36.5% (19)	19.2% (10)	23.1% (12)	11.5% (6)	5.8% (3)	0% (0)	3.8% (2)
Feedback of detecting logical errors was sufficient (reports of incorrect results).	5.13	28.8% (15)	15.4% (8)	25% (13)	11.5% (6)	11.5% (6)	5.8% (3)	1.9% (1)

- RQ1: *How do students perceive the method of automated assessment, and how it contributes to improving their programming skills.*

The first research question was answered through a questionnaire with the following results based on the evaluation of the feedback obtained after the end of the semester on a sample of 52 first-year students. It can be stated that:

- 81% of students perceive the **connection between the content** of lectures and AA, 11% disagree with this statement,
- 77% of students **understand the assignments** formulated in the language at a level corresponding to university students and consider them comprehensible, 11% disagree with this statement,
- automated assessments help students **understand** new content for 69% of students, 13% disagree with this statement,
- automated assessments help students **practice** content and are sufficient for 77% of students, 10% disagree with this statement,

- RQ2: *How do students perceive the environment of the VPL module.*

It can be stated that:

- with the statement that **the environment is easy to use**, agree 88% and disagree 8% of students,
- the **functionality of the editor** were sufficient for 69% of students; 15% of students disagreed with this statement,
- the **evaluation speed** were sufficient for 90% of students; 6% of students disagreed with this statement,
- feedback of **detecting syntax errors** were sufficient for 79% and insufficient for 10% of students,
- feedback of **detecting logical errors** were sufficient for 69% and insufficient for 19% of students.

Based on the questionnaire results, it can be stated that AA represents a technology, which brings positive results from the introductory courses in teaching programming. Students perceive this tool highly positively, and they are aware of the benefits it brings for them. It can be assumed that the successful implementation of AA modules or systems will increase the quality of training of IT specialists.

VPL is a useful and highly positively perceived system whose main advantages are integration into the LMS Moodle and modularity, which allows its parts in other (independent) systems. VPL components are used in the Priscilla system, which integrates AA with other elements typical for nowadays smart education (Skalka & Drlik, 2018).

Thanks to collecting all submitted assignments for every user, VPL provides a database that allows identifying problems of students and students who may have educational issues (Drlík et al., 2017; Skalka et al., 2020).

Collaborative techniques recede into the background in this phase of programming learning. Discussion forums were used as a supporting element in solving the assignments, enabling users to ask and answer questions in all roles (student, teacher). However, due to the gradual increase of difficulty of the assignments and the methodical support from the teacher in the teaching, their use was rare. Collaborative skills are fully developed in the next phases (next semester of study). Students solve tasks in a team, evaluate and comment on each other's assignments, and are also scored for helping their classmates.

Acknowledgements This research was funded by European Commission under the ERASMUS+ Programme 2018, KA2, grant number: 2018-1-SK01-KA203-046382 "Work-Based Learning in Future IT Professionals Education", Ministry of Education of Slovakia, grant number 004UKF-2-1/2021 "Preparation and development of teaching courses in English with a focus on artificial intelligence in the form of blended-learning", and Ministry of Education of Slovakia, grant number: 2020/8148:34-A1101 "Support for the development of practical skills of UKF students in Nitra".

References

Bosse, Y., & Gerosa, M. A. (2017). Why is programming so difficult to learn? *ACM SIGSOFT Software Engineering Notes, 41*(6). https://doi.org/10.1145/3011286.3011301

Chao, P. Y. (2016). Exploring students' computational practice, design and performance of problem-solving through a visual programming environment. *Computers and Education, 95*. https://doi.org/10.1016/j.compedu.2016.01.010

Drlík, M., Švec, P., Kapusta, J., Munk, M., Noskova, T., Pavlova, T., et al. (2017). Identification of differences in university e-environment between selected EU and non-EU countries using knowledge mining methods: Project IRNet case study. *International Journal of Web Based Communities, 13*(2). https://doi.org/10.1504/IJWBC.2017.084416

Galan, D., Heradio, R., Vargas, H., Abad, I., & Cerrada, J. A. (2019). Automated assessment of computer programming practices: The 8-years UNED experience. *IEEE Access, 7*. https://doi.org/10.1109/ACCESS.2019.2938391

Gomes, A., Carmo, L., Bigotte, E., & Mendes, A. (2006). Mathematics and programming problem solving. In *3rd e-learning conference--computer science education* (pp. 1–5).

Hug, T. (2005). Microlearning: A new pedagogical challenge. In *Proceedings of microlearning conference 2005*.

Keuning, H., Jeuring, J., & Heeren, B. (2018). A systematic literature review of automated feedback generation for programming exercises. *ACM Transactions on Computing Education, 19*(1). https://doi.org/10.1145/3231711

Le, N.-T. (2016). A classification of adaptive feedback in educational systems for programming. *Systems, 4*(2). https://doi.org/10.3390/systems4020022

Rodríguez-del-Pino, J. C., Rubio-Royo, E., & Hernández-Figueroa, Z. (2012). A Virtual Programming Lab for Moodle with automatic assessment and anti-plagiarism features. In *Conference on e-Learning, e-Business, Entreprise Information Systems, & e-Government*.

Skalka, J., & Drlik, M. (2018). Priscilla – Proposal of system architecture for programming learning and teaching environment. *IEEE International Conference on Application of Information and Communication Technologies*. Retrieved from https://publons.com/publon/27387754/

Skalka, J., & Drlík, M. (2018). Conceptual framework of microlearning-based training mobile application for improving programming skills. *Adv. Intell. Syst. Comput., 725*. https://doi.org/10.1007/978-3-319-75175-7_22

Skalka, J., & Drlik, M. (2020). Automated assessment and microlearning units as predictors of at-risk students and students' outcomes in the introductory programming courses. *Applied Sciences (Switzerland), 10*(13). https://doi.org/10.3390/app10134566

Skalka, J., Drlik, M., & Obonya, J. (2019). Automated assessment in learning and teaching programming languages using virtual learning environment. *Proceedings of IEEE global engineering education conference (EDUCON2017)*. Retrieved from https://doi.org/10.1109/EDUCON.2019.8725127

Skalka, J., Drlik, M., Obonya, J., & Capay, M. (2020). Architecture proposal for micro-learning application for learning and teaching programming courses. In *IEEE global engineering education conference, EDUCON* (Vol. 2020-April). Retrieved from https://doi.org/10.1109/EDUCON45650.2020.9125407

Staubitz, T., Klement, H., Renz, J., Teusner, R., & Meinel, C. (2016). Towards practical programming exercises and automated assessment in Massive Open Online Courses. In *Proceedings of 2015 IEEE international conference on teaching, assessment and learning for engineering, TALE 2015*. Retrieved from https://doi.org/10.1109/TALE.2015.7386010

Syahanim, M. S., Shukur, Z., & Judi, H. M. (2018). Scaffolding model for efficient programming learning based on cognitive load theory. *International Journal of Pure and Applied Mathematics, 118*(7), 77–83.

Evaluation of Primary School Mathematics Education: Applied Research Results

Viktor Gorokh, Liliia Hrynevych, Eugenia Smyrnova-Trybulska, Vasyl Tereshchenko, and Tetiana Vakulenko

1 Introduction

Traditionally, Ukrainian school mathematics education has always been considered quite strong. However, in recent years, more and more Ukrainian experts have openly reported disappointing trends in this field, primarily referring to the results of the External Independent Evaluation (EIE) (Bakhrushin, 2019). Undoubtedly, many conclusions drawn from the analysis of the results of the EIE in mathematics can be trusted to some extent (taking into account the limitations of EIE data). At the same time, we have to admit that the post-factum statement of the unsatisfactory state of mathematics school education in Ukraine, that is, when young people have completed their secondary education, cannot dramatically affect the situation, so to speak, for over than 10-year process of teaching mathematics to students in school. Such objective data (as those obtained from EIE results) on the quality of mathematics school education would be much more valuable, if they had been collected earlier, in order to provide both educators and administrators with room for maneuver aimed at eliminating negative trends or reinforcing positive ones.

Thus, the task of creating such a system of assessment of the quality of education at the level of Ukrainian school education, including mathematics education, which would provide an opportunity to obtain up-to-date information on the issue from at least primary school, has become urgent. And in these terms, the national long-term

V. Gorokh · V. Tereshchenko · T. Vakulenko
Ukrainian Center for Education Quality Assessment (UCEQA), Kyiv, Ukraine

L. Hrynevych
Borys Grinchenko Kyiv University, Kyiv, Ukraine

E. Smyrnova-Trybulska (✉)
Department of Humanistic Education, University of Silesia in Katowice, Katowice, Poland
e-mail: esmyrnova@us.edu.pl

E. Smyrnova-Trybulska et al. (eds.), *Microlearning*,
https://doi.org/10.1007/978-3-031-13359-6_13

Monitoring Study of the Quality of Primary Education (hereinafter – MSQPE) aimed at evaluating the "Levels of Reading and Mathematical Competencies of Primary School Graduates", launched in 2016 on the initiative of the Ministry of Education and Science of Ukraine, can be reasonably considered as one of the elements of the relevant system.

The first cycle of the MSQPE was conducted in 2017–2018, and its results, after thorough processing and analysis by the experts of the Ukrainian Center for Educational Quality Assessment (UCEQA), were presented to the public as a five-part report in late 2018 – early 2019 (Report on the results of the first cycle….).

However, despite the fact that the experts of the UCEQA have done a considerable amount of work on data analysis of the first cycle of the MSQPE, many aspects concerning the quality of mathematics education at primary school level require further research, since, as the experience of international comparative studies of the quality of education (Savchenko et al., 2020) shows, the data can be an object of extremely thorough analysis, helping to find ways to improve the situation in the field of school education, including mathematics education.

The purpose of this article is to outline the most urgent problems in the field of Ukrainian primary mathematics education, based on the results of the first cycle of MSQPE 2018 in the aspect of the goals and objectives of the reform of Ukrainian school education called the New Ukrainian School.

The researchers' hypothesis is that the use of the methodological approaches that provide meaningful mathematical activity accessible to students, even in the initial stages promoted in the NUS Reform will facilitate students' learning progress and will result in better learning outcomes.

The conclusions drawn in the paper are based on the results of the first cycle of the National Monitoring Study of the Quality of Primary Education held in 2018 (MSQPE).

2 Literature Review

Since the publication of the MSQPE first-cycle reports on the level of mathematical competencies of primary school leavers (December 2018), only few informative publications (Bakhrushin, 2019) of the same nature have appeared. The authors of these materials have generally summarized the most revealing data obtained from the MSQPE without going into detail or offering their own analysis of the data presented in the report. At the same time, the articles referred to in one way or another stated that "in general, the results of the monitoring provide a lot of useful information for finding ways to improve mathematics education in secondary school. Therefore, a more detailed analysis should be carried out, taking into account their joint impact" (Bakhrushin, 2019).

Mogens Niss, Danish secretary of ICMI during the 1990s, addresses the issues directly in his paper entitled "Quantitative Literacy and Mathematical Competencies." Niss argues for a broad PISA-like definition of "mathematical" literacy that would encompass most of what other authors in this volume refer to as "quantitative" literacy. In particular, Niss argues, if the objectives of mathematics education were organized around competencies such as reasoning, modelling, and communicating mathematically – rather than, for example, around content such as algebra, geometry, and calculus – school graduates would be far better able to navigate thoughtfully the turbulent waters of democratic debate and decision making (See pp. 217–222.) (Steen, 2003, p. 212).

> Niss defines "mathematical competence" as the ability to understand, judge, do, and use mathematics in a variety of intra- and extra-mathematical contexts. Necessary, but certainly not sufficient, prerequisites for mathematical competence are extensive factual knowledge and technical skills. (Niss, 2003, p. 218)

The relationship between mathematical competences in European depiction of the core curriculum (CC) and the standards of graduation exam requirements (SGER) was presented on the Fig. 1 (Heba et al., 2014, p. 254).

A closer analysis has given rise to the following eight competencies: (1) Thinking mathematically (mastering mathematical modes of thought); (2) Posing and solving mathematical problems; (3) Modelling mathematically; (4) Reasoning mathematically; (5) Representing mathematical entities; (6) Handling mathematical symbols and formalisms, (7) Communicating in, with, and about mathematics; (8) Making use of aids and tools (including information technology) (Niss, 2003, pp. 218–219).

In contexts of a study of mathematic competences in contemporary conditions, it is important to revisit the distinction between procedural and conceptual knowledge and review well-known pedagogical theory and mathematical practice, for example Dewey, Maslow (Österman & Bråting, 2019).

Computer-aided teaching of mathematics with the GRAN-1W program package was analyzed by Zhaldak et al. (2004). International team of experts Hohenwarter, Hohenwarter, Kreis and Lavicza prepared a comprehensive study and assessment teaching and learning calculus with free dynamic mathematics software GeoGebra (2008).

Research in the area of Computers in Early Childhood and Primary School Mathematics was conducted by Clements (2002), Skvortsova and Britskan (2018).

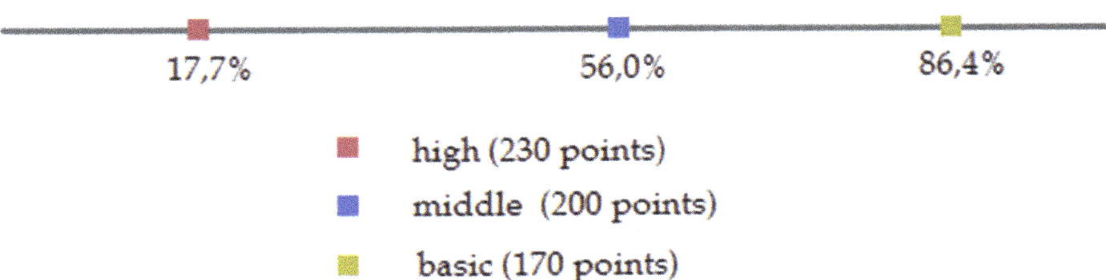

Fig. 1 The 2018 primary school leavers' (%) achievement of defined levels of mathematical competencies in the scale of 100–300. (Adapted from "Report on the results of the first cycle of a nationwide monitoring study of the quality of primary education "State of formation of reading and mathematical competencies of graduates of primary schools of secondary education institutions" 2018, Part II, p. 40)

"The computer can offer unique opportunities for learning through exploration, creative problem-solving, and self-guided instruction. Realizing this potential demands a simultaneous focus on curriculum and technology innovations" said Clements (2002, p. 174), reflecting on research by Hohmann (1994).

Scientists and experts from different countries continue analyzing and discussing mathematical literacy identification. Niss stressed "… the very notion of mathematical literacy is not well defined, especially as several related concepts, such as numeracy, quantitative literacy, mathematical proficiency, and mathematical competencies, are in general use as well…" (2012, p. 409).

Other authors in their research devoted to scientists of the future and an analysis of talented students' interests noted: "Nowadays, scientists not only need to be creative, resourceful, and inventive regarding their research questions and need to understand their field and research methods, but also need to know how to teach, how to catalog, … and much more" noted Höffler et al. (2019, p. 1).

The importance of mathematics education for the progress and security of the state is now being recognized in all countries and economies seeking to succeed. Researches have proven that mathematics competences are the key to forming computer literacy and programming skills, which are of high importance in the modern world. Ukraine is no exception in understanding the necessity of mathematics; that is why the issues of improving the quality of school mathematics education, finding ways to restore the prestige of mathematics and its status as one of personal and social value are now at the center of state educational policy (Decree of the President of Ukraine No 31, 2020).

Finding the answers to these questions is a difficult task. After all, against the background of great achievements in the field of elitist teaching of mathematics (*Note.* Students, who study at Kyiv, Kharkiv, Lviv, and Dnipro gymnasiums), mass school mathematics education in Ukraine, unfortunately, is in decline, which is proved, in particular, as noted above, by the results of EIE (Official report … 2016, Volume II, Official report … 2017, Volume II ; Official report … 2018, Volume II).

3 Research Methodology

As mentioned above, the material for scientific reflection in this article was the results of the first cycle of a nationwide monitoring study of the quality of primary education "State of formation of reading and mathematical competencies of graduates of primary schools of secondary education institutions", held in 2018. According to the authors of the study, the great value for the development of the methodological basis of the monitoring research was the experience of domestic and foreign experts on the organization and conduct of educational monitoring, preparation of cognitive, contextual and procedural materials, collecting, processing and analysis of data, etc (Report on the results … 2018: in 5 parts. Parts I – p. 34).

The background and bases of Research Methodology were in particularly IRT (Item Response Theory) theory and different types of IRT mathematical models, in particular, the IRT models included are the three-parameter logistic model, the two-parameter logistic model, the one-parameter logistic model, and the Rasch model (Battauz, 2015): (a) G. Rush's one-parameter model (Rash, 1993); (b) A. Birnbaum's two-parameter model; (c) A. Birnbaum's three-parameter model (Birnbaum, 1968). Using the IRT theory lets us see how correct answers depend on the latent characteristics (Baker, 2001).

For data processing and analysis based on the results of the main stage of the monitoring study, all calculations were performed in three information environments: Excel, R, and SPSS. The R package equateIRT implements item response theory (IRT) methods for equating different forms composed of dichotomous items (Battauz, 2016). R is easy to build thanks to the Comprehensive R Archive Network (CRAN) website. According to the classical test, theory packages were downloaded to calculate psychometric characteristics according to classical test theory and perform test analysis based on IRT models. The packages CTT, psych, psychometric, ShinyItemAnalysis, ltm, mirt, equateIRT were used. Packages such as reshape, difNLR, haven, fBasics, tinytex, ggplot2, and others were used to process the data and build different charts. SPSS is a software application for statistical data processing, designed for conducting applied research in the social sciences (Report on the results … 2018: in 5 parts. Parts I – p. 85). The monitoring study's methodology and instruments were developed following the best foreign and national practices. For instance, the study's general structure of the study and its instruments were developed based on the comprehensive work written by Greaney and Kellaghan (2008). The authors reviewed several national systems of the monitoring of education and some international surveys in education. They discussed the main issues in building educational assessment systems on different levels of education. Besides, some significant provisions on the relevant issues were shown according to such Ukrainian scientists (Liashenko, 2013). Because the Ukrainian system of education differs considerably from most of the European ones, the study's development required analyzing the national educational context. The works of Babyn et al. (2011) devoted to the Ukrainian system of education and the theory of national assessments were the study's background. In the Report, the terms "cognitive material", "context material" and "instructional material" are used in the following terms. *Cognitive materials* are test tasks that have been provided to the students participating in the monitoring study to measure the level of reading and mathematical competence of the respective participants. *Contextual materials* – questionnaires that were used to gather information from the participants in the monitoring study (year 4 students and teachers) regarding the educational (within the school) and extracurricular environment. *Instructional materials* – instructions, process charts, guidelines developed to ensure the standardized conduct of testing and questionnaires in the WSO involved in the administration of the processes, processing of monitoring materials by persons. (Report ….2018: in 5 parts. Parts I – p. 37). The instruments used in the research were student and teacher questionnaires and cognitive tests. Each student completed two 40-min tests and a 20–30-min-long questionnaire.

The 2018 MSQPE student sample included 9077 primary school students (fourth graders), who represented 484 classes of different types of educational institutions of Ukraine. A sample was designed with the use of PPS Model (Probability Proportional to School Size), the student sample is representative for the population of 361,841 students, which is more than 91% of the general population of Ukrainian fourth graders. Among the exclusions there are students studying in a minority language, students with special education needs, and students living under the military intervention in Ukraine. According to the monitoring study design, 4501 primary school students took part in the mathematics assessment Report on the results of the first cycle of a nationwide monitoring study of the quality of primary education "State of formation of reading and mathematical competencies of graduates of primary schools of secondary education institutions" 2018: in 5 parts. Part, Part II, p. 27–32).

MSQPE is a sample-based study, based on cross-national survey research. MSQPE methodology is described in detail in Volume 1 of the MSQPE first-cycle reports (Report MSQPE, Volume I).

All comments presented in the next section are author's reflections based on the goals and methods outlined in their research. It is important to emphasize that the majority of the authors participated in the project (National Monitoring Study of the Quality of Primary Education held in 2018 (MSQPE) and in the next section of the article important reflections, comments and conclusions are presented.

4 Results and Discussion

There is no doubt that school education is a long process where the results of the previous stage of students' education directly affect the success of learning the material in the subsequent stages. Therefore, students' success at the stage of completing of compulsory secondary education can, to some extent, indicate how well the student has mastered the curriculum, and to form the relevant competencies at the earlier stages of education – in basic and primary schools.

Here are just a few examples that clearly demonstrate that, even with some standard benchmarking tests aimed at testing basic math skills, comprehensive secondary school graduates show low levels of mathematical competencies.

For instance, Table 1 shows Year 11 students' results in solving test items on simplifying mathematics expressions (Hereinafter, we do not provide full test tasks. All the examples below refer to the multiple-choice test tasks with five answer options).

The test items on the topic "Functions" are equally challenging for school leavers. For example, only 38.9% of the EIE 2018 participants found the area of definition of the function $y = \frac{x+1}{x-2}$, and every other participant of EIE 2017 in mathe-matics was not able to find the point of intersection of the graph of the function $y = 2x - 2$ with the x-axis (Official report on the results of results of the external independent assessment in 2017, Volume II, p. 192; Official report on the results of the external independendwent assessment in 2018, Volume II, p. 205.)

Table 1. Year 11 students' results in solving the test items on simplifying mathematics expressions during EIE

EIE held in (year)	An expression to be simplified in a math test	The correct answer	Number of EIE participants who completed the task correctly (%)
2017	$1 - \sin^2\alpha - \cos^2\alpha$	0	57.7
	$\frac{a^2+16}{a-4} - \frac{8a}{a-4}$	$a - 4$	49.6
2018	$\frac{2a+2}{2}$	$a + 1$	52.9
	$a(a + 2b) - (a + b)^2$	$-b^2$	46.3
	$1 - \sin\alpha \, \mathrm{ctg}\alpha \, \cos\alpha$	$\sin^2\alpha$	36.5

Note. The data are adapted from "Official report on the results of the external independent assessment in 2017, Volume II, p. 192–193; Official report on the results of results of the external independent assessment in 2018, Volume II, p. 203–210".

The test participants also showed disappointing results in solving test items on simple percentage calculation. These results clearly demonstrate that many school leavers do not have basic practical mathematical skills, absence of which makes is difficult to cope with everyday real-life issues. For example, here are two mathematical problems.

> EIE 2010: The issuance of a succession certificate is subject to a state duty of 0.5% of the value of the inherited property. How much state duty will the heir have to pay if the value of the inherited property is 32,000 UAH?

The correct answer to this test item was chosen by only 61.9% of the EIE participants, at the same time, every sixth secondary school leaver agrees to pay a 10-fold state fee in exchange for freedom from mathematical thinking (Official report on the results of results of the external independent assessment in 2010, p. 85).

> EIE 2011: The magazine was originally priced 25 UAH. Two months later the same magazine cost 21 UAH. By what percentage was its price marked down?

Every other test participant was not able to choose the right answer to this problem, and every fifth thought that the price was reduced by 4%. The statistics of the answer choice by the EIE participants for this problem involuntarily makes one recall the well-known sad anecdote about the "new" Ukrainian, who told how he was making money: "I buy the product for two dollars apiece, and sell for four. That's 2 percent I earn for living" (Official report on the results of results of the external independent assessment in 2011, p. 78).

As the examples show, the situation is really disappointing. Of course, if we were talking about the results of the stage of completion of secondary basic education (Year 9), then we could still expect that in the next two years of schooling students would be able to improve their knowledge and skills in mathematics. However, the situation is more complicated, and the abovementioned test items relate to the mathematical content provided by the mathematics syllabus for Years 5–9 and were completed by Year 11 students, that is, by those who have completed comprehensive secondary education and most of them will no longer have the opportunity to study mathematics systematically.

As a result, without having mastered basic mathematical concepts in comprehensive school, these school leavers will potentially fall into the category of those whose further mathematical education will be problematic. And this is extremely dangerous in conditions where the proper level of formation of mathematical competencies is recognized as one of the key requirements for a person's competitiveness in today's civilization of information technologies.

Considering such negative effects in education, including mathematics, a long-term education reform, the New Ukrainian School, was launched in Ukraine in 2016. The main purpose of this reform is transformation of the education in Ukrainian school from knowledge-based into competency-based, so that it would equip the modern person with all necessary knowledge and skills for life in the twent-first century. Naturally, the reform was started from the initial level of education. Thus, in accordance with the Concept of the New Ukrainian School (The Concept of the implementation of the state policy in the sphere of reforming of comprehensive secondary education "New Ukrainian School" for the period up to 2029), a new State Primary Education Standard (On approval of the State Standard for Primary Education) was introduced in 2018, in which the requirements for compulsory learning outcomes are set out, taking into account the competency-based approach to learning. The new State Primary Education Standard is based on several key competencies, including mathematical competencies.

The new State Standard specifies the purpose of the mathematics education as developing mathematical and other key competencies; developing (critical) thinking, the ability to recognize and model processes and situations of everyday life that can be solved using mathematical methods, and the ability to make deliberate choices.

The main focus, as you can see, is shifted to competencies. However, this does not in any way mean that academic mathematical knowledge is losing its value in this approach. Not at all, since there is no doubt that no competencies can exist without knowledge. This is clearly emphasized in the European Commission documents, where competencies are defined as a combination of knowledge, skills and attitudes, where: (a) knowledge – facts and figures, concepts, ideas and theories which are already established und support the understanding of a certain area or subject; (b) Skills – ability and capacity to carry out processes and use the existing knowledge to achieve results; (c) Attitudes – disposition and mind-sets to act/react to ideas, persons or situations (Proposal for a Council Recommendation on Key Competencies for Lifelong Learning).

The foregoing is important in view of the fact that teaching mathematics to achieve new goals in the context of the implementation of the New Ukrainian School reform should be carried out with great care, taking into account both recent trends and traditions and practices that have been common for more than a decade. Because, as ever, today, despite the tremendous technological changes that have taken place in the world recently, both the utilitarian (pragmatic) component of mathematics education and the intellectual development of the individual remain the aspects, highlighted by Servais (1957) at the UNESCO Conference, that determined the future of the mathematics education, and in terms of up-to-date education they can be defined as competencies and scientific knowledge components.

It is only natural that the prudence and completeness of achieving the goal of mathematics teaching in primary school, defined by the new State Standard, should be monitored, so that, if necessary, it is possible to adjust both the content of mathematics education and the methods of teaching mathematics. For this reason, at the initial stage of implementation of the Concept of the New Ukrainian School in practice in 2018, the nationwide monitoring study of the quality of primary education was first conducted since the independence of Ukraine (1991) (Report MSQPE, Volume I).

One of its purposes was to study the level of mathematical competencies of 2018 primary school leavers, who studied under the old State Standard for Primary Education dated 2011, and to examine how these results related to some factors of socio-economic and psychological-pedagogical nature.

In order to achieve the stated goals, the MSQPE team has created an appropriate cognitive instrument – mathematics tests that can provide a qualitative measurement of the level of mathematical competencies, and a contextual instrument – questionnaires for students who took mathematics tests and teachers who taught these students.

Developing the cognitive instrument, the study authors considered two aspects that structure mathematical competencies: content and cognitive (Table 2).

For the purposes of the study, taking into account the provisions of the national standards of primary education and mathematics syllabi, programs of international comparative studies of the quality of education in mathematics in primary school, and the traditions of teaching mathematics in Ukrainian primary schools, mathematical content was structured into the following categories (sections): numbers; geometric shapes and geometric values; measurement; data processing – the details of which are the main mathematical topics and mastering of which is important for the development of mathematical competencies, are presented in Table 3.

In turn, cognitive skills within the study are structured into the following categories: knowing; applying; and reasoning. The category of *knowing* covers facts, procedures and concepts that primary school graduates should possess. The ability to operate with mathematical terms and notions and the knowledge of mathematical facts are the basis for mathematical thinking. In turn, the knowledge of the

Table 2 Measurements of mathematical competencies of primary school leavers

Aspect	Definition
Content	Defines the mathematical content that students need to master when learning mathematics at primary school
Cognitive	Defines the thinking processes that students need to develop and apply, both in solving mathematical problems and in solving real-life problems

Note. The data are adapted from "Report on the results of the first cycle of a nationwide monitoring study of the quality of primary education "State of formation of reading and mathematical competencies of graduates of primary schools of secondary education institutions" 2018, Part II, p. 17"

Table 3 Mathematical content

Content category	Mathematical topic
Numbers and Expressions	Writing and reading natural numbers; comparison of numbers
	Operations on natural numbers
	Text tasks
	Ordinary fractions. Find the fraction of the number and the number of its fraction
	Letter expressions, equations, inequalities
Geometric Shapes and Geometric Quantities	Geometric shapes
	Perimeter and area
Measurement	Measurement of segment length, body weight, capacity (volume). Converting units
	Time measurement
	Money management
Data processing	Reading data from tables, charts
	Using information presented in tables and charts to answer questions beyond the direct data reading
	Organizing and displaying data using tables, bar charts

Note. The data are adapted from "Report on the results of the first cycle of a nationwide monitoring study of the quality of primary education "State of formation of reading and mathematical competencies of graduates of primary schools of secondary education institutions" 2018, Part II, p. 19"

Table 4 Cognitive categories of mathematical competencies

Cognitive category	Definition
Knowing	A primary school graduate's awareness of mathematical facts, procedures, terms and notions
Applying	A primary school graduate's ability to apply knowledge and understand ideas to solve basic (standard) tasks
Reasoning	A primary school graduate's ability to solve non-standard tasks related to unfamiliar situations, complex contexts, and multi-step tasks

Note. The data are adapted from "Report on the results of the first cycle of a nationwide monitoring study of the quality of primary education "State of formation of reading and mathematical competencies of graduates of primary schools of secondary education institutions" 2018, Part II, p. 20"

procedures (sets of actions and rules of their implementation) is necessary to solve the routine tasks that a person faces in their everyday life. The category of *applying* describes students' ability to apply knowledge and understanding of ideas to solve basic (standard) tasks. Such tasks are standard exercises that students perform in mathematics lessons, and can be purely algorithmic (for example, columnar) or textual, describing simple situations using simple contexts. The category of *reasoning* goes beyond standard tasks and covers unfamiliar situations, complex contexts, and multi-step tasks. Such tasks require more complex reasoning for students, although they do not require students to have mathematical knowledge and skills that go beyond the curriculum. The essence of these categories is presented in Table 4.

A scale of 100–300 was used to report the results of assessing the level of mathematical competencies of primary school graduates based on the results of the MSQPE. It identifies two main benchmark levels of students' mathematical competencies – *basic and high* which correspond to 170 and 230 points, respectively, as well as the average threshold (200 points) though its value does not correlate with any average value of the monitoring study participants' performance.

Table 5 summarizes the verbal descriptions of basic and high levels of mathematical competencies, formulated by experts on the basis of the analysis of both the specifics of the test instrument and the test results.

In MSQPE 2018 the number of students who participated in the testing, in which the described cognitive instrument was used, was 4501. A two-stage stratified PPS (Probability Proportional to School Size) design was used to generate a sample of study participants, which provided equal probability for each primary school leaver to be included in the sample population. The sample of primary school leavers who took the math test was representative of the main traits and weighted by casualties, "regular school" (number of students in Year 4 class is over 15) and "small school" (number of students in the Year 4 class is from 7 to 15). The representativeness error was no more than 2%.

According to the results of the testing within the framework of the MSQPE, in 2018, almost 18% of primary school leavers demonstrated a high level of mathematical competencies, which allows them to solve multi-step mathematical problems that go beyond the standard and cover not well known or new situations. In

Table 5 Description of the levels of mathematical competencies

The level of mathematical competencies	Description
Basic	At the basic level, students should demonstrate a certain awareness of mathematical concepts and procedures related to the following context categories: 'Numbers and Expressions', 'Geometric Shapes and Geometric Quantities', 'Measurements', 'Data Processing'; perform simple calculations with positive integers; apply mathematical knowledge to solve simple problems related to real-life situations which are familiar to them. Students can follow clearly described procedures. They are able to choose and apply simple strategies for solving problems. At this level, students can only use information from one source and consider the tasks using the information given.
High	At the high level, students should have mathematical concepts and procedures related to the following content categories: 'Numbers and Expressions', 'Geometric shapes and Geometric Quantities', 'Measurements', 'Data Processing'; apply mathematical knowledge to solve problems that go beyond standard ones and cover less familiar and new situations and are presented in more complex contexts. At this level, students can purposefully work with the task and use well-developed skills to reason and draw conclusions, to use information from one or more sources.

Note: The data are adapted from "Report on the results of the first cycle of a nationwide monitoring study of the quality of primary education "State of formation of reading and mathematical competencies of graduates of primary schools of secondary education institutions" 2018, Part II, p. 25"

turn, over 86% of primary school leavers have reached the basic level of mathematical competencies. Thus, about 14% of students who completed their primary education had difficulties solving simple mathematical problems that relate to their real-life situations (Fig. 1).

According to the analysis of the MSQPE 2018 data, primary school leavers demonstrate the best results in solving the test problems related to the topics 'Numbers and Expressions' (62% of correct answers), and the most difficult for them are the tests that refer to such content section as 'Data Processing' (51% of correct answers). Fifty seven percent of students answered test questions related to the 'Geometric shapes and Geometric quantities' correctly.

It is worth mentioning that every sixth test item used in the study was related to the category of 'Geometric shapes and Geometric quantities'. The attention given to the geometry component of mathematical competencies is intentional. According to psychological studies, the initial intellectual activity (thinking) of a child is mostly geometrical. Sharygin, a prominent teacher, a scientist and an 'advocate' of science, said:

> Geometry is the primordial kind of intellectual activity both of all mankind and of the individual. The world science began with geometry. Without being able to speak yet, a child learns the geometrical features of the world. Lots of achievements of ancient geometricians (Archimedes, Apollonius) are surprising to modern scientists, despite the fact that they had no algebraic apparatus. Pursuing the analogy between the human's and the individual's, I must point out that geometric skills of young and middle-aged children almost never depend on the level of their mathematical proficiency. (Sharygin, 2007, p. 47)

According to the results of MSQPE 2018, a significant proportion of Ukrainian primary school leavers have a sufficiently developed geometric intuition and know basic geometry. For example, the data on Year 4 students' answers to one of the geometry problems is given below (Fig. 2).

In 2018, 22% of primary school leavers correctly solved the *Reasoning* mathematical problem. The results of solving this test item vary greatly depending on the groups of test participants: 66% of the study participants who reached the high score level (230 points) were able to solve this test item, and only 5% of the students who scored 170–200 points provided the correct answer.

The average complexity of the test tasks of different cognitive categories used in MSQPE 2018 varied more significantly in comparison with the indicators of their performance by the participants of MSQPE 2018. The primary school leavers demonstrated the highest scores for solving *Applying* test items (78% of correct answers) whereas *Reasoning* cognitive test items were the most difficult for the students (only 40% of correct answers).

In addition to obtaining information about mathematics performance of primary school leavers across the population in general, the MSQPE also observed, as noted above, the link between mathematics performance of primary school leavers and a number of socio-economic and psycho-pedagogical factors.

MSQPE mathematics assessment results showed that the difference between boys' and girls' performance is not statistically significant. Thus, at the level of primary school there is no evident dependence of mathematics performance on

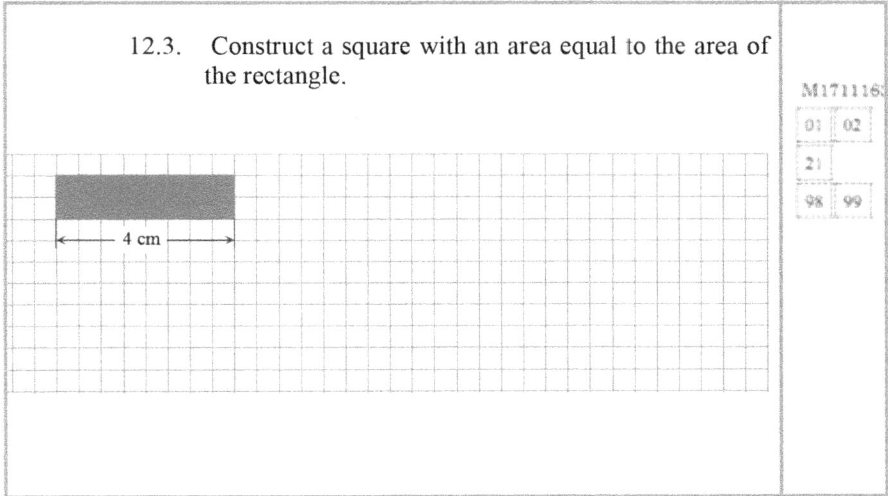

Fig. 2 MSQPE: item on geometric reasoning. (Adapted from "Report on the results of the first cycle of a nationwide monitoring study of the quality of primary education "State of formation of reading and mathematical competencies of graduates of primary schools of secondary education institutions" 2018, Part II, p. 45)

gender: on average, the boys scored 203.3 points in mathematics whereas the girls scored 202.5 points in this test.

At the same time, the data received indicate that there is a significant correlation between the students' mathematics performance and the location of the school in which the students completed their primary education. The students who went to city schools scored the highest average result (208.9 points) in mathematics. The students who attended primary schools in bigger towns scored a little less (203.1 points), and those who went to school in smaller towns scored even lower result (197.6 points). The students who attended school located in villages scored the lowest average result (190.3 points).

The correlation between the percentage of primary school students who reached certain levels of mathematical competencies and the type of settlement where their school is located is shown in Fig. 3.

Differences in mathematical performance of primary school leavers in 2018 depend also on the type of the school where they completed their primary education. Thus, students who studied at primary schools of general education with extensive learning of some subjects (until full implementation of New Ukrainian School Reform these schools will have been called lyceums and gymnasiums) and colleges, educational complexes and specialized schools have a significantly higher score point in mathematics (208.7, 208.8 and 211.7 respectively) than students of comprehensive secondary schools (198.5 points).

However, as the analysis of the MSQPE 2018 data revealed, today one of the most important factors affecting students' achievements in developing their

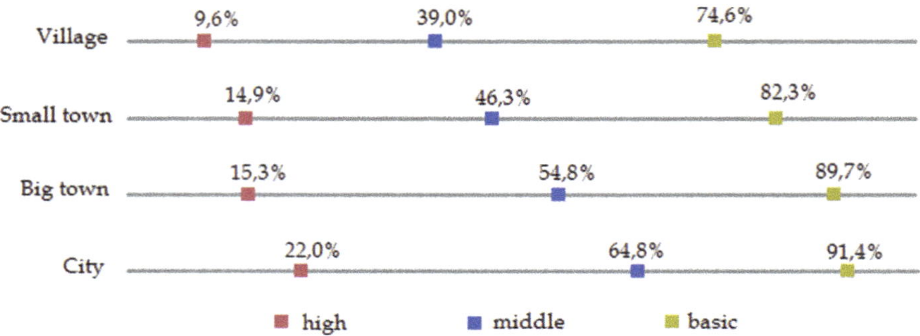

Fig. 3 How the level of mathematical competencies of primary school leavers (%) correlates with the type of locality where their school is located. (Adapted from "Report on the results of the first cycle of a nationwide monitoring study of the quality of primary education "State of formation of reading and mathematical competencies of graduates of primary schools of secondary education institutions" 2018, Part II, p. 56)

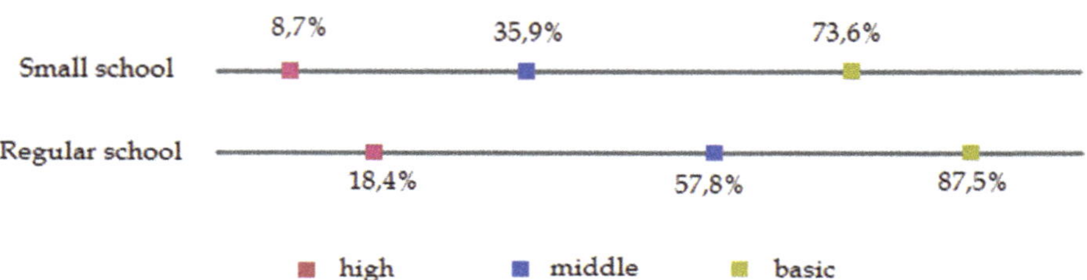

Fig. 4 The levels of mathematical competencies of primary school leavers (%) who attended small and regular schools, in the scale of 100–300. (Adapted from "Report on the results of the first cycle of a nationwide monitoring study of the quality of primary education "State of formation of reading and mathematical competencies of graduates of primary schools of secondary education institutions" 2018, Part II, p. 55)

mathematical competencies is the number of students studying at a school: primary school students who attended small schools (the number of students in the Year 4 class is from 7 to 15), showed significantly lower results than the students of regular schools (the number of students in the Year 4 class is more than 15) (Fig. 4).

Figure 4 shows the results of solving mathematics test items offered to Year 4 students in one of the test books (Report MSQPE, Volume II). As we can see, regardless of the content or cognitive dimension that characterizes each of the 25 test items, the students' performance was different and the gap between the scores correlated with the size of their schools.

The results of doing tasks related to the *Reasoning* cognitive category proved to be significantly different, which is a rather dangerous tendency for the modern age of information, because, according to the researchers, the role of mathematics in the information society is significantly changing. The use of mathematics ceases to be limited just serving primarily physics and the needs of technical sciences, it begins to perform a civilizational role, becoming a means of forming of a human's thinking culture (Gandel & Zholtkievich, 2001).

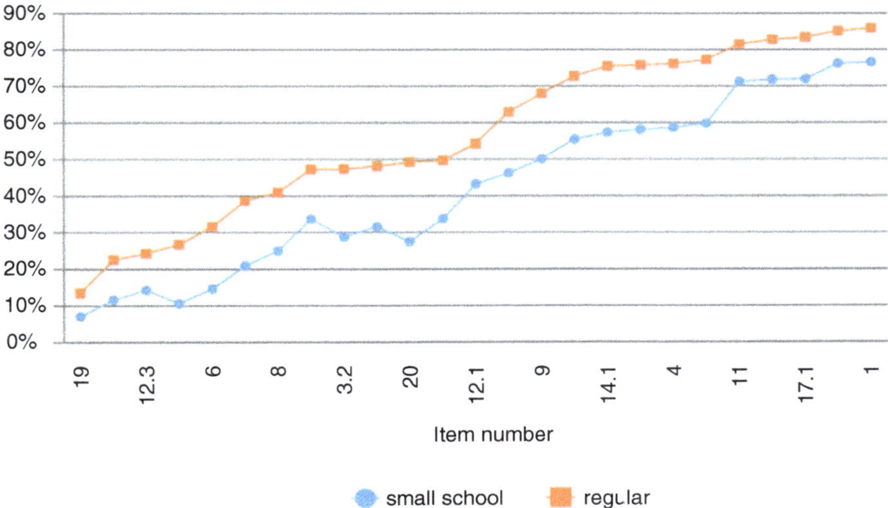

Fig. 5 Percentage of correct answers to test tasks provided by primary school leavers who attended small and regular schools in 2018. (Adapted from "Report on the results of the first cycle of a nationwide monitoring study of the quality of primary education "State of formation of reading and mathematical competencies of graduates of primary schools of secondary education institutions" 2018: in 5 parts. Parts I – V. Retrieved from http://testportal.gov.ua/zvity-dani-2/)

That is, if we now have problems related to students' ability to perform *reasoning* tasks at the primary school level, then in the future, we can get citizens who are unable to think at a sufficient level of abstraction to solve the challenges and problems they will face in their real life.

The test task that caused the widest gap between the results of students of small and regular schools is provided below (Fig. 6)

In regular schools, 26.7% of students solved this mathematics problem, and in small schools – only 10.7% did.

Thus, the results of MSQPE 2018 confirm Andreas Schleicher's (Schleicher, 2018), conclusion that there is no international data to prove that reducing class sizes is the best way to improve learning outcomes (Report MSQPE, Volume II). However, when interpreting the MSQPE results, it should be borne in mind that small schools are predominantly located in rural areas, and consequently, the learning outcomes may be adversely affected by other factors, such as the lower qualifications of teachers working in such schools, etc.

5 Some Comments on PISA Results

Ukraine took part in PISA 2018 and the results of the Programme were published on 3 December. Some facts shown in the PISA 2018 National Report were shocking for local stakeholders in education. Among those are low results in Mathematics: 36%

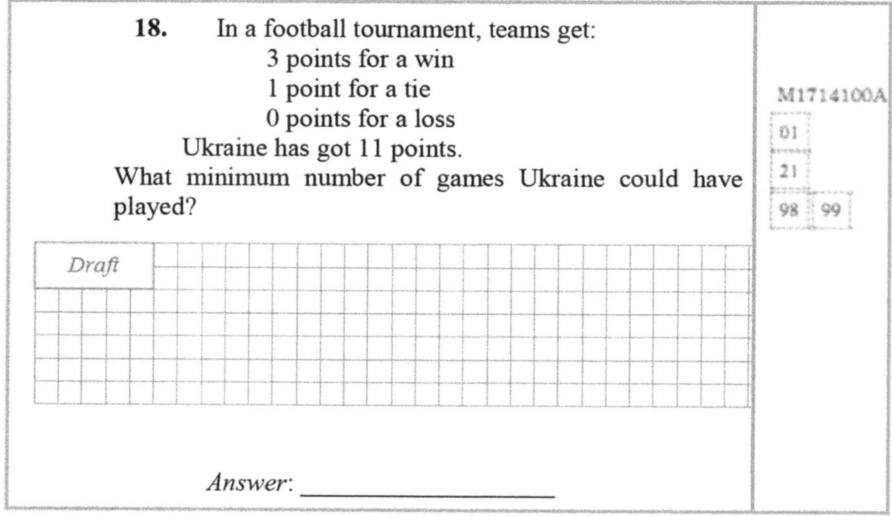
18. In a football tournament, teams get:
3 points for a win
1 point for a tie
0 points for a loss
Ukraine has got 11 points.
What minimum number of games Ukraine could have played?

Draft

Answer: ___________________

M1714100A
01
21
98 99

Fig. 6 MSQPE: item on mathematics reasoning. (Adapted from "Report on the results of the first cycle of a nationwide monitoring study of the quality of primary education "State of formation of reading and mathematical competencies of graduates of primary schools of secondary education institutions" 2018, Part II, p. 156)

of Ukrainian students do not reach the basic level of mathematics knowledge. They have problems with tasks that require simple solution strategies, percentages, fractions and decimal numbers (Mazorchuk et al., 2019, pp. 54–58).

PISA is the worldwide study on the quality of education in which Ukraine first participated fully in the cycle of 2018.

The study evaluated 15-year-old students. A total of 600,000 students in 79 countries were surveyed. Student tests lasted two hours. In Ukraine, nearly 6000 students were assessed and interviewed in 250 educational institutions. Ukrainian students took the tests in writing. PISA does not test whether students have mastered the content of the curriculum, but rather assesses how students are able to use their knowledge, skills and competences in real life. This study shows the weaknesses and strengths of the education system (National Report on PISA 2018 Results, p. 76).

The Table 6 includes some data on PISA results. Countries ranked in Mathematics

We note that Polish students performed better in exams in Mathematics Science and reading. Probably this is only the first experience and results less from procedural knowledge and conditions, which is well-known in other countries. Among other causes could include a reduction in the number of hours on mathematics and other science subjects, still insufficient and uncommon application of innovative and active teaching methods. Further extensive cross-sectional studies are needed.

Table 6 PISA results. Country ranked in Mathematics

	2018			2015		
	Reading	Mathematics	Science	Reading	Mathematics	Science
Ukraine	466	453	469	–	–	–
Poland	512(+6)	516(+12)	511(+10)	506(+3)	504(+5)	501(+3)

Note: The data are adapted from Schleicher (2019) and Mazorchuk et al. (2019)

6 Conclusions and Suggestions for Future Research

The results of the study show that some of the mathematical content, basic for mathematics education in primary school, is not sufficiently mastered by primary school leavers, and this can lead to even more negative results in the future. The researchers' hypothesis that the use of the methodological approaches providing meaningful mathematical activity accessible to students, even in the initial stages promoted in the NUS Reform will facilitate students' learning progress and will result in better learning outcomes was confirmed.

The additional conclusions are as follows:

- The data and illustrations provided by the study demonstrate today's negative tendency in Ukraine: at the primary school level it is evident that advantaged and disadvantaged students have different opportunities to develop their mathematical competencies. PISA 2018 data confirm some negative tendencies in secondary school Mathematics education.
- It is also clear that attention should be paid to the mathematics teaching methods in Ukraine. Some basic Mathematics concepts are not well taught in primary school, which leads to deep gaps in Mathematics knowledge later on. National and international research on education reveals the necessity to review approaches in Mathematics education.
- According to the results of MSQPE 2018, it can be stated unequivocally that the state should pay special attention to the category of small schools, in particular in the perspective of administrative decisions aimed at contributing to the elimination of this negative tendency in the context of the implementation of the ideas of the New Ukrainian School.

The MSQPE results are considered by the authors as base-line results, which will allow for tracking the differences in the students' performance while the New Ukrainian School Reform (NUS Reform) is implemented (Report MSQPE, Volume I).

Among the contemporary educational theories of math learning and teaching it takes an important place is the Polya's classic work "How to Solve It: a New Aspect of Mathematical Method" (Polya, 1985), which is still ranks high on various lists of most read and most referenced publications. The researchers from different countries analyses and continue research in area of implementation of the Polya's methods. Carifio (2015) underlines. that "Polya claims that true problem solving is accompanied by the cognitive activities of mobilization, organization, isolation and combination, and by the meta-cognitive evaluations of relevancy, proximity, and quality. These meta-cognitive evaluations occur as a result of monitoring cognitive activities…" (p. 105)

Mathematical skills emphasize by experts e.g. among the main parts of the computer programmer skills. There are Learning concepts and applying them to other problems; Mathematical skills (Many aspects of programming require an understanding of math beyond the basic level. To become proficient at programming, you will need to have a thorough understanding of algebra and arithmetic.); Problem-solving capability; Communication skills; Writing skills; Inquisitiveness (Computer Programmer Skills..).

We agree with Autor (Potapova, 2020), who „looks at innovative strategies for teaching mathematics which use elements of microlearning". The expert stressed that „a kind of new learning format, which is developed using a series of short learning materials and short tasks that make up a mini-course". Could to support the researcher about her conclusions about „microlearning not only opens up new pedagogical possibilities, but also increases the effectiveness of learning and improves educational outcomes. It is **compatible** with modern information and communication models and can be easily adapted to meet individual learning needs" (2020, 127).

The researchers concludes that "Emphasizing in the children, the development of office content, skill to interpret, know and solve mathematical problems from everyday situation to students" (Mateus-Nieves et al., 2021).

We confirm opinion of expert that „by incorporating all the components of microlearning into mathematics teaching, it is possible to engage a large population of learners, increase satisfaction and interest in the lesson and positively influence the learning experience" (Potapova, 2020, p. 127).

The mathematic and teaching of this subject has some own specific features. „It offers a wide range of educational resources, approaches and methods that develop critical and innovative thinking. Typical learning activities are problem analysis, problem proving, problem finding, etc" (Poptaova, 2020). Some of these activities can be designed as micro-learning units (Skalka & Drlík, 2018).

The research, conducted by Alqurashi (2017) „discusses the main three elements in creating an effective microlearning environment, which are: content pedagogy, and technology. It explores the knowledge of how carefully-selected content can be a successful element in microlearning". The Fig. 7 illustrated the microlearning model, included the main components and features, described based on Alqurashi (2017), Hug (2005) and Mikhailov (2018).

In the conditions of not very effective traditional mathematics training, as evidenced by research results, Microlearning may be a good alternative.

Coursmos, Grovo, Panopto stand out among the most common micro-learning tools today (Alqurashi, 2017). The further research could be focuses on the development of the microlearning environment and using for mathematics learning support.

Fig. 7 Microlearning model, included the main components and features. (Adapted from Alqurashi (2017) and Hug (2005) and Mikhailov (2018))

References

Alqurashi, E. (2017). Microlearning: A pedagogical approach for technology integration. *Turkish Online Journal of Educational Technology, 11*, 942–947.

Babyn, I. I., Hrynevych, L. M., Likarchuk, I. L., Lytvyn, A. V., Mykhailichenko, M. V., Sovsun, …, Shynkaruk, V. D. (2011). *Analytical report on the state of monitoring the quality of education in Ukraine*. In I. L. Likarchuk (Ed.), Kiev: Center for Test Technologies and Monitoring the Quality of Education: IBO. Retrieved from http://timo.com.ua/sites/default/files/materials/Analit_dopovid_ctt_.pdf (In Ukraine)

Baker, F. B. (2001). *The basics of item response theory*. ERIC Clearinghouse on Assessment and Evaluation, University of Maryland.

Bakhrushin, V. (2019, February 3). As evidenced by some results of the monitoring research in mathematics. *New Ukrainian School*. Retrieved from http://nus.org.ua/view/pro-shho-svidchat--deyaki-rezultaty-monitoryngovogo-doslidzhennya-z-matematyky/ (In Ukrainian)

Battauz, M. (2015). equateIRT: An R package for IRT test equating. *Journal of Statistical Software, 68*(7), 1–22. https://doi.org/10.18637/jss.v068.i07

Battauz, M. (2016, June 6). *The R Package equateIRT: A Tutorial*. Retrieved from https://dokumen.tips/documents/the-r-package-equateirt-a-tutorial.html.

Birnbaum, A. (1968). Some latent trait models and their use in inferring an examinee's ability. In F. Lord & M. Novick (Eds.), *Statistical theories of mental test scores*. Addison-Wesley.

Carifio, J. (2015). Updating, modernizing, and testing polya's theory of [Mathematical] problem solving in terms of current cognitive, affective, and information processing theories of learning, emotions, and complex performances. *Journal of Education and Human Development, 4*(3), 105–117. https://doi.org/10.15640/jehd.v4n3a12

Clements, D. H. (2002). Computers in early childhood mathematics. *Contemporary Issues in Early Childhood., 3*(2), 160–181. https://doi.org/10.2304/ciec.2002.3.2.2

Computer programmer skills: Definition and examples. https://www.indeed.com/career-advice/resumes-cover-letters/computer-programmer-skills

Decree of the President of Ukraine №31. (2020). *Announcement of the 2020/2021 academic year of the Year of Mathematical Education in Ukraine.* Retrieved from https://www.president.gov.ua/documents/312020-32165 (In Ukrainian).

Gandel, Y. V., & Zholtkevich, G. N. (2001). On the role of mathematics in the information society. *Universitates, 3*, 32–36. (In Russian).

Greaney, V., & Kellaghan, T. (2008). *Assessing national achievement levels in education.* National Assessments of Educational Achievement. Vol. 1. World Bank.

Heba, A., Kapounova, J., & Smyrnova-Trybulska, E. (2014). Theoretical conception and some practical results of the development of mathematical competences with use of elearning. *International Journal Continuing Engineering Education and Lifelong Learning, 24*(3/4), 252–268. https://doi.org/10.1504/IJCEELL.2014.063098

Höffler, T. N., Köhler, C., & Parchmann, I. (2019). Scientists of the future: An analysis of talented students' interests. *International Journal of STEM Education, 6*(29).

Hohenwarter, M., Hohenwarter, J., Kreis, Y., & Lavicza, Z. (2008). Teaching and learning calculus with free dynamic mathematics software GeoGebra. *TSG 16: Research and development in the teaching and learning of calculus* (pp. 1–9) 11th International Congress on Mathematical Education (ICME 11), Monterrey.

Hohmann, C. (1994). Staff development practices for integrating technology in early childhood education programs. In J. L. Wright & D. D. Shade (Eds.), *Young children: active learners in a technological age* (p. 104). National Association for the Education of Young Children.

Hug, T. (2005, May 6–8). Micro learning and narration. Exploring possibilities of utilization of narrations and storytelling for the designing of "micro units" and didactical microlearning arrangements. Paper presented at the fourth Media in Transition conference, MIT. https://www.researchgate.net/publication/237558117_Micro_Learning_and_Narration_Exploring_possibilities_of_utilization_of_narrations_and_storytelling_for_the_designing_of_micro_units_and_didactical_micro-learning_arrangements. Accessed 10 Sep 2017.

Liashenko, O. I. (Ed.) (2013). *Organizational and methodological support of monitoring research on the quality of general secondary education.* Monograph: Pedagogichna Dumka (In Ukraine)

Mateus-Nieves, E., Castillo, C., & Ferney, E. (2021). Instrumentalization vs instrumentation of microlearning in a math class. *International Journal of Development Research, 11*(04), 46156–46162. https://doi.org/10.37118/ijdr.21620.04.2021

Mazorchuk, M., Vakulenko, T., Tereshchenko, V., Bychko, G., Shumova, K., Rakov, S., …, Kuznetsova, J. (2019). *National Report on PISA 2018 Results. Ukrainian Center for Education Quality Assessment*: Ukrainian Center for Educational Quality Assessment. Retrieved from http://pisa.testportal.gov.ua/wp-content/uploads/2019/12/PISA_2018_Report_UKR.pdf (In Ukrainian).

Mikhailov, V. (2018). Microlearning – Features, advantages and disadvantages. *Education.* https://edu-russian.ru/mikroobuchenie-osobennosti-preimushchestva-i-nedostatki.html

Niss, M., (2003). Quantitative literacy and mathematical competencies. In B. L. Madison (Ed.), *Quantitative Literacy: Literacy: Why numeracy matters for schools and colleges* (National Council on Education and the Disciplines) (pp. 215–220). Mathematical Association of America.

Niss, M. (2012). Mathematical literacy. In S. J. Cho (Ed.), *The Proceedings of the 12th international congress on mathematical education, intellectual and attitudinal chal-*

lenges 8 July – 15 July, 2012, COEX (pp. 409–414). Springer Open. doi: https://doi.org/10.1007/978-3-319-12688-3_31

Official report on the results of results of the external independent assessment in 2010/Ukrainian Center for Educational Quality Assessment. Kyiv. (2010). Retrieved from http://testportal.gov.ua/wp-content/uploads/2017/01/Report2010.pdf (In Ukrainian).

Official report on the results of results of the external independent assessment in 2011/Ukrainian Center for Educational Quality Assessment. Kyiv. (2011). Retrieved from http://testportal.gov.ua/wp-content/uploads/2017/01/Report2011.pdf (In Ukrainian).

Official report on the results of results of the external independent assessment in 2016 (Volume II)/Ukrainian Center for Educational Quality Assessment. Kyiv (2016). Retrieved from http://testportal.gov.ua/wp-content/uploads/2017/01/ZVIT_ZNO_2016_Tom_2.pdf (In Ukrainian).

Official report on the results of results of the external independent assessment in 2017 (Volume II) / Ukrainian Center for Educational Quality Assessment. Kyiv (2017). Retrieved from http://testportal.gov.ua/wp-content/uploads/2017/08/ZVIT_ZNO_2017_Tom_2.pdf (In Ukrainian).

Official report on the results of results of the external independent assessment in 2018 (Volume II) / Ukrainian Center for Educational Quality Assessment. Kyiv. (2018). Retrieved from http://testportal.gov.ua/wp-content/uploads/2018/08/ZVIT-ZNO_2018-Tom_2.pdf (In Ukrainian).

On approval of the State Standard for Primary Education: CMU Resolution dtd 21/02/2018, No 87. Retrieved from https://www.kmu.gov.ua/ua/npas/pro-zatverdzhennya-derzhavnogo-standartu-pochatkovoyi-osviti

On the results of External Independent Assessment in 2018: Decision of the Board of the Ministry of Education and Science of Ukraine dtd 27.09.2018 № 9/1-20. Retrieved from http://testportal.gov.ua//wp-content/uploads/2018/10/Pro-pidsumky-provedennya-ZNO-u-2018-rotsi-Karandij-V.A.-27.09.18.pdf (In Russian)

Onishchenko O. (2019). Why is the tsarina sad. What did the elementary school monitoring said? *The mirror of the week*. 4. Febeuary 2–8 2019. Retrieved from https://dt.ua/EDUCATION/chomu-carivna-tuzhit-301425_.html (In Ukrainian).

Österman, T., & Bråting, K. (2019). Dewey and mathematical practice: Revisiting the distinction between procedural and conceptual knowledge. *Journal of Curriculum Studies, 51*(4), 457–470. https://doi.org/10.1080/00220272.2019.1594388

Polya, G. (1985). *How to solve it*. Princeton University Press.

Potapova, T. V. (2020) The use of elements of microlearning in the study of mathematics. In N. O. Ponomareva (Ed.), *Innovative pedagogical technologies in digital school: collection. Thesis of participants of the II scientific-practical. conf. of young scientists*, Kharkiv, May 14–15 2020/Kharkiv. nat. ped. Univ. GS Frying Pan. Kharkiv: KhNPU, 2020, pp. 127–129.

Proposal for a Council Recommendation on Key Competencies for Lifelong Learning. {COM(2018) 24 final}/European Commission. Brussels, 17.1.2018 {SWD(2018) 14 final}, p. 7. Retrieved from https://eur-lex.europa.eu/LexUriServ/LexUriServ.do?uri=SWD:2018:0014:FIN:EN:PDF

Rash G. (1993). *Probabilistic model for some intelligence and attainment tests* [Basic ideas of IRT]. Mess Press.

Report on the results of the first cycle of a nationwide monitoring study of the quality of primary education "State of formation of reading and mathematical competencies of graduates of primary schools of secondary education institutions" 2018: in 5 parts. Parts I – V. Retrieved from http://testportal.gov.ua/zvity-dani-2/ (In Ukrainian).

Savchenko, O. Y, Baibara, T. M., Besedina, A. V., Bibik, N. M., Lapteva, L. I., Lunko, N. I., …, Prokopenko, N. V. (2020). *TIMSS 2007. Part 1. National survey results*. Kyiv, NVU Publishing Group, 400p. ISBN 978-966-552-249-2.

Schleicher, A. (2018). *Best class in the world: How to build a 21st century education system*. Chronicle, p. 296 (In Ukrainian).

Schleicher, A. (2019). PISA 2018. *Insights and interpretations*. OECD Publishing.

Servais W. (1957). *Teaching mathematics in secondary schools* (M. Kayner, Trans.). *Mathematics education.* Part 1. (pp. 22–31). Retrieved from https://math.ru/lib/book/djvu/mp2/mp2-1.djvu (In Ukrainian).

Sharygin, I. F. (2007). Does the 21st century school need geometry? *Mathematical Education, 3*(8), 37–52. (In Russian).

Skalka, J., & Drlík, M. (2018). Conceptual framework of microlearning-based training mobile application for improving programming skills. In: M. Auer, & T. Tsiatsos (Eds.), *Interactive mobile communication technologies and learning. IMCL 2017.* Advances in Intelligent Systems and Computing, vol. 725. Springer. https://doi.org/10.1007/978-3-319-75175-7_22

Skvortsova, S., & Britskan, N. (2018). Training for future primary school teachers to use the learning apps service in teaching mathematics. *International Journal of Research in E-learning., 4*(1), 59–77. https://doi.org/10.31261/IJREL.2018.4.1.05

Steen, L.A. (2003). Numeracy in an international context. In B. L. Madison (Ed.). *Quantitative literacy: Literacy: Why numeracy matters for schools and colleges.* (pp. 211–213) National Council on Education and the Disciplines. Mathematical Association of America.

The Concept of realization of state policy in the sphere of reforming of comprehensive secondary education "New Ukrainian School" for the period up to 2029, approved by the decree of the Cabinet of Ministers of Ukraine dtd December 14, 2016. Nr 988-p. Retrieved from https://www.kmu.gov.ua/ua/npas/249613934

Zhaldak, M., Goroshko, Y., Vinnychenko, Y., & Smyrnova-Trybulska, E. (2004). Komputerowe wspomaganie nauczania matematyki pakietem programów GRAN-1W (część I) *Matematyka i Komputery,* [Computer-aided teaching of mathematics with the GRAN-1W program package (part I) *Mathematic and Computers,*] 18, 8–12.

Index

E. Smyrnova-Trybulska et al. (eds.), *Microlearning*,
https://doi.org/10.1007/978-3-031-13359-6

Milton Keynes UK
Ingram Content Group UK Ltd.
UKHW020611301023
431580UK00003B/12